IDEAS ON
INSTITUTIONS

IDEAS ON INSTITUTIONS

analysing the literature on
long-term care and custody

Kathleen Jones and A. J. Fowles

Routledge & Kegan Paul
London, Boston, Melbourne and Henley

First published in 1984
by Routledge & Kegan Paul plc
39 Store Street, London WC1E 7DD, England
9 Park Street, Boston, Mass. 02108, USA
464 St Kilda Road, Melbourne,
Victoria 3004, Australia and
Broadway House, Newtown Road,
Henley-on-Thames, Oxon RG9 1EN, England
Set in Baskerville 11pt by Hope Services, Abingdon
and printed in Great Britain by
T. J. Press (Padstow) Ltd, Padstow, Cornwall
© Kathleen Jones and A. J. Fowles 1984

Library of Congress Cataloging in Publication Data

Jones, Kathleen, 1922–

Ideas on institutions.
Bibliography:p.
Includes index.
1. Institutional care — Addresses, essays, lectures.
2. Long-term care facilities — Addresses, essays, lectures.
3. Social service literature.   I. Fowles, A. J.
II. Title.
HV59.J66   1984   362'.0425   83-17824
British Library CIP data available

ISBN 0-7100-9721-2 (pbk.: v. 1)

CONTENTS

84123

PROLOGUE

When civilisation grew in the western world, it grew behind walls — in castles and monasteries and small crowded cities; and the outcasts lived in the forests — madmen and idiots, lepers and escaped slaves, outlaws and felons, some victims and some predators. The gate and the drawbridge were signs of safety, because freedom was dangerous.

Then the position was reversed. The forests were felled, and the Rule of Law was established; and the victims and the predators were in their turn confined behind walls, in hospitals and asylums, in poorhouses and workhouses, in gaols and bridewells. Sometimes this was done out of kindness, and sometimes out of fear; but as society grew harsh with industrialisation, the result was often much the same in either case: an institutional system which held a captive population. Many people tried to make it more humane, but the system proved curiously resistant to improvement.

In the second half of the twentieth century, the institutional walls were breached. Social scientists advocated the abolition of the institution, because they thought the system was beyond reform. Politicians and civil servants promoted community care, because they hoped it would be better, and knew it would be cheaper. Room was found in the cities for the harmless and the tolerable; but there remained the problem of 'the mad and the bad' — the people the community could not or would not tolerate.

Then the money began to run out.

As economic recession deepened, fear increased and compassion evaporated. Cuts in public expenditure meant that resources for both institutional and community care were restricted; and politicians and civil servants began to argue that the social experiments of earlier years were an unnecessary extravagance. Society became harsher and more punitive. There was mass unemployment and trouble in the cities, and the community was not (if it ever had been) either welcoming or supportive. The rich began to barricade themselves behind walls again, protected by electronic security devices to keep out the predators, while the victims were left to get on as best they could. The Rule of Law became the Rule of Law and Order, and there was a fresh enthusiasm for building and filling prisons. In the old institutions, the chronic or long-stay populations remained in steadily worsening conditions — the hard core of the problem; and 'institutional or community care?' began to look like a zero sum game, because there were no right answers.

INTRODUCTION

One of us has experience of research in mental hospitals and mental handicap hospitals, and the other has experience of prison research. We share a concern about people who have to live in institutions[1] for long periods of time, and about what institutions can do to them.

We both think that institutional living will continue in the western world on a considerable scale, despite the energetic efforts of many public authorities to reduce or abolish it; that many institutions are now substantially worse than they were twenty years ago, despite energetic attempts to make them better; and that there are common features in apparently disparate types of institutional care and custody which made it useful to explore ideas across the administrative boundaries of particular services.

This review of the major literature of the past two decades has been written to clear our own minds on a difficult and tangled subject. Some of the books we examine are strident and polemical. They have often been uncritically rejected by practitioners, who found them unhelpful, and uncritically accepted by academics and their students, who have turned such concepts as 'total institution', 'institutional neurosis' and 'carceral power' into catch-phrases. In this literature can be found sweeping statements, massive generalisations, and some fairly shoddy reasoning; but also disturbing insight, sound scholarship and lively argument — and there are some important ideas and principles which can be used as a basis for further research. Much of the work has not previously been subjected to sustained and coherent analysis.

1

We have selected the writers who seemed to us to have made major contributions either in terms of what they had to say, or in terms of their impact on the reading public (which is not always the same thing). We have tried to state their cases fairly, to examine their professional backgrounds, their ideologies, their methods and their conclusions, and to sift out what we have learned from their work.

The collection begins with the writing of Erving Goffman, Michel Foucault and Thomas Szasz, all of whom published their first major studies on the institutional theme in 1961. They were to shatter a consensus in which liberal penologists assumed that the purpose of imprisonment was to reform, and that understanding and counselling could turn offenders away from a life of crime, while liberal psychiatrists placed their faith in psychodynamic group therapy and good staff relations. Benign prison governors and benign medical super-intendents were told that they and their staffs were agents of social control; that prisoners and mental patients lived in social worlds of which they knew little or nothing; that prisons created criminals, and mental hospitals created mental illness. Goffman's devastating insights made a wider analysis possible, and punctured many institutional pretences. Foucault's powerful attacks, at first imperfectly understood in the English-speaking world, added a tone of deep scepticism and despair. Szasz, the libertarian psychotherapist, portrayed psychiatric examination as the modern equivalent of the Inquisition.

The first three demolition experts were two North Americans (neither born in the United States: Goffman was born in Canada, and Szasz in Budapest) and a very Parisian Frenchman. They differed in experience, in knowledge bases, and in intellectual interests. All they had in common was the belief that institutional life was dehumanising; but the note, once struck, reverberated across the Atlantic and the English Channel. Concepts and new phrases were taken up, applied and misapplied, used and misused by subsequent writers. We have tried to avoid writing a history of ideas — a complex and difficult task across three countries and twenty years — and to stay close to the original writing in each case.

The movement was taken up in Britain in a form which to our knowledge has no parallel in the United States or in

France: a series of empirical studies which documented the evidence of institutional living in detail, illustrating the theoretical points and providing a wealth of factual data to back them. From this body of material, we have selected four outstanding examples for Part II: Russell Barton's *Institutional Neurosis*, which suggested the existence of a new disease entity; Peter Townsend's *The Last Refuge*, a monumental study of old people in residential care; Terence and Pauline Morris's *Pentonville*, a study of a London prison which became a classic in criminology; and *Sans Everything*, a symposium by a somewhat mysterious organisation called AEGIS (Aid for the Elderly in Government Institutions), which paved the way for a series of official hospital inquiries in the 1970s.

Part III crosses the Atlantic again, and shows the movement going in different intellectual directions. We have included David Rothman's two historical studies of how and why the United States constructed institutions, and how and why reform movements failed. N. N. Kittrie's *The Right to be Different* introduces a new perspective — a wide-ranging legal attack on the compulsory treatment of a variety of 'deviants', including the mentally ill, juvenile delinquents and drug abusers. The last three selections all come from the field of penology: Stanley Cohen and Laurie Taylor's *Psychological Survival* is a disturbing analysis of the lives of long-term prisoners in a maximum security wing. Haney, Banks and Zimbardo, three Stanford psychologists, set up their own 'simulated prison' in California to study the effects of prison conditions in the personalities of prisoners and their guards; and King and Elliott studied Albany Prison in the Isle of Wight, to find out how a promising therapeutic experiment went wrong.

With the exception of Michel Foucault, whose writings are now easily available in English, our writers are all British or North American. The anti-institutional movement has spread to many other countries. In Italy, for example, the work of Franco Basaglia[2] and Melossi and Pavarini's *Carcere e fabbrica*[3] follows similar lines, sharpened by Italian attempts to abolish mental hospitals altogether. In concentrating on British and American texts, we do not wish to imply that there is not equally important work to be found elsewhere;

but our knowledge and our linguistic powers are limited.

The theme of the intellectual attack on institutional care is one in which a number of other themes inevitably become interwoven: the development of community care in Britain, and of 'deinstitutionalization' in the United States, and the policy reasons for both; the professional conflict between lawyers and psychiatrists; the growing disenchantment with social therapy, and the increasing use of behaviour modification and drug treatments; the development of patients' rights and prisoners' rights movements; the demoralisation and the increasing unionisation of institutional staffs. These are themes which must be developed outside the confines of the present study; but we will briefly substantiate our statement that institutions are a matter for continuing concern.

In 1982, we carried out a survey[4] of trends in the residential populations in England and Wales of five types of institutions: mental hospitals, mental handicap hospitals, penal establishments (prisons, Borstals and detention centres), geriatric hospitals and units, and homes for the aged and handicapped. In 1960-1, the total population was 366.8 thousand. In 1978-80, despite all the efforts made to develop community care, it had risen to 380.0 thousand. While the increase in institutional accommodation was smaller than the increase in total population (the figures were 3½ per cent and 6 per cent respectively) the reality was very far from the massive run-down anticipated by academics and policy-makers alike. The major change was in the type of accommodation: the population of local authority homes, chiefly for old people, had increased by 80 per cent, but it was difficult to determine how far this reflected the pressures of an ageing population rather than a move from traditional kinds of institutional care. We were also doubtful about the policy implications of the change. There are some good small homes, but there are also some large ones which are very 'institutional' in character. The change may be more a matter of switching from central government to local government financing than providing a better quality of life for residents.

In the same period, the mental hospital population had decreased by some 42 per cent, and that of mental handicap hospitals by 24 per cent; but the population of geriatric hospitals and units had increased slightly, and the prison population had risen by over 60 per cent. Even if all local authority homes were excluded from the calculation, nearly a quarter of a million adults in England and Wales were still living in institutions.

Where detailed figures were available for length of stay in the traditional institutions, they indicated an increasing bifurcation between a small, rapidly changing, short-stay population, and a large long-stay population as remote from normal living conditions as ever; and the long-stay population was less likely to be rehabilitated than in the past, because such alternatives as the community had to offer had already been tried before admission, and had failed.

In the United States over the same two decades, the mental hospital population decreased by a staggering 72 per cent, chiefly as a result of the development of Community Mental Health Centers; facilities for mental retardation decreased by 21 per cent; but the population of federal and state prisons rose by over 40 per cent.[5] There is no detailed information on the population of local jails, which are thought to hold about four times as many prisoners as federal and state prisons taken together.[6] Meanwhile, the term 'transinstitutionaliz- ation' has been coined to describe the condition of those transferred from state facilities to private nursing homes, hostels and 'after-care' facilities, often of very dubious quality and standards.[7] Community Mental Health Centers are run- ning out of federal funding — and some are developing in- patient beds, while the mental hospital is frequently spoken of as necessary 'back-up'.

Institutions are changing, but they are not disappearing; and the changes may be more a matter of what Andrew Scull has called 'word-magic',[8] than of improvement in conditions. The failure of the liberal promise, together with increasing economic stringency, has opened the way for harsher philos- ophies and less humane policies. The diversification of types of care across the public and private sectors means that it is more difficult than in the past to monitor conditions; and official statistics now give only a very inadequate guide to what is happening.

This study of the literature is a first contribution towards building a new framework for thinking about institutions.

PART I
The springs of protest

1 GOFFMAN: THE RADICAL

The publication of Erving Goffman's *Asylums* in 1961 introduced a sociological dimension into a discussion previously dominated by practitioners. A cross-service approach stressed the similarities in apparently disparate kinds of institutions — prisons, concentration camps, mental hospitals, even convents and army barracks. Goffman stood existing formulations — even liberal and humane formulations — on their heads, because he emphasised the importance of inmate perceptions rather than the perceptions of senior staff in management roles.

Two curious features stand out: the first is that Goffman is not really interested in institutions as such. Jason Ditton's *The View from Goffman* (1980) provides a bibliographic exegesis of his work, with a series of commentaries, and it is plain that his main thread of interest is in symbolic interactionism. The analysis which has provided so much groundwork for discussion on institutional mangement is almost incidental to a developing body of work which runs from Goffman's MA dissertation on 'Some Characteristics of Response to Depicted Experience' (1949) through his PhD thesis on 'Communication Conduct in an Island Community' and such well-known works as *The Presentation of Self in Everyday Life* (1959), *Behaviour in Public Places* (1963), and *Interaction Ritual* (1967) to *Frame Analysis* (1974). Goffman comments, provides startling insights, and passes on to other preoccupations. Only *Stigma* (1963) touches an allied theme.

The second feature is that, while many people quote Goffman on institutional life, there is little in the way of serious analysis of what he said. Jason Ditton notes that 'Typically, Goffman is cited by many yet examined by few'[1] and if this is true of his work as a whole, it is even more true of the somewhat specialised field of institutional care. People who run institutions seldom have much background in sociological theory. Sociologists, for their part, have little practical knowledge of, or experience in, the problems of running institutions. The majority take the view that institutions are power structures arising from a particular system of social control. They may be referred to in order to illustrate the defects of that system, but they are of no particular interest in their own right. Goffman's thinking crosses these two worlds.

Goffman and the radical view

Erving Goffman was writing from within a sociological tradition which is usually traced back to the work of Edwin Lemert in the early 1950s,[2] and which reached systematic exposition in Howard Becker's edition of *The Other Side* in 1964.[3] The Becker volume includes Kai Erikson's 'Notes on the Sociology of Deviance',[4] which provides a succinct summary of the argument. Erikson argues that deviant behaviour is only properly understood in an interactionist perspective. It can be defined as

> conduct which is generally thought to require the attention of social control agencies — that is, conduct about which 'something should be done' . . . Deviance is not a property *inherent* in certain forms of behaviour; it is a property *conferred upon* these forms by audiences which directly or indirectly witness them.

Erikson points out that most people conform to social expectations most of the time. When the community elects to bring sanctions against one of its members for misbehaviour

> it is responding to a few deviant details set within a vast array of entirely acceptable conduct. Thus it happens that a moment of deviation may become the measure of a person's position in society. He may be jailed or hospitalised,

certified as a full-time deviant, despite the fact that only a fraction of his behaviour was in any way unusual or dangerous. The community has taken note of a few scattered particles of behaviour, and has decided that they reflect what kind of person he 'really' is.

The social control mechanism which leads to institutionalisation is arbitrary and class-biased, penalising the poor, the black and the immigrant. Erikson is less interested in what happens to the deviant than in what the deviant represents: he has a symbolic importance, showing us 'the difference between the inside of the group and the outside'. Deviance, he argues, does not disrupt societal stability: it preserves it, reinforcing group norms and providing 'on-going drama at the edge of group space'.

Institutions such as prisons and mental hospitals therefore do not cure deviant behaviour: they perpetuate it, gathering 'marginal people into tightly segregated groups' and reinforcing their sense of alienation from the rest of the community. The basic contention is that the rest of us need prisons in order to be good, and mental hospitals in order to stay sane.

By the time Goffman wrote 'The Moral Career of the Mental Patient', these new ideas were becoming current in American schools of sociology. They were revolutionary in the literal sense of the term, since they challenged the conventional wisdom about the function of prisons and mental hospitals. Goffman provided the first major cross-service analysis in this vein, focussing on the mechanics of deprivation and detention apparently common to a number of types of institution which had previously only been considered separately. He rejected the official staff perspective, choosing instead to adopt the perspective of the inmates as a corrective to the volume of official writing. Despite all that has been written in the quarter of a century since this paper was originally delivered, little has been added to his analysis in the way of elaboration. It still stands as basic to a study of institutional life, and to much of the discussion in our subsequent chapters.

The book, which was originally published by Doubleday of New York in an Anchor Books edition, consists of four papers: 'On the Characteristics of Total Institutions', 'The Moral

Career of the Mental Patient', 'The Underlife of a Public
Institution' and 'The Medical Model and Mental Hospitalisation'. Each of these takes up a particular facet of a coherent
argument on institutional processes.

Total institutions

Goffman introduced the term 'total institution' and defined
it more carefully than many of his imitators have done. A
'total institution' is 'a place of residence and work where a
large number of like-situated individuals, cut off from the
wider society for an appreciable period of time, together lead
an enclosed, formally administered round of life'.[5]

All institutions are not total institutions, though 'every
institution has encompassing tendencies'; but some institutions, such as homes for the blind or the aged, mental hospitals, prisons, concentration camps, army barracks, boarding
schools and monasteries or convents, are 'encompassing to a
degree discontinuously greater than the ones next in line'.

Goffman's concept of the 'total institution' can be represented as follows: there is a continuum from open to closed
institutions, but there is a break towards the closed end,
separating off a group of closed, or nearly closed, institutions
which can be described as 'total'.

In fact, both the completely open institution and the completely closed institution are abstractions. No institution is
ever completely open: if it were, it would have no distinguishing characteristics at all. No institution is ever completely
closed. If it were, it would die off. Open systems theory has
taught us that all human systems are dependent to some
extent on their immediate environment, and that they cannot
survive without it. A mental hospital or prison imports staff,
inmates, policy, material supplies and public reactions from
the outside world; it exports staff on completion of contract,
inmates on completion of stay or sentence, empirical material
which may affect policy, the product of work programmes
(mailbags, assembled electric switches, carpentry, scrubbing
brushes, fancy paper hats, those curious toys which are made
in occupational therapy, and so on), garbage, and stories of
strike, threat and crisis which form the basis of public reactions.

All sorts of people cross the boundary: inspectors, professional superiors, inmates' visitors, research workers, workmen, students, policemen, magistrates and others. But these considerations do not invalidate Goffman's argument about the relatively closed or 'total' institution. His contention is that this group of institutions has features in common: he qualifies it by adding that none of these features is specific to them, and that not all of the features may be found in any one of them. What he proposes is not a list of features to be identified in all cases, but a constellation of features which tend to occur in most cases, and which have some relation to each other. He is embarking on a sort of verbal cluster analysis. What he describes as a 'total institution' will probably not fit any real-life institution exactly. It is a Weberian ideal type against which the practices of real-life institutions may be measured.

It is important to clarify this definition, because the term 'total institution' has become something of a catch-phrase, and is often applied unthinkingly to particular prisons or mental hospitals. Goffman is much more scholarly than some of his imitators, and his frame of reference is precisely defined.

'Total institutions' have four main characteristics: batch living, binary management, the inmate role, and the institutional perspective.

'Batch living' describes a situation where 'each phase of the member's daily activity is carried on in the immediate company of a large batch of others, all of whom are treated alike, and required to do the same thing together'. It is the antithesis of individual living, where there are large areas of life which may be pursued on a basis of personal choice. It is characterised by a bureaucratic form of management, a system of formal rules and regulations, and a tight schedule which allows little or no free time. It allows the inmate no freedom of movement between different social groups, and no choice of companions: he lives with the same group of people, selected and defined by outside authority, twenty-four hours a day, without variety or respite. This is contrasted with 'a basic arrangement in modern society. . . . the individual tends to sleep, play and work in different places, with different co-participants, under different authorities, and without an over-all rational plan.'[6] In the institutional situation, individuals are not merely constrained by, but are violently attacked by, the system. They live under surveillance, and any infraction of the rules 'is likely to stand out in relief against the visible, constantly examined compliance of the others'.

Goffman is not clear which came first, the 'large blocks of managed people' or the staff who manage them; but 'each is made for the other'. 'Total institutions' typically consist of these two groups of people, the managers and the managed — staff and patients, prison officers and prisoners, teachers and pupils.

This is 'binary management': 'Two different social and cultural worlds develop, jogging alongside each other with points of official contact, but little mutual penetration.'[7] The managers have power, and social distance is their weapon. They exercise this most tellingly in withholding information, so that the managed exist in 'blind dependency', unable to control their own destinies. The very fact of being an inmate is degrading: 'Staff tend to feel superior, and righteous. Inmates tend . . . to feel inferior, weak, unworthy and guilty.'[8] Because the two groups do not and cannot know each other as individuals, they set up antagonistic stereotypes. Staff tend to see all patients or prisoners or pupils as being alike — 'bitter, secretive and untrustworthy'. The managed draw similar hostile pictures of the managers. The two groups may use a special tone of voice in talking to each other, and informal conversation and social mixing may be frowned upon by both sides.

How do ordinary people, with their own way of life and personal networks and round of activities, become inmates? Goffman thinks that this is not a process of 'acculturation', which involves moving from one culture to another, but of 'disculturation' or 'role-stripping' so powerful that the individual who is subjected to it may be rendered incapable of normal living when he returns to the community. He has been reduced from a person with many roles to a cypher with one: the 'inmate role'.

Much of this process is achieved through admission procedures, which Goffman sees as 'a series of abasements, degradations, humiliations and profanations of self' — a mortification process. Institutions are 'the forcing houses for changing persons'. To become an inmate involves a total break with the past, symbolised by the acquisition of a new name or number, uniform clothing, and the restriction or confiscation of personal possessions. All this may be done in a highly ritualised admission procedure in which the inmate may be forced to recite his life history, take a bath, possibly without privacy, and submit to weighing, finger-printing, intrusive medical examination and head-shaving. The overt reason for these activities is administrative necessity: the real purpose is role dispossession. The bath, in particular, is a highly symbolic ritual, involving physical nakedness as the midpoint of a process of abandoning one life for another. 'The new arrival allows himself to be shaped and coded into an object that can be fed into the administrative machinery of the establishment, to be worked on smoothly by routine operation.'[9] The new clothes are likely to be standard issue, the property of the establishment. Combined with a loss of 'personal maintenance equipment' such as combs, shaving sets or cosmetics, they create a new and humiliating appearance. The process is one of personal defacement.

As the stay is prolonged, so the loss of personal identity becomes more marked. There may be systematic violation of privacy through the practice of group or individual confession. The inmate's defences may be repeatedly collapsed by a process called 'looping', where the mere fact of defence is taken as proof of guilt.[10] There may be 'indignities of speech or action' — inmates are forced to beg humbly for a glass of water or a light for a cigarette, to move or speak in a markedly deferential way indicating their lowly status. They may be beaten, or subjected to electric shock treatment, or physically contaminated — there are some particularly nasty examples drawn from concentration camps and political prisons.

Control may be kept by means of a system of rewards and punishments, petty by outside standards, but assuming Pavlovian dimensions in a situation of deprivation. Rules may not be made fully explicit. The inmate cannot appeal to them for protection, and he may break them unwittingly, and be punished for it. Like Kafka's K., he exists in a half-world of guilt and apprehension. He has no privacy, no rights, and no dignity.

How does the inmate survive these attacks on his personality? Goffman suggests four types of 'secondary adjustment'[11]:—

(i)   the inmate may withdraw, cutting himself off from contact;
(ii) he may become intransigent, and fight the system;
(iii) he may, in a vivid phrase, become 'colonised', paying lip-service to the system like the inhabitant of some African or Asian country awaiting the day of independence;
(iv) he may become converted, genuinely accepting the institution's view of himself, and what is acceptable behaviour.

The last of these is not really survival, but a kind of personal extinction. Curiously, and on the face of it illogically, it is the only adjustment acceptable to the authorities of the institution. Any attempt by the inmate to immunise himself against the destructive forces focussed on him will be seen as non-co-operation, and may be used as an excuse to detain him longer.

He may develop a 'line', a sort of edited account of how he came to be an inmate, repeated to his fellows and to anyone else who will listen with increasing self-pity. He may have a sense of 'dead and heavy-hanging time' — of life wasted, and the months or years ticking away without gain or satisfaction. Against these reactions, the authorities offer 'the institutional perspective': a view of life which denies his individual perspective and validates the institution's existence. It is promoted by such means as the house magazine, the annual party, the institutional theatrical, the Open Day and the Sports Day, which create an artificial sense of community. These formal events offer certain minor possibilities of role release for the inmate — recognised and routinised liberties, forbidden in normal circumstances, may be allowable; but the total effect is to reinforce the power of the institution, and the 'assault on the self': 'These ceremonial practices are well suited to a Durkheimian analysis: a society dangerously split into inmates and staff can through these ceremonies hold itself together.'[12]

The moral career of the mental patient

The second essay is a dynamic and original elaboration,

of what Goffman has to say about the 'inmate role'. Mental patients (like doctors or lawyers or politicians) have careers, though the course is downwards rather than upwards. First comes the pre-patient phase: something is wrong, the individual is somehow out of gear with his social setting and the people around him. At this stage, there may well be alternative definitions of the situation, and possible alternative outcomes. Then comes a precipitating factor, which may be outside the patient's control:-

> a psychotic man is tolerated by his wife until she finds herself a boy friend . . . an alcoholic is sent to a mental hospital because the jail is full, a drug addict because he declines to avail himself of psychiatric treatment on the outside . . .[13]

At this point, the 'betrayal funnel' comes into operation: the pre-patient goes for an interview with a psychiatrist or some other professional in the understanding that he is a free individual, and then finds that his relatives or friends have a prior understanding with that person from which he is excluded. He is passed from hand to hand, often with reassurances that he should see another doctor or that he is only in need of a rest, until the time when the sponsoring relative 'nonchalantly goes back . . . into a world . . . incredibly thick with freedoms and privileges' while he is left 'in a psychiatric ward, stripped of almost everything'.

He is put through the admission procedure, forced to humble himself, taught the consequences of rebellion or disobedience or mere questioning. He is induced to see himself as a failure, someone who has suffered a social collapse:—

> Once lodged on a given ward, the patient is firmly instructed that the restrictions and deprivations he encounters are not due to such blind forces as tradition or economy — and hence dissociable from self — but are intentional parts of his treatment, part of his need at the time, and therefore an expression of the state that his self has fallen into.[14]

The fact that he is in a mental hospital is taken as *prima facie* evidence that he is the kind of person mental hospitals exist to treat. There is a particularly valuable section on case records, and the way in which they are framed to support this contention. The record will not include data on those occasions in his life when he has coped honorably and effectively with difficulties, nor will it include a rough sampling of all the difficulties he has faced, and the ways in which he has coped with them. Instead, it will concentrate exclusively on his failures or alleged failures, often with a lavish use of social labelling, judgmental attitudes and inferences as to his motivation which would be considered libellous in any other setting.

Staff conferences and 'the most informal of levels, the lunchtime and coffee-break small-talk of staff' add gossip to distorted fact, till the hospital is systematically producing and circulating precisely the kind of information about the patient which he would normally like to hide, embroidered with stereotypes and distortions. The patient suffers a kind of moral fatigue in which his real personality may collapse, and he becomes increasingly capable of the kind of acts and motives which are being attributed to him. 'He can learn at least for a time . . . the amoral acts of shamelessness.'

The underlife of a public institution

In the third paper, Goffman returns to the theme of 'secondary adjustment', the ways in which people in institutions survive by making adaptations to the system. This time, he is thinking less of major adjustments by patients — withdrawal, intransigence, colonisation, conversion — than of the small ways in which both staff and inmates may make the system serve their personal ends. These add up to the 'underlife' which runs alongside the official life sanctioned by rules and regulations. Staff may make use of patients as baby-sitters, gardeners and handymen, send them on errands, 'liberate' food intended for the inmates from wards or kitchens, sleep on night duty or misappropriate patient funds. Patients, denied these opportunities, have to be content with 'make-dos', using toilet paper for Kleenex, scavenging from the refuse dumps, hoarding small articles, getting an extra helping of some favourite food, manoeuvring themselves into hospital work which provides minor satisfactions — new books for the library assistant, extra food for those who work in the kitchens, better-fitting clothes for those in the clothing store. Such practices may be half-legitimated in the sense that they are well-known and tolerated, though not officially acknowledged.

In this long and rather wandering paper, Goffman touches on a number of other features of institutional under-life: the 'piston effect' which makes it easy for any member of staff introducing a new activity for patients to claim that it is a therapeutic success, because patients will be enthusiastic about almost anything that gets them off the ward for an hour or two; the social use of space, whereby certain areas are explicitly or tacitly agreed to be out of bounds to certain people, while others are used for free assembly, and those who seek privacy may still find it in odd corners; the demarcation of personal territory in day wards and dormitories, and the use of pin-ups, photographs and small personal articles to define it; the practice of 'stashing', or carrying one's personal possessions around in a handbag, kitbag or pillow-case, because there is no adequate locker space, and soap or food or clothes or money might be stolen; practices of smuggling, sale, barter and gambling which help to create an illicit power structure. Complex patterns of economic and social exchange are identified and illustrated.

'When existence is cut to the bone,' Goffman writes, 'we can learn what people do to flesh out their lives.' These are means of self-defence against the destructive forces of the institution, against the 'assault on the self'; and Goffman ends with the sombre thought that 'Our status is backed by the solid buildings of the world, while our sense of personal identity often resides in the cracks.'[15]

The medical model and mental hospitalisation

The final paper, more elegantly constructed, is subtitled 'Some Notes on the Vicissitudes of the Tinkering Trades'. It is based on the concept of the 'repair cycle' and on an analogy between putting a possession, such as a car, in for repair, and putting oneself in for repair. In each case, there is a process — observation, diagnosis, prescription, treatment. The faulty machine is run through, the malfunctioning pin-pointed, a repair takes place, the machine is run again to check that it works satis-factorily, and it is returned 'as good as new' or something like it. In the case of a mechanical possession we take it for granted that the workshop will stop any further damage, that the object still belongs to its owner, and that the repair can be carried out at a time convenient to him. There is a 'framework of rights and duties' forming 'a kind of matrix of anxiety and doubt'. The client wonders whether the repairer is competent, whether he will act in the client's interests or his own, and whether his fee will be reasonable or exorbitant. The repairer or server wonders whether the client has confidence in him, whether he has 'shopped around' and whether he will pay the charges when the work is done.

The difficulties of this relationship are greatly increased when the object to be serviced is one's self, for 'the client is very interested in what is happening to his body, and in a good position to see what is being done'. One solution for the medical repair man is 'the wonderful brand of non-person treatment' in which he greets the patient and says goodbye to him in normal fashion, but in between treats him as though he were an object left behind by its owner. If bad news has to be given to a patient, this is usually done in the presence of a relative, and an interesting split occurs: the relative becomes the client, while the patient remains an object.

This is particularly the case when the doctor's diagnosis involves mental hospital admission, for the service to be given may be a service to relatives or neighbours rather than to the patient himself. So the patient is processed into hospital, where the psychiatrist claims to treat the whole person, but does not regard him as a person, and indeed may leave him largely to the care of nurses and attendants. His social roles stripped away and his behaviour patterns altered, he has no opportunities of demonstrating normal functioning. 'A re-fraction of conduct thus occurs, the walls of the institution acting like a thick and vaulted prism.'

In order to obtain treatment, the patient has to learn how to present himself:–

a contrite admission of illness stated in modestly untech-nical terms, and a sincerely expressed desire to undergo a change of self through psychiatric treatment. In short, there is a psychiatric line the patient must follow if the psychiatrist is to be affirmed as a medical server.[16]

The 'unschooled' patient is much more likely to respond to his situation by being angry or reproachful or pleading to go home; but these reactions invalidate the psychiatrist's professional position. In order to defend it, he is likely to regard any one of them not as a direct communication, but as evidence of illness: so psychiatrist and patient are 'doomed by the institutional context to a false and difficult relationship'. Some psychiatrists, recognising this, turn from individual therapy to family therapy, group therapy, research or paper work or staff groups in order to escape; but the best way for the psychiatrist to solve his problem is 'to leave the state mental hospital as soon as he can afford to'.

The paper ends with some reflections on 'the danger mandate' — the view that there are some aspects of human relationships so difficult or dangerous that only a qualified psychiatrist is able to undertake them — and a shrewd passage on hospital double-talk: both concepts illustrate ways in which the expertness of the doctor is reinforced at the patient's expense. The 'danger mandate' discounts the contribution of nursing and other staff, while double-talk involves a constant series of judgments favourable to the institution. The ward door is locked 'to give the patient a sense of security'. Regimentation is 'therapeutic regularity'. The forced taking of drugs to give the hospital authorities the opportunity to reduce night staff is called 'sedation' or 'medication'. The removal of a patient's teeth is called 'treatment for biting', and a hysterectomy is described as 'treatment for sexual promiscuity': 'In all of these cases, the medical action is presented to the patient and his relatives as an individual service, but what is being serviced here is the institution.'[17]

Goffman's contribution

Empirical findings cannot disprove Goffman's assertions, for the 'cluster analysis' method means that he is immune from disproof. If he had claimed that *all* mental hospitals (or other types of institution) followed certain practices, or that *no* mental hospitals followed other, more desirable practices, one could bring real-life experience to bear on what he says; but the statement that none of the features he describes is specific to institutions, and that not all of them may be found in any one institution, lifts him above argument and rebuttal into the realms of abstract theory. There is no hypothesis capable of being tested; yet seldom can abstract theory have been so firmly buttressed with practical example. The method enables him to see what he wants to see, and to ignore what he does not, without fear of criticism. It is, to say the least, ingenious.

The analysis focussed and articulated the experience of many people who had lived and worked (whether as patients or as staff) in institutions. The picture of bureaucratisation and depersonalisation, of the substitution of institutional values for human values, was powerful, compelling and true. It was all the more powerful because the story was told without any apparent sense of moral outrage: this was what life in an institution was like, and nothing much could be done about it. 'If all the mental hospitals in a given region were emptied and closed down today, tomorrow relatives, police and judges would raise a clamor for new ones; and these true clients of the mental hospital would demand an institution to satisfy their need.'[18]

But if the picture is true, it has to be said that it is not the whole truth; and of course, Goffman did not intend it to be. His aim was to set up a model against which reality could be measured, rather than to describe reality itself. Readers (and there were many of them in the sociology departments of universities and polytechnics) who assumed that all institutions were 'total institutions' and that he had provided a full description of their operation missed the point. Reformers who complained that he took no account of the many improvements in mental hospitals in the 1950s — the therapeutic community systems, the training schemes, the open door policies, the parole policies — similarly missed the point; but the book may nevertheless have been damaging because it was widely misunderstood. One publisher advertised it under the headline 'What really goes on in mental hospitals?'

Though the book is primarily theoretical, the supporting

evidence for Goffman's arguments are drawn from two kinds of sources, and both are curious in nature. There is mention in the introduction of first-hand research, but the empirical base is extremely narrow. It consists of one year's work, in 1955-6, in St Elizabeth's Hospital, Washington, D.C. spent as 'assistant to the athletic director'. This post apparently allowed Goffman to spend his time with the inmates in participant observation without being identified with the staff world. His aim was to redress the balance by ignoring staff views as so many other accounts had ignored inmates' views. Dr Winfred (misprinted 'Winifred') Overholser read his manuscript and 'made helpful corrections regarding some outright errors of fact', but he cannot have learned much about hospital policy, or about the problems of running it. It is horrifying to learn that patients scavenged from the refuse bins, but one wants to know why. Was it because the meals served were inadequate in quantity? Because the nurses stole the food? Because the cooks overestimated the patients' requirements? Because some patients over-ate for emotional compensation? Were the refuse bins general rubbish bins or (slightly less horrifying) pig bins? Here is a limited but very important aspect of hospital life on which it would be interesting and of practical value to have a tracer study showing the handling of provision accounts and food all the way from the Hospital Treasurer through to the serving of the meal and the refuse bin; but Goffman does not undertake this. He delivers his findings — patients eat the food out of the refuse bins, this is a secondary adjustment — and passes on to another subject.

St Elizabeth's Hospital, Washington is an unusual institution. Its catchment area is the District of Columbia. From the outside, it is not unattractive — built in parkland some way out of the capital city, and constructed on the villa system. One member of staff described it recently as the hospital which takes 'every nut who wants to kill the President, and every nut who thinks he is the President'. Perhaps that is staff mythology; what is possibly more relevant is that the catchment area is something like 90 per cent black, and that the hospital population reflects this. In 1955-6, when Goffman worked there, the wards were still racially segregated — a fact which he does not mention.

The experience at St Elizabeth's forms the basis of analysis of mental hospitals. It is backed by citations from written sources, but Goffman's method and orientation allow him to abstract from these sources only what he wants, which is the critical material. He is under no obligation to quote all the constructive policies or to balance his account with extracts from the work of social psychiatrists who reject the medical service model and try to build on good human relationships.

Evidence about other kinds of institutions comes from documentary sources. This has advantages — the book is extremely full in documentation, and the experiences quoted, drawn from wide reading, vividly support the main arguments; but the disadvantage is that his sources are highly selective. The reader is often asked to view an experience through the eyes of a highly articulate and very atypical observer. The source for the account of life in the Royal Air Force is T. E. Lawrence's *The Mint* — and Lawrence — ex-colonel, hero of the Desert War, friend of sheiks and prime ministers and archbishops — must surely have been the most unusual recruit ever to join the RAF. 'Abbeys, convents, monasteries and other cloisters' (Goffman is exceedingly vague on religious detail) are seen in the light of the Rule of St Benedict, and Kathryn Hulme's *The Nun's Story*; the account of a remarkable woman, but a failed nun. Prison is seen through the eyes of Brendan Behan (but in fact Behan was in Borstal, which is not the same, and again Goffman is vague on detail), and boarding school through the eyes of George Orwell, son of an Indian High Court judge, but in every sense a rebel from the English class system. All these writers, and others quoted, are 'outsiders' — people who refused to fit into a particular system, and whose reaction was one of intransigence. Too angry to internalise their conflicts, too tough to be forced into conformity, they represent the defiance of the human spirit against the System. Their struggles are important, sometimes archetypal, but they are special people, and their hypersensitive reactions are not necessarily those of the average inmate. How many mute inglorious T. E. Lawrences are there in the RAF?

A further criticism concerns Goffman's sociological method. The use of an ideal type approach is justifiable, but it has one major disadvantage: it focuses attention on the similarities between institutions (many of them deplorable) and it does not allow for the exploration of differences between them. Goffman does mention that he is 'establishing common features with the hope of highlighting significant differences later', but this promise of a second approach never materialises.

There is a thesis in *Asylums* which is never explicitly stated, but which is repeatedly assumed without question: that inmates are put into institutions not because they want to go there or need to go there, but because other people put them there. Like so much else in Goffman's work this is true (in the sense that it does happen), but not universally true. The view that society conspires to foist its own ills on the so-called prisoner or patient, who is scapegoated into the institution, assumes that the social functioning of all or most such people is normal before 'society' and the institution exerted their evil influences. This view ignores the reality, the pain and the destructiveness of grossly abnormal behaviour. Perhaps it is significant that such views (shared by a number of other writers to be discussed later) only became current after the development of the psychotropic drugs in 1953-4. These drugs suppress many of the behavioural symptoms of mental illness. Since they are very widely prescribed in the industrialised world, it is unlikely that any observers who were not working in mental hospitals before that date, or who have not visited mental hospitals in developing countries (where few drugs are in use today) have much appreciation of what an untreated case involves in the way of personal disintegration. No observer who has either of these experiences is likely to doubt the reality of mental illness, or the need for treatment.

Goffman looked at mental hospitals, loosed his shafts of insight, and moved on to other fields of study. Within his own frame of reference, the work is complete, and his approach entirely justifiable. Those of us who try to use it for practical purposes have to realise that it is not, and was not intended to be, a guide to action. Within our frame of reference, it must be recognised as partial evidence: it outlines an ideal type (which is an extreme case), it concentrates on inmate views and ignores policy issues, it is based on highly selective data, it stresses similarities and ignores differences, and it shows little understanding of the problems of severely abnormal behaviour, or of running a stigmatised and under-financed service. All the same, sometimes wayward, and frequently misunderstood, Goffman provides in *Asylums* our best guide to the power of the institution, and the power of the individual to resist it.

2 FOUCAULT:
THE EXCAVATOR

Goffman's *Asylums* was translated into French in 1968, when a reviewer from the *Revue Française Sociologique* found it 'essentiellement nord-americaine'.[1] French social scientists were by that time much more concerned with the work of Michel Foucault, who produced his strange and highly symbolic *Histoire de la Folie* in 1961.[2] This study percolated slowly into the consciousness of the English-speaking world until 1965, when the first English version was published in New York under the title *Madness and Civilisation*.[3] Two very different and equally original contributions to the institutional debate thus crossed the Atlantic in opposite directions.

Though Goffman's work is very frequently referred to by other scholars, he has, strictly speaking, no followers. What he wrote was complete in itself. It could be quoted and illustrated, but it could not be either amplified or tested. Foucault, on the other hand, has a number of imitators. Once the technique of digging into history and coming up with new interpretations was established, revisionist historians such as Rothman, Ignatieff or Scull[4] could do the same.

Like Goffman, Foucault is not really interested in institutions or institutional care: the subject provides him with illustrative material for other themes. The publication of the *Histoire de la Folie* was followed fourteen years later, in 1975, by *Surveiller et Punir*, translated as *Discipline and Punish*.[5] The two books may be conveniently taken together as representative of Foucault's thinking about 'the carceral city', referring respectively to mental hospitals and prisons, but they represented only a small part of his literary output over this period. Foucault's main concern is with what he calls 'the archaeology of knowledge' (carefully differentiating this from the history of ideas). His choice of a title for his Chair at the Collège de France in 1970 was 'Professor of the History of Systems of Thought'. His translator and commentator Alan Sheridan writes, 'One senses the effort that went into the exact choice and placing of words.'[6]

'Encore, ne parlera-t-on pas de Foucault,' says Philippe Robert in a review of research material on prisons.[7] 'Let us not speak of Foucault.' When one considers Foucault's reputation as a philosopher, the sweeping and dismissive nature of many of his statements, and the sheer readability of his books, it is remarkable how little he is reviewed, and how little criticised. He is either dealt with respectfully on his own ground, the august and somewhat arid reaches of French and German philosophy, or dismissed as exaggerated, pretentious and inexplicable. Because he is sweeping and dismissive, he is difficult to catch in mid-flight, so to speak. How does one pin down a writer who swoops across the centuries, rarely giving dates (and giving rather unexpected dates when he does, usually referring to events in France or in the Rhine provinces); who seldom cites other authors, apart from long-dead Frenchmen, and whose publishers often fail to provide footnotes? Peter Lazlett, attempting this difficult task for *New Society*, found him puzzling, enlightening, baffling, muddling and stimulating, and ended a review of *Discipline and Punish* by saying 'We lay down this book knowing almost nothing about why, how or even when all the fascinating changes he discusses actually happened.'[8]

We can question whether some of them ever happened on a sufficient scale to justify Foucault's claim to historical significance.

The analysis of unreason

The *Histoire de la Folie* was Foucault's doctoral thesis, largely written during his 'period of silence' when he was in self-imposed exile in Uppsala, Warsaw and Hamburg. In academic terms, it did not fit into any recognisable area of study, and the University of Paris finally accepted it as a work in the History of Science.

The full title is *Folie et déraison: histoire de la folie à l'âge classique*, and the English title is somewhat misleading, since most of the book is about 'unreason' — lyrical outbursts, flights of fancy, artistic expression and unorthodox behaviour — rather than about 'madness'. Foucault's aim is to go back beyond the late Middle Ages — the time at which he argues that a split occurred in the western world between reason and unreason — and to restore unreason to what he regards as its rightful place in human experience.

The opening theme is simply stated: until the end of the Middle Ages, the outcast of western society was the leper. Leprosy, brought home from the Middle East by the Crusaders, was the symbol of the strange and unacceptable. When it finally waned, the leprosaria were used for the confinement of 'poor vagabonds, criminals and "deranged minds" . . . the cities of the damned had found a new population'. The fear of 'grinning Death' was replaced by the fear of unreason. There follows a memorable and evocative passage on Stultifera Navis, the legendary Ship of Fools or 'drunken boat' which 'glides along the calm rivers of the Rhineland and the Flemish canals', and is the subject of a painting by Hieronymus Bosch. But the fools, criminals and vagabonds were not to remain free: by the seventeenth and eighteenth centuries, the Ship of Fools was no longer in motion: 'Behold it moored now: made fast among things and men. Retained and maintained. No longer a ship but a hospital.'[9]

'It is common knowledge,' Foucault tells us, 'that the seventeenth century created enormous houses of confinement.' This statement is followed by a reference to 'absolute power . . . lettres de cachet and arbitrary measures of imprisonment', and tied to a place, a date and an event: Paris, 1656, the foundation of the Hôpital Général. This was an administrative reorganisation of several existing establishments, including the Salpétrière, Bicêtre and the Hôpital de la Pitié, to form a resource for the poor of Paris 'of both sexes, of all ages and from all localities, of whatever breeding and birth, in whatsoever state they may be, able-bodied or invalid, sick or convalescent, curable or incurable'.[10] This 'Great Confinement' was copied in other French cities,

and spread all over Europe. It was an instrument of contain-
ment, a 'third order of repression', complementing the work
of the police and the courts. By the late eighteenth century,
'confinement had become the abusive amalgam of heterogeneous elements'; but the system 'disappeared throughout
Europe at the beginning of the nineteenth century' to be
replaced by the even more sinister régime of 'moral treatment'
as developed by Pinel and Tuke. This was a 'moral imprisonment', since the inmates of institutions were pressurised into
controlling their own emotions, rather than having them controlled by external restraints; and it led in time to the assault
on human personality represented by psychoanalysis, since
'all nineteenth century psychiatry really converges on Freud'.
The book ends with a panegyric to unreason, in which
Nietzsche and Van Gogh figure prominently.

The historical assertions of this remarkable work are so
much at variance with the interpretations of historians, and
with what we understand of recorded fact, that it would take
a very long time to deal with them fully. We might start by
pointing out that medieval leprosaria were very small – half a
dozen lepers living outside a particular town, rather than
hundreds living in regimented colonies; or that Sebastian
Brant's *Narrenschyff*, one of the chief sources quoted for the
'Ship of Fools' argument, is not about 'madness' or 'mental
illness', but about the very common vices of Brant's fellow-
citizens in Strasbourg – drunkenness, arrogance, narrow-
mindedness and meddling in other people's affairs;[11] that
Hieronymus Bosch's painting, 'The Ship of Fools', which is
in the Louvre, is about the vices of the religious Orders who
dominated the town of 's-Hertogenbosch from which the
painter derived his name, chiefly concentrating on gluttony
and lechery. The only 'fool' in the more restricted sense of
the term is a jester who sits in the ship's rigging.[12]

The basic misunderstanding has been repeated by subsequent writers. For instance, N. N. Kittrie cites the *Narrenschyff* as evidence of 'ritual exclusion' in Northern Europe
in the Middle Ages, telling us that 'entire ships were chartered,
and insane persons were entrusted to seamen to be dropped
off in uninhabited places',[13] while two Canadian planners,
M. J. Dear and S. M. Taylor, inform their readers that 'Frequently the mad were handed over to boatmen, who then

disembarked with their "ship of fools", ultimately intending to drop off their cargo in uninhabited places.'[14] In both accounts, the reference is to Foucault. Two American writers, Winifred Barbara Maher and Brendan Maher of Harvard University, have recently carried out research in depth on the 'Ship of Fools' story. They wrote to Foucault, asking him to amplify his sources, and were referred to the Waller Collection in the library at Uppsala. They consulted the librarian at Uppsala, the chief of the History of Medicine Division in the US National Library of Medicine, and the staff of some of the major nautical museums of Europe. Their conclusions are that

> No record (in the form of diaries, ships' logs, marine
> records generally etc.) exists of any actual voyages of such
> ships . . . We began by doubting that the practice of load-
> ing the small and costly vessels of the 14th and 15th cen-
> turies with lunatics would have recommended itself to even
> the most sanguine of shipmasters . . . the current references
> to ships of fools as part of the treatment of the mentally
> ill are wholly without foundation.[15]

Thus is history invented.

At the other end of Foucault's historical panorama, one can argue that nineteenth century psychiatry, so far from 'converging on Freud', was chiefly concerned with the management of the industrial poor, with scant attention to personality factors – an argument which Foucault himself uses elsewhere in his discussion, suggesting that the asylum 'imitated the punishment of criminals, using the same prisons, the same dungeons, the same physical brutality'.[16] The curious nature of Foucault's analysis (one must not call it 'reasoning', because this is a hymn to unreason) may be illustrated in depth by taking two examples from the chapter entitled 'The Birth of the Asylum'.

Foucault on Tuke and Pinel[17]

As Foucault says, we know the images. William Tuke, backed by the Society of Friends, set up an establishment called The

Retreat in York in 1792 where lunatics might be treated with
kindness and gentleness, according to Quaker principles.
Philippe Pinel, in the same year, struck off the chains from
the lunatics in two Paris hospitals, the Salpêtrière and Bicêtre.
Foucault writes satirically of

> the patriarchal calm of Tuke's home, where the heart's
> passions and the mind's disorders slowly subside; the lucid
> firmness of Pinel, who masters in a word and a gesture the
> two animal frenzies that roar against him as they hunt him
> down . . . The legends of Pinel and Tuke trasmit mythical
> values.[18]

It may be that Foucault is more concerned with the legend
(what subsequent generations made of the actions of Pinel
and Tuke) than what actually happened; but he says that it is
necessary to get behind the images. If that is his aim, then
recorded fact has something to offer to interpretation, and
his own interpretations may be tested against the records.

Foucault states that the Retreat was 'an instrument of
segregation . . . a moral and religious segregation which sought
to reconstruct around madness a milieu as much as possible
like that of the Community of Quakers'.[19] This is a mis-
reading. The Retreat was like a community of Quakers
because it was a community of Quakers. It was founded as a
result of the investigation of the Society of Friends into the
case of Hannah Mills, a Quaker girl who died in the York
Asylum, and was intended only for their own members.

Foucault goes on to allege that 'the fear instituted at the
Retreat is of very great depth'. The work of the Retreat is
very fully documented: records include the case-books, the
accounts, the Visiter's Book (sic) and several other major
sources. Foucault appears only to have consulted Samuel
Tuke's account, *A Description of the Retreat*, published in
1813. Tuke's chapter on 'Medical Treatment' has to be read
as a whole. It is basically a rejection of the accepted medical
methods of his time, which included bleeding, purging,
mechanical restraint and intimidation, and a plea for gentleness, warmth, good food and fresh air as the main methods of
treatment.

The regime at the Retreat was based on 'soft and mild

persuasion', and Tuke explicitly rejects 'the terrific system of management'[20] by which he means management by terror or intimidation. Foucault's argument seems to be based on two passages, quoted as follows:–

(i) The principle of fear . . . is considered as of greatest importance in the management of patients.[21]

(ii) There can be no doubt that the principle of fear in the human mind, when moderately and judiciously executed . . . has a salutory effect on society.[22]

In Tuke's original version, passage (i) continues: 'But it is not allowed to be excited, beyond that degree which naturally arises from the necessary regulations of the family.' Passage (ii) continues: 'But where fear is too much excited, and where it becomes the chief motive of action, it certainly tends to contract the understanding, to weaken the benevolent affections, and to debase the mind.' This is very partial reporting by Foucault. It is also likely that he genuinely misunderstands what Tuke was saying: the Quaker is probably not referring in the passages to terror or intimidation, but to 'the fear of the Lord' — the inculcation of a sense of religious awe leading to obedience.

Foucault then proceeds to quote four examples of repression practised at the Retreat, all of which are open to objection:–

(a) the celebrated case of the 'maniac' who arrived on the doorstep in manacles and a straitjacket, and was immediately freed. Samuel Tuke notes 'the maniac was sensible of the kindness of his treatment: he promised to restrain himself'. Foucault takes this as evidence of the remorseless application of the principle of internal control.[23] The practical alternatives were keeping the restraints on, or risking injuries to the staff. Why does Foucault consider the exaction of a promise of good behaviour to be the unkindest of the three?

(b) Foucault alleges that 'work comes first in "moral treatment" as practised at the Retreat'.[24] The patients at the Retreat did not work. The Retreat was (and still is) a fee-paying establishment. In William Tuke's day, patients were encouraged to read 'soothing works of the classics and mathematics' and forbidden novels as over-exciting, but the factory paradigm which Foucault was later to develop in *Discipline and Punish* is totally inappropriate to a residence for middle-class Quakers.

(c) The instance of the Lady Superintendent's tea-parties, where Foucault invites us to see the patient treated with anxiety-provoking social distance, 'incessantly cast in the role of the unknown visitor'.[25] Afternoon tea was a social occasion, and the Lady Superintendent (not 'the directors and staff', which implies an ominous surveillance), simply treated the patients in the style to which they were accustomed. Foucault admits that these were 'social occasions in the English manner', and then totally perverts their significance.

(d) The incident in which a patient threatened an attendant with a large stone:–

> The keeper stopped, looked the patient in the eyes; then advanced several steps towards him, and 'in a resolute tone of voice, commanded him to lay down the stone'. As he approached, the patient lowered his hand, then dropped his weapon; he then submitted to be quietly led to his apartment.[26]

Can this really be construed as the imposition of 'the stifling anguish of moral responsibility'?

Foucault continues by alleging that, in the Retreat as in Bicêtre 'the medical personage . . . becomes the essential figure of the asylum'.[27] As already noted, the Tukes were strongly anti-medical in their views. The Retreat doctor, Dr Fowler, was a visiting physician, not a psychiatric director. Foucault quotes as evidence of his power Samuel Tuke's statement that 'the physician sometimes possesses more influence over the patients' minds than *the other attendants*' (emphasis added).[28] This is a misunderstanding of the English class system. 'Attendants' were servants, not directors, and the classification of the doctor as an attendant implies a low status.

Foucault is correct in saying that William Tuke placed great emphasis on the concept of the family at the Retreat. He described himself as 'the father of the family' and regarded the Retreat as an extension of his own household. It is difficult to see what more beneficent model he could have employed in the 1790s. This did not amount to 'minority under family tutelage, a juridical status in which the madman's civil status is alienated'.[29] While Quaker families were doubtless somewhat patriarchal by modern standards, they were extended families, containing adults as well as children, and they were extremely supportive of their members.

Finally, Foucault ignores a factor of great importance to the Quaker community — the belief in the 'Inner Light' which illumines every individual, so that he knows instinctively what is good behaviour. This concept, somewhat analogous to Kant's Categorical Imperative, involves respect for the individual, and a trust in the ultimate goodness of human personality which is a notable feature of Quaker communities. Foucault is fully entitled not to share this belief; but to attack it as repressive would require a much more sophisticated theological and psychological approach than he provides.

The York Quakers of the late eighteenth century are perhaps a rather specialised sub-culture. It is understandable that an agnostic who is also a Frenchman may fail to grasp the finer points of Quaker belief or the significance of afternoon tea. When he comes to deal with Pinel, he is on his home ground, for both are Parisians with a training in the field of psychopathology; but again there are gaps and misinterpretations in the story as he describes it.

Foucault rehearses the 'famous' story of the confrontation between Dr Pinel and 'le paralytique Couthon', President of the Paris Commune. The 'two animal frenzies' he describes in his reference to the image of Pinel's work are the twin dangers of unchained madness, as represented by the lunatics, and the fury of the Commune, which in 1792 had the guillotine rising and falling daily; but unfortunately, the real point of the story is entirely missed.

Philippe Pinel was a medical man, trained at Toulouse. Before the Revolution in France, he flirted with a number of the current fashions in medical practice. He was acquainted with Mesmerism (then a public entertainment at Court), and wrote a number of semi-philosophical treatises, including one on whether the insane were more so in the winter than in the summer. René Semelaigne, his son-in-law and biographer, describes him as rather a timid man. There was nothing in his record to suggest a burning social zeal.

Semelaigne tells the story in detail.[30] When the French Revolution occurred, Pinel found himself in a very awkward political situation. As physician in charge of the Salpétrière and Bicêtre, two of the fortress-like buildings which attracted public suspicion and hatred in Paris, he had to keep the goodwill of both the Assemblée Nationale and the Paris Commune. 1793, the year of his appointment, was not a good year in which to fall foul of either. The Assemblée Nationale wanted the lunatics freed for political reasons — 'Man is born free, but is everywhere in chains,' wrote Rousseau. Medicine, like every other avenue of national cultural and intellectual life, was to exhibit the revolutionary spirit, and Pinel was to symbolise the Revolution by striking off the chains.

Couthon, who was a paraplegic, was President of the Paris Commune, and the Paris Commune was afraid of the lunatics. Couthon warned Pinel: 'Malheur à toi si tu nous trompes, et si parmi tes fous tu caches des ennemis du peuple.' Subsequently he had himself carried down to Bicêtre to jeer at the physicians: 'Ah, ça, citoyen, est-ce que tu es fou toi-même de vouloir déchainer de pareils animaux?' The use of 'tu' to a professional man shows the force of his contempt.

Pinel was in considerable danger. In the event, he obeyed the Assemblée, and invented (probably rather speedily) a system of orderly asylum management which would control the lunatics and so enable him to avoid Couthon's threats.

Of the first five patients released from their chains, according to Semelaigne, only two ultimately went free. One was 'un officier anglais sequestré depuis quarante ans' who must have been rather elderly to have been an enemy of the people, and who was allowed to go back to England. The other was a priest who believed that he was Christ, and had been excommunicated. Pinel ordered the attendants and the other patients to treat him with silence; and for some reason, this angers Foucault, who spends two pages on the humiliation and indignity involved in robbing the priest of his illusion. While he was confined and chained, he could enact Christ's passion. Once freed 'a prisoner of nothing but himself, the sufferer was caught in a relation to himself that was of the order of transgression, and in a non-relation to others that was the order of shame'.[31]

One can only ask what Foucault would have done. Would he have found it more Christian to keep the man in chains in order to perpetuate his Passion?

Of the other three patients released in the symbolic striking off of chains, one was near death, and died soon after. One was a soldier who went back to his regiment and was later readmitted for passing himself off as a general. The last was a scholar who died on the guillotine.

Foucault is right in that Pinel was probably not a great philanthropist. He seems to have been a prudent man who managed to survive, and who developed a system which he called 'traitement morale'. This had little in common with 'moral management' as practised at the Retreat. The Tukes were encouraging the Inner Light, the knowledge of good and evil, of right and wrong behaviour, in their patients. They distrusted the emotions, which they thought better kept under control than explored or expressed. 'Morale' in French is not the equivalent of 'moral' in English. A more accurate translation would be 'treatment through the emotions' or 'non-physical treatment'. It is this mode of treatment which enrages Foucault. He calls it 'the play of mirrors' — turning the madman's emotions back on himself, using reason to challenge unreason:-

> the asylum . . . placed the mirrors in such a way that the
> madman, when all was said and done, inevitably surprised
> himself, despite himself, as a *madman*. Freed from the
> chains that made it a purely observed object, madness lost,
> paradoxically, the essence of its liberty, which was solitary
> exaltation; it became responsible for what it knew of its
> truth; it imprisoned itself in an infinitely self-referring
> observation; it was finally chained to the humiliation of
> being its own object. Awareness was now linked to the
> shame of being identical to that other, of being com-
> promised in him, and of already despising oneself before
> being able to recognise or to know oneself.[32]

This is wonderful rhetoric, and it reads even better in French. More importantly, it may say something which is deeply true about the personal plight of those who suffer from mental illness; but as a criticism of the system which

Pinel introduced, it will not do — it ignores the fact that the striking off of chains was primarily a symbolic political act, ignores the fact that Pinel struck off the chains under orders from the Assemblée Nationale, which was at odds with the Paris Commune, ignores the plight of the 'timid' Pinel, caught between two political forces and understandably anxious to keep his own head, and treats as a system of therapeutics what can have been no more than a sensible device to manage the patients so precipitately released from physical restraint. René Semelaigne describes the new régime in the Salpétrière and Bicêtre, and there is much more about teaching old ladies to knit and offering them the consolations of religion than there is about intolerable emotional confrontations.

Foucault's perspective

If Foucault has some of the basic facts wrong, can we trust the interpretation which he places upon them? The rational answer would appear to be that we cannot, that his case falls to the ground; but Foucault has his answer ready. Like Goffman, he is an expert in evading detailed criticism. He is not writing a history — 'histoire' in French includes not only historians' history, but also any kind of narrative, account, anecdote or even fable; and he is basically a Structuralist — concerned not with 'the facts' but with the underlying structures behind the facts, and the way in which facts *as perceived by others*, generate images. Anyone who criticises Foucault's interpretation therefore has the task of challenging his assertions about what other (unnamed) people have made of the facts — an impossible exercise.

Professor Donald Macrae[33] sums up Structuralism as involving three positions:—

(i)   appearance in human conduct and affairs is not reality;
(ii) reality is structured;
(iii) this structuring is code-like.

The Structuralist critique is typically synchronic, crunching together events and ideas from apparently disparate periods and disparate cultures in an attempt to find new patterns of significance. It is basically anti-historical, and no amount of patient dating and detailed refutation will shake the argument.

Foucault's own choice of 'the archaeology of knowledge' as a title for his area of study shows a determination to excavate ideas rather than events. It is a method which has produced some remarkable new insights in linguistics, through the work of Chomsky and others, but even if the method is sound, we may properly enquire whether Foucault is digging in the right places.

The attack in *Madness and Civilisation* is often subliminal. Through powerful images and symbols, fearful, exciting or acutely painful, Foucault reaches the emotions of his readers directly, without the intervention of rational thought. The splendid image of the Ship of Fools, calmly gliding, then tragically made fast, captures our imagination at the outset. It may be that in the symbol of the ship (often used in medieval literature, with a variety of symbolism attached to it) Foucault has found a code; but the significance which he attaches to the Ship of Fools is not what Brant had in mind, and both are different from what Hieronymus Bosch had in mind. It may be that, in Donald Macrae's apt phrase, Foucault has been 'deceived by a mere clang'.[34] Rather than uncovering a basic pattern, he has only dug up a superficial similarity.

To begin to understand how and why this strange book was written, we need to clear away some of the confusions caused by translation, and to know something of Foucault's own intellectual development.

As already noted, most of the book is about unreason rather than 'madness', and the original title reflects this. 'Folie' in French has whimsical connotations entirely absent from the English term: 'folâtrer' is to sport or frisk about, rather than to suffer from insanity; but the problem is that the English language makes a distinction where the French language does not. Alan Sheridan reveals this when he notes that it is difficult to translate into French King Lear's remark to his fool — 'Ah, fool, I shall go mad'. In French, this becomes 'Ah, fou, je deviendrai fou'.[35] While Sheridan sees this as replacing a nuance by a pun (which is fair enough in literary terms), the implication of replacing 'fool' (a very broad category, including most if not all the human race) by 'madman' (a very narrow category) is very much greater for social scientists. It may be that the reintroduction of the term

'madness' for 'mental illness' in some schools of sociology
derives from just this confusion. (It also derives from a dis-
satisfaction with medically oriented explanations of bizarre
behaviour, but that is another story).

Foucault himself seems unaware of the possibilities of
confusion. Not only does he confuse Brant's fools, who are
weak, stupid or vicious, with the 'lunatics' of the period;
towards the end of the book, he shifts to talking specifically
about people categorised as mentally ill in the nineteenth or
twentieth centuries without any sense of incongruity.

Foucault's own life experience gives some clues to his
writing. He began his literary career by taking his licence de
philosophie in the Ecole Normale Supérieure. The ENS is one
of the grandes écoles of France, of very high intellectual
standing. Foucault was taught philosophy largely in a Hegelian
framework. In revolt against Hegel, he turned to Marx, and
became a Communist. From Marx and Althusser he turned to
psychology, and then to psychiatry. He took a Diploma in
Psychopathology, and in the early 1950s, spent three years
observing practice in mental hospitals. In 1954, he published
his first book, *Maladie Mentale et Personnalité*, which is a
curious hybrid — part very orthodox abnormal psychology,
part Marxist analysis. Alan Sheridan finds in it 'a distinct
sense of self-mutilation, of the professional setting aside all
personal feeling as he dons his white coat', and comments
'No-one who did not know . . . would guess that Foucault
could have written such passages. It was only a matter of
time before the straitjacket would snap, and its wearer take
his revenge.'[36] After writing it, Foucault went into the wilder-
ness, accepting relatively undemanding teaching posts outside
France while he hammered out his ideas. He came back with
the *Histoire de la Folie*. Successive exposures to different kinds
of knowledge and ideological commitment had finally fused
into an individual approach; but if we look at the structure of
Foucault's own knowledge-base, it is not too difficult to dis-
cern the reaction against Hegelian philosophy in his insistence
on the validity of the unorthodox; the neo-Marxist influence in
his views on the enslavement of the industrial proletariat; the
influence of Lévi-Strauss and other Structuralists on his general
mode of attack; and the vehement rejection of the psychiatrists
whose practice he studied for three formative years.

The analysis of punishment

These considerations give us at least a base-line for evaluating *Surveiller et Punir*. There are further problems of translation, because *Discipline and Punish*, the English title, is not the equivalent — though Foucault is said to have suggested it himself. 'Surveiller' is to watch, superintend or supervise, not to discipline in the modern sense of the word. The translator's note points this out, and mentions other difficult points of rendering, such as the fact that there is no English equivalent for 'supplice', the public spectacle of the torture and death of a criminal, or for 'la question', the procedure for the extraction of confessions by interrogation.

Foucault was 35 years old when he published the *Histoire de la Folie*, and nearly 50 when he published *Surveiller et Punir*. The latter book is more mature, more coherent, and more closely related to historical fact. Though most of the references are to eighteenth-century or early nineteenth-century penologists, such as Mably, Beccaria and Jeremy Bentham, the writer is clearly aware of the development since 1961 of other types of anti-institutional writing, particularly the work of Goffman. The attack is therefore sharper and more precise. It is also notably more apt to dwell on pain, and the details of torture — a theme briefly touched on at the end of the *Histoire de la Folie*, where there is an appreciative passage on the writings of the Marquis de Sade.

The book begins with a particularly horrifying and gruesome death — that of Damiens the regicide in 1757 — described at length; and it is reasonable (a word Foucault would not respect!) to consider why he found it necessary or appropriate to include this material. Is it mere sensationalism, the desire to shock and seize the reader's attention? Or is it something which goes deeper — a calculated attempt by a writer with a Diploma in Psychology and a Diploma in Psychopathology to arouse painful emotions in the reader which can be played on later? We have already noted the subliminal attack in the *Histoire de la Folie*: that was gentle by contrast. This time, the reader is plunged at the outset into a situation of horror in which he must identify with one or more of the parties. Does he feel for the victim or the executioner, groan or cheer with the crowd? At the end of a bare three pages of text, he is likely to have played all the parts, to be irretrievably snared in that web of pain and guilt which lies at the heart of penology. The death of Damiens is not merely a successful literary device. It is an exercise in the psychology of the reader.

The main theme of the book is as follows: by the end of the eighteenth century, 'the gloomy festival of punishment was dying out'. The public spectacle of torture and execution was replaced by imprisonment, 'the most hidden part of the penal process'. The body of the criminal was no longer dismembered in a long and painful ritual before the coup de grâce: it was scrupulously preserved in the half-living state of incarceration. Rationing of food, sexual deprivation, corporal punishment and solitary confinement affected the body directly, but the main assault was on the soul (âme) of the prisoner. Judgment became individualised: sentence was carried out not in relation to the criminal act, but in relation to the criminal individual and his personality:—

> the passions, instincts, anomalies, infirmities, maladjustments, effects of environment or heredity; acts of aggression are punished, but also through them, is aggressivity; rape, but at the same time perversions; murders, but also drives and desires.[37]

Judges develop a sense of shame about punishing: 'the psychologists and the civil servants of moral orthopaedics proliferate on the wound it leaves'.

> A whole army of technicians took over from the executioner, the immediate anatomists of pain: warders, doctors, chaplains, psychiatrists, psychologists, educationalists: by their very presence near the prisoner they sing the praises that the law needs.

The guillotine — then in occasional use in France — is shrugged off very lightly: 'a death lasts only a moment . . . contact between the law, or those who carry it out, and the body of the criminal is reduced to a split second'. The real punishment lies in incarceration. What appears to be penal leniency is really a technique of power, developed for social control of a most complete and insidious kind.

Public execution, the 'supplice', was another technique of power — the affirmation of the triumph of the sovereign over the wrong-doer. It was an overt political act; but it sometimes misfired because the populace, called to the scene to witness, and by implication to fear, the sovereign's vengeance, might side with the condemned man. Incarceration is a more efficient weapon, because it takes place in secret. In modern capitalist society, 'humane' punishment is a weapon of the ruling class — 'humanity is the respectable name given to this economy and to its meticulous calculations'.[38]

This is not orthodox Marxist analysis — the assumption that any humanitarian movement is 'false consciousness', a deluded bourgeois reaction which merely delays the day of the Revolution by blunting the edge of class conflict: it is an assertion that humanitarianism is a deliberately chosen weapon for pursuing the class conflict. We might ask why, if the ruling class is so clear and so malevolent in its intentions, it does not employ the cheaper and more efficient weapon of the guillotine more often, rather than expending money and effort on rehabilitation; but the answer to this is that the prison is an instrument of terror: a lasting example to would-be criminals and dissidents, hidden and yet visible, enduring in its effects.

The 'meticulous calculations' for achieving this end are set out in detail. The difficulty is that Foucault often writes in the historic present, and the reader has trouble in deciding whether particular references are to the present day, or to the Code Napoléon at its most rigorous. Both time and space in the Structuralist critique are simply dimensions like any other, to be taken into account or ignored at will. Like Lévi-Strauss, who often makes a virtue of the unexpected juxtaposition in time and space, Foucault sometimes disturbs his readers by this device, but too often confuses them.

There is a long and fairly ordered critique of the views of eighteenth and nineteenth century writers on penology, punctuated by occasional reversions to the theme of execution which serve no apparent analytical purpose, and seem to be designed only to reactivate the emotions aroused by the execution of Damiens. There is an account of Bentham's Panopticon and of the Philadelphia system of confinement, and a detailed analysis of 'hierarchical, continuous and functionalised surveillance': the control of time, the control of space, the control of movement. These techniques of discipline — 'a political anatomy of detail' — are then explored at length for nearly a hundred pages, almost a third of the book, in settings other than the prison, notably the school and the factory. The factory is regarded, in Marxist fashion, as the paradigm of class control. In the last three chapters, Foucault returns somewhat abruptly to the theme of the prison in an attack on what is variously described as 'the carceral city', 'the carceral continuum', 'the carceral pyramid', 'the carceral network' and 'the carceral system'.

Prisons do not eliminate or reduce crime, Foucault argues: they breed it. Prisons are necessary to define the delinquent and dangerous elements in society, to provide the basis for a system of political surveillance. Police, prisons and delinquents form 'an ensemble . . . a circuit that is never interrupted'. Judges have no integrity of judgment: 'Their immense appetite for medicine . . . is constantly manifested — from their appeal to psychiatric experts to their attention to the chatter of criminology.'[39]

Prison exerts 'a power of normalisation' and this book 'must serve as a background to various studies of the power of normalisation and the formation of knowledge in modern society'. It is a poor ending to a powerful, if politically slanted, analysis.

In the *Histoire de la Folie*, the final note is one of Nietzschean despair — institutions are always instruments of repression in every country and every century. The outward manifestations alter, but the underlying structure remains unchanged. In *Discipline and Punish*, the conclusion is more overtly Marxist than in *Madness and Civilisation*. In a delicate reference to the coming revolution, Foucault says that he can hear at the heart of the carceral city 'the distant roar of battle'.

Madness and Civilisation is the work of a man who has been close to the orthodox treatment of the mentally ill, is repelled by it, and passionately wants to state an alternative thesis. He was young, and rich in rhetoric, and caught in the cross-currents of European philosophy. Fourteen years later, when he produced *Discipline and Punish*, he was a very different person — a senior and respected scholar able to define his own intellectual field of study, with a number of philosophical works behind him — the *Naïssance de la Clinique* (1963) in which he extended his critique of modern medicine; *Les mots et les choses* (1966), a philosophical account of the order and development of knowledge; *L'Archéologie du savoir* (1969), which develops the Structuralist critique more fully, and some lesser works.

The mature Foucault is more reasoned in his arguments, more political in his judgments, more skilful in his use of a distinctive (and highly quotable) terminology; but the impress of a powerful and lively mind, outraged by oppression and the threat of oppression, stretches across the years. Foucault is not a historian, and cannot be judged as one: he is an image-maker, employing precisely those techniques of arousing the emotions which he deplores in Tuke and Pinel; and he is a Gallic image-maker. Though curiously he never mentions the Bastille, the emotions which he arouses are those which inspired the Paris mob on 14 July 1789.

Olympian, aloof and sometimes arrogant, Foucault lives in an intellectual world of his own making. Despite a formidable battery of scholarship, his main contribution to knowledge comes through dazzling literary devices and polemic, through challenge rather than through understanding. He attacks orthodox concepts of the nature of mental illness and crime, dismisses all humanitarian instincts with a deep and unremitting scepticism, and sees the development of prisons and mental hospitals as nothing more than a conspiracy by the powerful against the powerless. As a corrective to the liberal-reformist view, this is valuable; as a total view, it has its weaknesses. Maurice Cranston, who is also a philosopher concerned with human rights, takes the view that Foucault's 'boldest statements about the past' are not 'backed up with any evidence', and that his method is too often that of argument by assertion.[40]

The recognition that benevolence is not always what it seems; that the subduing of the dissident elements in society played a part in nineteenth-century social reform as well as the noble sentiments expressed by reformers; that the building up of large institutional populations of vulnerable people can arouse sadistic instincts in those who manage them; and that the perpetuation of routine-laden and repressive systems is an offence against human personality; required a prophet, and Foucault fills the role. Perhaps prophets have to exaggerate in order to be heard.

3 SZASZ:
THE ICONOCLAST

Dr Thomas Szasz is a practising psychoanalyst who flatly denies the existence of mental illness, the validity of psychiatry as a branch of medicine, and the necessity for mental hospitals. He is particularly opposed to what he calls 'institutional psychiatry', and to the compulsory detention of patients, which he regards primarily as a means of social control. In a literary career of some twenty years, he has written fourteen books[1] and a very large number of papers and articles on these and allied themes.

Szasz stands so far outside the world of the mental hospital that he has nothing constructive to contribute to a study of what goes on inside it. In that sense, his work could be considered marginal to the theme of institutional care and custody: he cannot be expected to take seriously the problems of a system which he argues should be swept out of existence. But his work is highly relevant because it represents the extreme limits of protest. No one else has argued in such absolute terms, in so many thousands of words, or over so long a period. A full acceptance of his case would end the discussion once and for all, because there would be nothing left to provide a frame of reference.

The argument presented in this prodigious literary output consists of a number of related propositions, and the groundwork is laid out in two early books, *The Myth of Mental Illness: foundations of a theory of personal conduct* (1961) and *Law, Liberty and Psychiatry: an inquiry into the social uses of mental health practices* (1963).

The Myth of Mental Illness was long in preparation. Szasz

47

tells us[2] that it is 'part autobiography', and that he started
work on it in 1954, while on active duty with the US Navy —
an assignment he seems to have found less demanding than
full-time psychoanalytic practice in Chicago. He says that the
publication of the book caused a furore. The Commissioner
of the New York State Department of Mental Hygiene
demanded that he should be dismissed from his post in the
State University of New York, Syracuse, because he did not
'believe' in mental illness. We are not told the details of this
controversy, but Szasz continued to hold his post.[3] He describes his own position as follows:—

> The problems . . . are easy to state, but, because of the
> powerful cultural and economic pressures that define the
> 'correct' answers to them, are difficult to clarify. They
> have to do with such questions as: What is disease? What
> are the actual and ostensible tasks of the physician? What
> is mental illness? Who defines what constitutes illness,
> diagnosis, treatment? Who controls the vocabulary of
> medicine and psychiatry, and the powers of physician-
> psychiatrist and citizen-patient?[4]

The particular form of mental illness he chose for analysis
is conversion hysteria, in which patients exhibit physical
symptoms for which there is no apparent organic explanation.
Szasz argues that conversion hysteria may be used as 'the
historical paradigm of the sorts of phenomena to which the
term "mental illness" refers' on three grounds: it is the problem which captured the attention of the early neuropsychia-
atrists, such as Charcot, Janet and Freud, and led to the
drawing of a distinction between neurology and psychiatry;
logically, hysteria is the condition which presents the physician with the problem of distinguishing 'the "real" or genuine
from the "unreal" or false'; and in psycho-social terms, it provides 'an excellent example of how so-called mental illness can
best be conceptualised in terms of sign-using, rule-following
and game-playing.. . . It is a game characterised by, among
other things, the end-goals of domination and interpersonal
control, and by strategies of deceit.'[5]
    Though present-day psychiatrists are apt to say that
hysteria is now comparatively rare, Szasz argues that much

of what is called 'mental illness' in the Western world and 'malingering' in Soviet Russia is of this kind. Attempts to deal with it in either socio-political context are basically forms of social control, and physicians should beware of becoming involved in this kind of activity. 'Among contemporary physicians, it is the psychiatrist who, more than any other specialist, has arrogated to himself the role of protector of the poor.'[6]

But medical men should stick to medicine. Szasz is distinctly ambivalent about the work of social workers, since within a few lines, he accuses them of being social control agents 'admirably suited for the purpose of keeping in line potentially discontented members (or groups) of society', and yet seems to grant them some sort of legitimacy in the role of 'attorneys for the poor'. What he is clear about is that psychiatrists are primarily physicians. Patients have no need to ' "cheat" their way to being humanely treated by means of faking illness', and physicians, with an advanced technology to master, 'may have neither time for nor interest in' the dubious activities he allocates to social work.[7]

The identification of social care with social control is worked out further in a chapter on 'The Ethics of Helplessness and Helpfulness' which traces the belief that those who are weak, disabled or helpless have a claim on society to the Judaeo-Christian ethic. The effect of this tradition is to create 'the religious game' — people are encouraged to define themselves as weak, disabled or helpless in order to elicit support from others. This is in itself undesirable; and the offer of help may cover discreditable motives:—

> The possibility that attitudes of 'kindness' towards 'poor patients' serve, by and large, the purpose of enhancing the doctor's self-esteem must be concealed at all costs. . . . We must scrutinise, therefore, all therapeutic attitudes traditionally ascribed to benevolence, keeping always in mind that such manoeuvres on the part of the therapist may serve only to depreciate and subjugate the patient . . .[8]

There follows a strong attack on the ethics of the Sermon on the Mount — 'these are the rules of irresponsibility and childish dependency'. 'Blessed are the poor in spirit' is

interpreted 'Man should be "poor in spirit", i.e. stupid, submissive: Do not be smart, well-informed or assertive!'[9] 'The
beliefs and practices of Christianity are best suited for slaves.
This is hardly surprising when one recalls the oppressed
milieu in which this creed emerged.'[10]

Christianity was a success because it democratised and
popularised Judaism, holding out the promise of rewards in
the next life for those who failed to be assertive in this life;
but although its demoralising influence in the creation of
'childish dependency' persisted, it also became the source
of a new kind of domination and oppression through the
Inquisition.

The Middle Ages in Europe were characterised by the
power of the Catholic Church, and the ritual persecution of
witches. Most witches were women, just as most of the
hysterics later defined by Charcot and Freud were women.

> Witches and sorcerers, recruited from the ranks of the poor
> and oppressed, played the role of scapegoats. They thus
> fulfilled the socially useful role of acting as social tranquil-
> lisers . . . by participating in an important public drama,
> they contributed to the stability of the existing social
> order.[11]

This was 'an inverted theological game', the darker side of
the search for sainthood and salvation. It has been replaced
by 'the medical game' involved in the diagnosis and treatment
of mental illness, and the scapegoating mechanisms once
involved in the witch hunts have an equivalent in the labelling
and persecution of the mentally ill.

But there is a better way of life, an ethos which avoids the
tangle of dominate-and-be-dominated. Just as the abolition
of slavery ended the paternalistic relationship between slave-
owner and negro, so it is possible to end the paternalistic
relationship between psychiatrist and patient:–

> Much of what passes for 'medical ethics' is a set of paternal-
> istic rules the net effect of which is the persistent infanti-
> lization and domination of the patient by the physician. A
> shift towards greater dignity, freedom and self-responsibility
> for the disenfranchised — whether slave, sinner or patient —

can be secured only at the cost of honest and serious commitment to an ethic or autonomy and egality. This implies that all persons are treated with respect, consideration and dignity.[12]

The cost of this for the formerly disenfranchised is that they must be expected 'to shoulder certain responsibilities, among them the responsibility to be maximally self-reliant and responsible even when ill or disabled'.[13]

Law, Liberty and Psychiatry continues the attack on 'false psychiatric liberalism . . . the danger of tyranny by therapy'. This is a collection of papers, published originally in twelve different journals, on the constitutional implications of hospitalising mental patients and the rights of the patient.

Mental health movements are seen as a threat to liberty, and the law as a means by which the threat may be contained. The approach rests on specifically American principles: the Declaration of Rights, the American Constitution, the ideals of the Founding Fathers. Liberty is 'an inalienable human right, second only in importance to the right to life'. Liberty is freedom, the state of being unfettered, 'the absence of restraints imposed by other persons upon our own freedom of choice and action — that and nothing more recondite'. For those 'oppressed by psychiatrists', liberty means freedom from psychiatric coercion.[14]

'Mental illness' is merely a name for 'problems in living', not a medical classification. It encourages a false belief — that human life would be harmonious, satisfying and secure if this alleged disease entity were conquered; but this is 'a wishful fantasy', raising the spectre of medical control. The slogan is 'Liberty against psychiatry', opposition to a mental health movement which, by explaining away aberrations of behaviour, represents an erosion of moral standards and the extension of the power of the state: 'hidden under a façade of medical and psychiatric jargon, and . . . buttressed by a self-proclaimed desire to help or treat so-called mentally ill persons'.[15] The importance of patients learning to stand on their own feet and to take responsibility for their own lives is stressed again, in a semi-theological vein: 'I believe, as do many others, that the burden of good and evil lies not too heavily but too lightly on the shoulders of modern man.'[16]

Involuntary commitment to a mental hospital involves a serious loss of personal responsibility, and of civil liberties. In many jurisdictions (by which Szasz seems to mean in many states of the USA), those who are so committed are considered legally incompetent, cannot vote, make legal contracts, marry or divorce, hold a licence to drive a motor vehicle, or prevent 'invasions of . . . person or body'.[17] The role of the psychiatrist in such cases is 'to exert social control on a socially deviant person'. This has nothing to do with medicine or medical principles. It involves usurping powers and duties which properly belong only to the agents of the criminal law. Psychiatrists are compared to jailers, punishing those who break the social code under a cloak of false benevolence.

The dangers of involuntary commitment are illustrated, rather oddly, by the case of King Ludwig II of Bavaria.[18] After a reign of considerable eccentricity and bizarre behaviour, this unfortunate monarch was confined in Berg Castle in 1886, where he killed his physician, and drowned himself in the castle lake. Szasz argues at some length that Ludwig was stripped of his powers and 'committed' by a psychiatric conspiracy on evidence from 'the stablemaster and other lackeys' because he was a barrier to Bismarck's ambition to unify the German states. It is not clear what Szasz thinks should have been done about King Ludwig. The point he is making is that his commitment was a political and legal affair rather than a medical one. This is 'false commitment' of a kind analogous to that practised today.

Though psychiatrists assure the general public that they are overworked and their hospitals understaffed, so that they 'are not looking for business', they are promoting 'the self-interests of psychiatry' rather than the fundamental values of individualism, liberty and self-government.[19] Just as they should steer clear of social work and social workers, so they should avoid entanglement with the criminal law. Liberal penology is attacked for being too closely attached to psychiatric concepts, and a fairly stark doctrine of punishment is propounded: people charged with offences are either guilty or not guilty. Criminal behaviour is not a mental illness. The human dignity of the offender demands that he should be treated as responsible for his actions, and suffer the penalty of them, rather than being 'discredited as a responsible human being'.[20]

The discussion of criminal responsibility is not directly relevant here, though some of the arguments employed by Szasz in drawing the hard line between psychiatric commitment and penal commitment were to be taken up later by N. N. Kittrie.[21] The corollary of denying the existence of mental illness and the benevolence of psychiatric intervention is to shift the weight of dealing with people who have 'problems in living' and break the law firmly into the penal sphere.

> What I am trying to say is that achieving dignity and individuality is always a personal affair. It can be facilitated or hindered; but in the end, each person must do it for himself.
> In a sense, an individual is the end product of the *decisions* he has made. He who fails to make decisions, for the consequences of which he is responsible, is not a person.[22]

With the publication of *The Myth of Mental Illness* and *Law, Liberty and Psychiatry*, the basic argument was expounded. Later books were to expand on different parts of the theme, which may be summed up as follows:

(i) mental illness is a myth
(ii) involuntary commitment is a crime
(iii) institutional psychiatry is social control.

Each of these apparently straightforward propositions conceals semantic problems which become increasingly complex as the volume of literature develops.

Mental illness is a myth

What does Szasz mean by 'myth', and what does he mean by 'mental illness'?

'Myth' has two possible interpretations. In popular speech, the term means something which is not true, a fictitious story. In the technical sense used by anthropologists and most theologians, it means a story which cannot be verified in literal terms, but which can be analysed to reveal important social truths. Is Szasz telling us that mental illness is a fiction, a condition which does not exist and has been invented? Or is he telling us that the condition does exist, but is not really an illness?

This is not easy to determine, because Szasz slips from one meaning to the other. He shows a frequent impatience with 'myths and ritual' in the religious sense, and his treatment of Jung in *The Myth of Psychotherapy*[23] suggests that he has little sympathy with the Jungian view of myths as social archetypes. Jung thought myths of profound relevance to the experience of individuals and cultures. Szasz sweeps them away brusquely, arguing that Jung, the 'pastor without a pulpit' escaped from the mythologies of Christian theology only to transfer them to 'psychiatric theology'. Further, he is categorical in his denial of the existence of mental illness: 'Let us launch our inquiry by asking, somewhat rhetorically, whether there is such a thing as mental illness. My reply is that there is not . . . this notion has now outlived whatever usefulness it may have had, and . . . it now functions as a myth.'[24]

On the other hand, the chapter of *Law, Liberty and Psychiatry* from which this statement is taken begins with a quotation from Gilbert Ryle to the effect that 'A myth is not a fairy story. It is the presentation of facts belonging in one category in the idioms belonging to another'; and the categorical statement that mental illness does not exist is soon followed by qualifications about 'problems in living'. These do exist. The argument is that they are not 'illness', which brings us on to the second problem.

In *Myth of Mental Illness*, Szasz argues that logical classification is basic to human understanding. Phenomena must, in logical terms, be either 'A' or 'non-A'.[25] Thus there is a distinction between real jewellery and paste jewellery, between a Cézanne painting and a forgery. In the same way, it is possible to distinguish between real illness and false illness, or malingering. The physician should be able to tell, on the basis of medical observation, whether a patient is genuinely sick, or confronting him with 'counterfeit bodily illness'. Charcot and Freud 'changed the rules of the game' to conceal this fundamental distinction. The assertion that hysteric patients were sick people was not a medical discovery, but a semantic strategy to confuse the distinction between bodily disease and 'difficulties in living'.[26]

The points come so thick and fast, and in such smooth succession, that it is difficult to disentangle them, and to see exactly what the reader is being asked to agree to; but concealed in this argument are at least three basic assertions: that all phenomena are either 'A' or 'non-A', and that therefore if bodily illness is 'A', mental illness is 'non-A'; that hysteria as diagnosed by Charcot and Freud is paradigmatic of all mental illness; and that the view of mental disorder as sickness was invented by Charcot and Freud, who thereby created a confusion.

The distinction between 'A' and 'non-A' is elementary in logic, but no student of philosophy who got past the first few pages of a textbook would contend that all phenomena could be categorised in this dichotomous fashion. The distinction between 'A' and 'non-A' applies only to contradictory or contrary terms, e.g. black is non-white, new is not old;[27] but there is nothing in logic to suggest that all pairs of terms are of this kind. 'Mental' is not contradictory or contrary to 'bodily'. Further 'non-A' does not imply 'counterfeit A'. Szasz is confusing the issue with his talk of paste jewellery and forged paintings, and building in a value-judgment. In strictly logical terms, if it were possible to argue that mental illness is 'counterfeit bodily illness', it would be equally possible to argue that bodily illness is 'counterfeit mental illness'. The introduction of concepts from logic does not in itself guarantee a logical argument.

The claim that conversion hysteria as diagnosed by Charcot and Freud is paradigmatic of all mental illness is made specifically in *The Myth of Mental Illness*, and the argument is then extended to all of mental illness; but this is not a correct use of 'paradigm'. A paradigm case is a case which exhibits in particular form the essential features of a general problem. Hysteria does not fulfil this function in relation to all forms of mental illness — it is a special case. Szasz himself says that hysteria is now rarely diagnosed. We have only his word for it that hysteria is 'really' malingering, and that all forms of mental illness are 'really' hysteria. In a later work, *Schizophrenia: the sacred symbol of Psychiatry* (1979) he argues on very different premises. We are told that patients diagnosed as schizophrenic, who comprise the bulk of the mental hospital population, are in hospital because their doctors have a kind of folk-memory dating from the days when most long-stay patients suffered from paresis (general paralysis of the insane): 'Psychiatry still speaks with the accents of neuro-syphilis on its lips.. . . . Thus has the image of the crooked spirochete making people mad been replaced, in the minds of many psychiatrists, by the image of the crooked molecule making them mad.'[28] In the earlier book, mental illness is associated with hysteria, and thus with malingering. In the later one, it is associated with syphilis, and thus with social stigmatisation. Both are forms of special pleading.

'Before Charcot's time,' Szasz says categorically, 'a person was said to be ill only if his body was physically disordered'.[29] This statement requires only the most summary form of re-buttal. Webster's Dictionary, a good American source, traces the etymology of the word 'sick' back to the Old Norse 'sjukr', meaning sick or distressed, and the Middle Irish 'socht', meaning depression or silence. Hippocrates recognised mental disorder as part of the sphere of medicine.[30] Aristotle pondered the relationship between the *psyche* and the *soma* at length;[31] Galen's doctrine of the four humours (choler, phlegm, bile and melancholy) involved a recognition of behavioural symptoms.[32] Greek medicine certainly involved some understanding of mental disorder and the mind-body relationship. Poynter and Keele, in a general history of Medicine, note:—

> Throughout history, there has been an awareness of the fact that a person can no more be understood merely in terms of his physical and chemical parts than can a Shakes-pearian sonnet in terms of its alphabet . . .[33]

> The history of the medical view of the relation between body and mind falls into three main epochs: in the first, disease is looked on essentially as a manifestation of sin; in the second, it is viewed as physical or chemical, with sec-ondary effects on the mind; and in the third period, during which the term 'psychosomatic' was introduced, it is viewed as 'anthropological', or involving the whole person.[34]

A totally mechanistic view of man, seeing the body simply as a machine unaffected by the personality and stresses of its tenant, has never been seriously propounded in medicine. As Goffman suggests in 'The Medical Model and Mental Hospitalization',[35] some physicians are apt to act as if it were true, because physical medicine would be easier to practise if it were more like servicing a car. It is a nuisance to have to consider the reactions of the driver at the same time; but any textbook of psychosomatic medicine will confirm that a mechanistic view is not truly scientific, because it flies in the face of the facts. Decades of solid research on the psychological factors in such conditions as asthma, diabetes, cardiovascular conditions and skin diseases contradict it.[36] The view put forward by Szasz caters to medical prejudices, but has no basis in medical knowledge.

The relationship of mental illness to physical illness was summed up by the Macmillan Commission in Britain in 1926 in the following terms:—

A mental illness may have physical concomitants; probably it always has, though they may be difficult of detection. A physical illness, on the other hand, may have, and probably always has, mental concomitants. And there are many cases in which it is a question whether the physical symptoms or the mental symptoms predominate.[37]

By ignoring the evidence of this relationship, Szasz, who frequently implies that he is on the side of the 'oppressed', is driving us back into the nineteenth century association of 'lunatics' with 'paupers' and 'criminals'. No one argues that mental illness *is* physical illness, and the relationship between the two is not fully understood; but there are no grounds for denying that a relationship exists.

The sweeping assertion that 'mental illness is a myth' therefore requires very careful qualification. If Szasz is saying that the symptomatology of mental illness is different from the symptomatology of physical illness, then he is superficially correct, though he is ignoring a good deal of evidence that the two are aetiologically related. If he is saying that mental illness is not a serious problem, being merely a matter of malingering or failure to stand on one's own feet, then he leaves a good deal of human misery unexplained, and impoverishes his own profession's capacity to deal with even the most gross of physical symptoms. If he is saying that this problem is a serious one, but that medical men ought not to deal with it, because it is beneath their notice, or because it involves dangers of social control, or because they may become tainted with the evils of benevolence, then we have to turn to other parts of his argument for further explanation.

Involuntary commitment is a crime

On this issue, Szasz takes a purely libertarian stance. Involuntary commitment to mental hospital is 'a grossly discriminatory sanction, injuring lower-class persons much more than upper-class persons'.[38] It is curious that, following this statement, we are given the case of King Ludwig, and the complaint that he was stripped of his royal prerogatives.

At the time when *Law, Liberty and Psychiatry* was published, the overwhelming majority of patients in American mental hospitals were compulsorily detained, and there was substance in the argument that psychiatrists often ignored the fact, as though it had no effect on the treatment situation, and that some hospitals at least offered an environment no more desirable than that of a prison:—

> The similarities between commitable mental illness and crime . . . emerge. In both, the person 'offends' society, and is therefore restrained. The motives for restraining the mentally ill person are ostensibly therapeutic, whereas for the criminal they are allegedly punitive. This distinction, however, cannot be defended satisfactorily. State hospitals have been notorious for their neglect, and indeed abuse of the mental patient.[39]

Szasz was to provide a good deal of ammunition for the American Civil Liberties Union in its campaign for the rights of the mental patient, and he writes in the context of that movement, with an emphasis on constitutional rights, the difficulty of defining 'dangerousness' to oneself or to others, and the need to avoid defining conduct as sick merely because it was inconvenient or troublesome. These points were well made in *Law, Liberty and Psychiatry*, though the effect of the attack was somewhat lessened by its very sweeping nature. Clearly if one believes that there is no such condition as mental illness, then all commitment to psychiatric hospitals is improper commitment. By calling it a 'crime', Szasz was using that term in an uncharacteristic way. Elsewhere in the book, he equates crime simply with breaking the law, which is presumed to be perfectly in accord with moral standards. In this reference, he implies that the law is wrong, for commitment is a legal process. What he is doing is to try to prevent the law, for which he has great respect, from becoming contaminated by psychiatric considerations. There is praise for the Wolfenden Committee in England (1957) which recommended that in most circumstances, homosexual conduct should not be subject to legal restriction: 'Contemporary American mental health legislation is moving in exactly the opposite direction. It seeks to impose close supervision on personal conduct, as if so-called mental sickness were a serious public health hazard.'[40] The enemy is 'the therapeutic state' which acts like a parent and infantilises the citizen.

The ACLU campaign has proceeded on two main fronts: the right to refuse treatment, and the right to receive treatment.[41] Szasz strongly advocates the former, but has no time for the latter. Nobody is entitled to treatment — it is part of the process of infantilisation.

> How could an enterprise as poorly defined as psychiatric treatment be considered a legal right? Who would decide what is therapeutic and what is noxious? It is widely accepted today that involuntary mental hospitalization may itself be therapeutic. But, might it not be harmful sometimes? Moreover might it not be therapeutic for some hospitalized mental patients to be set free? These are crucial considerations. For if we define as 'therapeutic' acts which restrict a person's freedom, we shall establish the conditions for therapeutic Fascism.

Institutional psychiatry is social control

In *The Manufacture of Madness* (1971), the practice of

'institutional psychiatry' is traced back to the medieval witch-hunts, with a return to the theme of the witch and the mental patient as scapegoats. 'The Age of Faith' in which people were persecuted and scapegoated as witches, has been replaced by 'The Age of Reason' which has substituted the concept of mental illness for that of heresy. The argument, developed from the idea of the 'inverted theological game' in *The Myth of Mental Illness* and touched on in other books along the way, is based on a comparison of 'messianic Christianity' as exemplified by the Inquisition and 'messianic Psychiatry'.

The account of a continuing persecution starts with medieval European society dominated by the Church, and traces the development of scientific ideas that set men's minds stirring and led them to challenge clerical authority. The Church reacted by declaring them the agents of Satan:—

the sorceress who healed, the heretic who thought for himself, the fornicator who lusted too much, and the Jew, who, in the midst of a Christian society, stubbornly rejected the divinity of Jesus — all were categorised as 'heretics', and thus was each, as an enemy of God, persecuted by the Inquisition.[42]

The massacre of witches and Jews became accepted social practice. In one period of six months at the end of the thirteenth century, a hundred thousand Jews were massacred in Bavaria. There are many references to the persecution of the Jews in periods from the thirteenth century through to the Second World War and the Nazi concentration camps, and this is treated as a continuous story in a way which associates psychiatrists first with the inquisitors, and later with the Nazis. The impression given, though never stated outright, is that psychiatry is anti-Semitic — and this is curious in view of the fact that many American psychiatrists are of Jewish origin, as indeed was Freud.

The treatment of the persecution of the witches is fairly superficial. The only primary source referred to is the *Malleus Maleficarum* or *Hammer of the Witches* (1486), a chilling enough account of the nature, proclivities and evil deeds of witches, with the appropriate means of examination, torture and execution. Though there are many transcripts of witch trials available, Szasz takes the rest of his material from such sources as Robbins's *Encyclopaedia of Witchcraft and Demonology* (1959) and Christina Hole's *Witchcraft in England* (1947). Szasz makes little reference to the growing literature on the sociology of deviance, which might have strengthened his case. In fact, though he trades on labelling theory at times, he specifically repudiates the approach of the deviancy theorists:—

Although I have used the sociological approach to deviance in this study, I have, whenever possible, avoided calling witches and mental patients 'deviants'. Words have lives of their own. However much sociologists insist that the term 'deviant' does not diminish the worth of the person or group so categorised, the implication of inferiority adheres to the word.[43]

For Szasz, the persecution of Jews and witches and the development of the mental health movement make up one stream of oppression in which there is no necessity for differentiation. The mental health movement threatens 'the persecuted Other':—

We have seen that whenever men wanted to degrade, exploit, oppress or kill the Other, they have always declared him to be not 'really' human. This has been the characteristic feature of human conquests, enslavements and mass murders throughout history . . . This was the basic issue in the systematic anti-Semitism of Spain and Germany; in the European witch-hunts; in American Negro slavery; and in the modern, virtually world-wide persecution of the mentally ill.[44]

This is the sinister heritage of the 'institutional psychiatrists'; but there is another of the now characteristic semantic changes in the use Szasz makes of the term 'institutional'. His emphasis on involuntary commitment, and the references to force and persecution, give the impression that he is referring to psychiatrists practising in hospitals on patients committed against their will. In fact, he means all psychiatrists who are supported out of public funds, and not in private practice:—

The most important economic characteristic of Institutional Psychiatry is that the institutional psychiatrist is a
bureaucratic employee . . . its most important social characteristic is the use of force and fraud. . . . Psychiatrists
employed by state mental hospitals, college health services,
military organisations, courts, prisons and others in similar
positions are, according to this definition, institutional
psychiatrists . . . institutional psychiatry is the characteristic abuse of medicine . . .[45]

The entire argument needs to be seen in its historical context. At the time Szasz began to publish his major books, the
mental health movement in the United States was very active.[46]
A much-publicised Federal Government Report, *Action for
Mental Health*, was published in 1961, and a new law made
possible the development of Community Mental Health
Centers, supported by federal funds. This development
brought psychiatric care (for the most part not hospital-
based, and not involving compulsion) within the reach of
many Americans, and one might have expected Szasz to wel-
come the movement as a major step towards reducing the
huge mental hospital populations. In fact, over the past
twenty years, the number of patients in mental hospitals in
the USA has been reduced by more than two-thirds; but
Szasz has no enthusiasm for the new movement, which he
sees as a sinister extension of state power: —

In my opinion, the 'mental health' — in the sense of
spiritual well-being — of Americans cannot be improved by
slogans, drugs, community mental health centers, or even
with billions of dollars expended on a 'war on mental illness' . . . The best, indeed the only, hope for remedying
the problem of 'mental illness' lies in weakening, not
strengthening, the power of Institutional Psychiatry. Only
when this peculiar institution is abolished will the moral
powers of uncoerced therapy be released. Only then will
the potentialities of Contractual Psychiatry be able to un-
fold . . .[47]

The new movement had been heavily criticised in *Ideology
and Insanity* (1970) as 'barely off the drawing boards' and

filled with 'high-flown phrases and utopian promises': 'Indeed, the only thing clear about it is its hostility to the psychiatrist in private practice who ministers to the individual patient: he is depicted as one who engages in a nefarious activity.'[48]

Contractual Psychiatry, the 'moral power of uncoerced therapy', means private practice. Community mental health — collectivistic, not individualistic — was developing rapidly, and at last liberalising the mental hospital system Szasz had justly criticised; but his response was to attempt to rally his academic colleagues to the medical (and entepreneurial) flag:

> Academic psychiatry now faces a two-pronged attack on its integrity: blandishments — consisting of vast sums of money, available to those willing to train cadres of mental health workers; and accusations — consisting of criticisms of those unwilling to lend their own, and their institutions' talents and resources to the waging of all-out 'war against mental illness' . . . the larger academic community and society in general, must recognise the nature and value of academic endeavours, and must protect them from encroachments by zealous social reformers.[49]

Contractual Psychiatry, otherwise called Autonomous Psychotherapy, is free from the taints of control and coercion because the patient seeks help freely with those troublesome 'problems in living' and pays for the service he receives. Szasz is businesslike about this: —

> The financial arrangement between therapist and client must be clearly understood and strictly followed . . . I discuss the fee with the patient, and explain my practice of rendering a statement at the end of each month . . . I do not accept clients for whom the cost of analysis is a significant economic hardship. Strained financial circumstances do not provide a suitable psychological atmosphere for this kind of therapeutic work.[50]

He had written earlier in *The Manufacture of Madness* 'Like other men, psychiatrists cannot be expected to act systematically against their own self-interest.'[51]

With *The Myth of Psychotheraphy* (1976) Szasz comes full circle, and denies the validity of psychotherapy as well:—

There is, properly speaking, no such thing as psychotherapy. Like mental illness, psychotherapy is a metaphor and a myth. Hypnosis, suggestion, psychoanalysis, whatever the so-called psychotherapy might be labelled, are names we give to people speaking and listening to each other in certain ways.[52]

By this time, the treatment is tired, and the conclusion only too predictable: 'The paradigmatic institutional method is involuntary mental hospitalisation. The paradigmatic physiochemical method is the use of drugs or electric shock. And the paradigmatic rhetorical method is psychoanalysis.'[53]

Words and meanings

Szasz is the most acrobatic and elusive of writers. We have questioned his use of such terms as 'myth', 'illness', 'paradigm', 'crime' and 'institutional', all of which are basic to his argument; and there are two other words which illustrate the same capacity to play upon meanings — 'game' and 'state'.

In *The Myth of Mental Illness*, there is a chapter on 'The Game-Playing Model of Human Behaviour', in which Szasz draws on the work of G. H. Mead and Piaget's ideas on children's games.[54] By the time he wrote *The Ethics of Psychoanalysis*, four years later, he was discussing Stephen Potter's ideas on 'gamesmanship',[55] and was developing models of the therapeutic encounter in terms of bridge and chess. These involve an analogy — the therapeutic encounter is *like* bridge or chess in that . . ., etc. But when he comes to write of 'the theological game', 'the medical game', 'the therapeutic game', he is using direct description, not analogy. By calling these activities 'games', he is implying that they are not undertaken seriously or honestly, and that they are somehow discreditable.

'State' has two meanings — one for an American and one for a European. Szasz employs both. The USA has state mental hospitals — that is, mental hospitals administered by individual states, which have their own programmes supported by some federal funding; yet Szasz writes of 'the therapeutic State' in a sense which suggests the menace of Nazi Germany or Soviet Russia, monolithic organisations dedicated to the suppression of human freedom. It is difficult to see the State of New York in this light.

There are perhaps more fundamental illogicalities in his writing: the tendency to cite the exceptional case as the norm, to write 'All . . .' when he means 'Some . . .', to stress similarities and ignore differences. Heresy equals mental illness, witch equals mental patient, persecution equals treatment. The result is often caricature rather than exploration.

Some of his writing has a high moral tone: there are appeals to liberty, to freedom, to dignity, to self-respect, to morality. The impression is given that his opponents, the idealists of the mental health movement, have none of these virtues in mind. They are portrayed as 'agents of force and fraud', near-Fascists who design only to enslave America. Szasz shows no evidence of ability to distinguish between Fascism and Communism: to him, both are collectivist, and both equally endanger the all-American virtues of true grit and self-sufficiency.

But behind the preaching is a very hard-nosed commercial approach. People are allowed to seek help with their 'problems in living', and Szasz is prepared to help them, provided that they are rich, and can pay up every month. Those who cannot pay are simply uninteresting to him. The cash nexus between doctor and patient has been metamorphosed into a sacred bond, preserving the patient's status.

Szasz is the most unabashed of capitalists; but it is a particular kind of American immigrant capitalism, in which memories of the torture chamber and the concentration camp and the political oppressions of the old world blend with a sense of almost unlimited economic opportunity in the new. He is not only making money. He is also exorcising his political ghosts.

Szasz was born in Budapest, and reached the United States at the age of eighteen, in 1938, the year the Nazis annexed Austria. Behind him, there is the folk-memory of a Hungarian — of the Catholic Church, a powerful force for social control in the days of the Austro-Hungarian Empire; of secret police, of arbitrary arrests, of techniques for changing people's minds and altering their personalities; and after he reached America, there was the Nazi occupation of Hungary, and then the Soviet occupation. His inability to distinguish between the two political philosophies becomes more comprehensible when one recalls that both meant the same to Budapest: armed occupation and a new kind of political oppression to replace the old.

One can only speculate on the origins of his fierce and oft-repeated assertion that psychiatry is not medicine, that mentally ill people are not ill. This is an old medical prejudice, but something of an in-joke, equivalent to the way physicians decry the work of surgeons, and surgeons of physicians. Few doctors would be prepared to put it in print, and the view must be unique among doctors who have taken a psychoanalytic training. Szasz is not only willing to put it in print, he has gone on doing so for twenty years, while still holding a Chair of Psychiatry at Syracuse and practising as an analyst. He tells us that *The Myth of Mental Illness* is 'part autobiography'. The inability to reconcile medicine and psychiatry, the systematic destruction of Freud and the neuropsychiatrists, may date from contradictions in training, from the very different orientations of the basic medical course and experience in psychoanalysis; but they may also owe something to European geography. Vienna, the centre of psychoanalysis and the location of Freud's discoveries, lies along the Danube to the north of Budapest, and was the centre of the Austrian oppression of Hungary. It is enough to suggest irreconcilable conflicts.

Szasz is neither an historian nor a sociologist, though he is prepared to bend history and sociology to his purposes. He is a medical practitioner of a very conservative kind, an analyst who distrusts psychoanalysis, a citizen who distrusts the state, and yet has faith in the law. What he has to tell us about institutions is almost wholly destructive, though his writings, and his part in the ACLU campaign, may have made some institutions more humane in his own country.

His besetting sin is over-statement; but it is also the secret of his readability. He does not trouble the reader with half-tones, with complex arguments, or with obscure and difficult points. The negative thesis is firmly stated and firmly adhered to, the evidence to the contrary ignored, and the reader carried along on a flood of persuasive argument. Almost every point could be challenged, qualified or doubted; but nihilism, after all, saves the pain of thinking.

PART II
The British empiricists

4 RUSSELL BARTON: THE MEDICAL INTERPRETER

What Dr Russell Barton had to say is easily described, though half of it is usually forgotten. Where it came from, and what it meant, are more difficult to determine.

William Russell Barton, consultant psychiatrist at a large mental hospital near London, wrote a small book entitled *Institutional Neurosis* which appeared in 1959. In it, he described a disease of the same name, and his thesis was simple: patients came into mental hospitals with one form of illness, and the hospital itself could give them another. Institutional neurosis was a distinct condition which could be diagnosed and treated. The first half of the book is taken up with a description of the symptoms and causes, and the second half is a prescription for treatment both in the hospital, and at a suitable stage in recovery, in the community.

The approach is overtly medical, and the monography modest in scope, amounting to only 63 pages. While it predates Foucault's work on mental illness, it gives the appearance of having captured some of Goffman's early ideas, adapting them to a medical purpose. Yet Russell Barton specifically disclaims any knowledge of Goffman's work in his preface to the second edition,[1] and he traces a much longer heritage — back to Myerson's description of 'prison stupor' in 1939, Bettelheim and Sylvester's work on 'psychological institutionalism' in 1948, and even 'Oblomovism' as described by Goncharov in 1858.[2] He does not claim to be advancing anything new, merely to be arranging existing ideas in an orderly manner.[3] A foreword by Dr Noel Gordon Harris, who says he does not 'like the title of the book very much', also praises the author for his courage in writing it, and says that it 'should have been written many years ago'.[4]

The task of tracing the origin of ideas is a difficult and often a fruitless one. It is quite possible that Goffman himself had read Myerson and Bettelheim and Sylvester: there were many pointers in the existing literature to the effects of institutional pressures on individuals, and Goffman never claims that his ideas have developed out of an intellectual vacuum. His distinctive, phenomenological style of writing relies on direct experience rather than on existing texts, but that does not mean that he was necessarily uninfluenced by them. So we are left with a puzzle: did two very different writers several thousands of miles apart independently pick up the same ideas and use them for very different purposes, or was there an unacknowledged link between them? Was the *Zeitgeist* at work, high-lighting ideas because the time was ripe for their acceptance; or was one writer heavily influenced, perhaps unconsciously, by the other?

A new disease entity?

It is first necessary to describe Russell Barton's development of the theme of 'institutional neurosis'. He says that he uses the phrase 'because it promotes the syndrome to the category of a disease rather than a process, thereby encouraging us to understand, approach and deal with it in the same way as other diseases'.[5] The clinical features of this disease are apathy, lack of initiative, loss of interest in the outside world, submissiveness and resignation. Patients take no interest in the future. Their personal habits and standards deteriorate. They often adopt a characteristic posture, shown in four pictures of elderly women patients on the cover of the book: 'the hands held across the body or tucked behind an apron, the shoulders drooped, and the head held forward. The gait has a shuffling quality, movements at the pelvis, hips and knees are restricted.'[6] Staff observation of this condition may give rise to such entries in patients' notes as 'Dull, depressed and solitary', 'Remains uncommunicative, withdrawn and unoccupied' or alternatively 'Has settled down well', 'Is co-operative and gives no trouble.'[7]

Not all people in institutions develop this condition, and some people outside may do so — 'probably hermits, some housewives and old age pensioners'.[8] In mental patients, the condition 'may be indistinguishable from the later stages of schizophrenia'.[9] It is more easily distinguished from depression, organic dementia and myxoedema, though the conditions may overlap. People in types of institutions other than mental hospitals may develop it. The final proof that it exists is that 'hospitals run by a staff aware of the neurosis and its aetiology are ceasing to produce it'.[10]

Institutional neurosis might perhaps be explained in terms of social conditioning or psychoanalysis; but Russell Barton finds it sufficient to point to 'clusters of factors' in the mental hospital environment which cause it to develop and which can be tackled on the ward.[11] There are seven such 'clusters':

1. *Loss of contact with the oustide world*: caused by locked ward doors, the 'begrudged and condescending granting of leave', poor facilities for visitors, difficulty in writing letters, and inability to make ordinary social relationships.

2. *Enforced idleness*: due to ward routines, lack of activities or meaningful work.

3. *'Bossiness of medical and nursing staff'*; 'My impression is that an authoritarian attitude is the rule rather than the exception'. Russell Barton notes 'the use of the imperative mood' in staff communications with patients, and the development of petty tyranny and bullying.

4. *Loss of personal friends, personal possessions and personal events*: in the mental hospital, the significance of these factors is replaced by a sense of institutional possessions and institutional events.

5. *Drugs*: the use of sedatives to produce apathy, and make patients easily managed. (The psychotropic drugs, which control extreme emotional reactions, had been developed earlier in the 1950s, and at the time Russell Barton wrote, many psychiatrists were heavily over-prescribing by modern standards).

6. *Ward atmosphere*: poor furniture, decoration and lighting, dirt, noise, smell and the appearance of other patients all produce a general environment of drabness and depression.

7. *Loss of prospects*: the difficulties of taking up the

patterns of family life again, loss of job prospects, problems of accommodation and making friends and fears of loneliness in the outside world could all produce an apathetic acceptance of hospital life.

The listing and description of these factors in itself suggested ways of reversing their effect. In the second part of the monograph, these are set out in the form of a chart for each patient,[12] with cross-headings listing the people who might help to bring change about. These include medical staff, nursing staff, occupational therapist, social worker, friends and volunteers, general practitioner and relatives. The intention is to produce a working document 'confronting individual members of staff with their role and contribution in combating institutional neurosis', and it is intended that this should be used in group discussion. The aim is to find out 'What can be done? Who should do what?'

Another chart, featuring a ladder,[13] shows an eight-stage procedure for getting patients back into the community. It runs from '0 — Patients sit around doing nothing' to '7 — People no longer attached to hospital: join League of Friends if they wish' via such stages as part-time work (for pay), full-time work outside the hospital while still living in, a transitionary period in a hostel, and living in lodgings with attachment to a hospital social club. There is some very practical material on subjects such as how to run ward meetings, how to partition off beds, the substitution of placebos for sedatives, and how to help women patients to improve their appearance with hairdressing and cosmetics. By this time, we are light-years away from the sociological concerns of Goffman or Foucault, but well into the preoccupations of a good consultant psychiatrist in the late 1950s, when the influence of such American writers as Stanton and Schwartz[14] and Greenblatt, Levinson and Williams[15] on the importance of social therapy was strongly felt.

Antecedents

Institutional Neurosis, despite its initial bow to scholarship, is basically a handbook for mental hospital staff — a 'how to do it' book which was to be deservedly popular with nurse tutors and social work teachers. Some fairly basic ideas are, as the author says, arranged in an orderly manner, and the psychology is excellent: a memorable title, a new disease entity, and two sets of simplified prescriptions which may easily be committed to memory. The interpretation and translation of ideas which were swirling around the fields of psychiatry and sociology (then much closer than they are today) should not be underestimated. However, despite the author's specific disclaimer, the book has been widely interpreted as a new contribution to thinking about institutional care, and the question of its intellectual origins needs to be pressed a little further.

Was the acknowledged debt to Goncharov, to Myerson and to Bettelheim and Sylvester justified? A re-reading of these sources suggests that the connections were tenuous. In *Oblomov*,[16] Goncharov describes a chronic state of lassitude and boredom in a man who had no will to enter on the struggle of living. Oblomov lived in his own very dirty flat. His decrepit man-servant, Zakhar, shuffled in and out, trying to draw his attention to his debts and the imminent threat of eviction. There was no lack of stimulus, only a failure to respond to it; and there were many visitors, each representing a different aspect of the outside world, and each in turn rejected. It may be seen as a picture of schizophrenia or depression or latter-day *mal de siècle*, but it is not a picture of the results of institutional living. Dr Myerson, a consultant in Boston State Hospital in the late 1930s, does use the phrase 'prison stupor',[17] but without any further reference to prisons. He describes hospital conditions as decreasing patients' motivation, diminishing their social contacts, and leaving them 'immersed in monotony'; but he is writing exclusively about schizophrenic patients, and his proposals for improving their condition are commonsense and orthodox; physiotherapy, exercise, sunshine, vitamin pills, some attention to clothing, and the arousing of motivation through 'praise and blame' — the giving or denying of sweets, cigarettes or ice-cream.

Bruno Bettelheim and Emmy Sylvester do use the phrase 'psychological institutionalism'[18] a condition they describe as 'a deficiency disease in the emotional sense'; but they are concerned with children — in institutions, in foster-homes or in 'disorganised family settings'. They regard 'psychological institutionalism' as 'a deficiency disease in the emotional sense' — which may have prompted the description of 'institutional neurosis' as a disease — but their writing makes it clear that they regard it as a form of emotional retardation in childhood, not as a disease entity which can develop in maturity.

The antecedents claimed for *Institutional Neurosis* therefore do not account for the new elements in it. On the other hand, there seems little doubt about the debt in some form to Goffman. The listing of 'prisons, displaced persons' camps, orphanages, convents and other institutions' seems a clear echo of Goffman's five-fold classification of 'total institutions'.[19] The disclaimer 'By no means all people in institutions develop it' (i.e. institutional neurosis) has a clear ring of 'none of the elements I will describe seems peculiar to total institutions'.[20] There is the recognisable 'cluster' technique,[21] and both Goffman and Russell Barton mention housewives as liable to suffer from similar psychological limitations to those to people in institutions.[22] The differences in the handling of the material are very basic — Goffman's grasp of his material was surer, his analysis struck keeper, and his purpose was subversive of the existing medical order in mental hospitals, while Russell Barton was a doctor with administrative responsibility, concerned with humanitarian schemes for patient management. Nevertheless, it seems probable that Goffman's thinking, if not his name, was accessible to Russell Barton when he was writing. Goffman's early papers circulated widely in the late 1950s, and some of his more striking phrases may have become common currency before *Asylums* was published.

There were other new ideas in the air, too: the ideas of community care which developed in the deliberations of the Royal Commission on Mental Illness and Mental Deficiency (1954-7) and became incorporated in the Mental Health Act of 1959; the recommendations of the World Health Organisation's Third Expert Committee on Mental Health (1953)[23] on the need for an open-door policy, and for a recognition of the importance of 'ward atmosphere'; the new practice of the therapeutic community, developed by Dr Maxwell Jones at the Henderson Hospital.[24] All these must have played some part in creating the climate of opinion which made it possible to produce *Institutional Neurosis*, and to use it for teaching purposes.

So some new ideas are given respectable antecedents (Oblomov and the rest) and turned to the purposes of humane medical control.

Was 'institutional neurosis' a new disease entity, or merely an arresting semantic label? Other psychiatrists, perhaps predictably, were to reject the idea that a new disease had been discovered, and that their hospitals caused it. There was a fair point in the argument that, since most of the long-stay patients in mental hospitals had a diagnosis of schizophrenia, and the symptoms of burned-out schizophrenia were apparently indistinguishable from those of 'institutional neurosis', what Russell Barton was describing was only the end-result of the original disease process. The argument was perhaps of the chicken-and-egg variety. The interaction between a self-isolating tendency in the individual and an environment which positively promotes self-isolation is still imperfectly understood.

Dr Noel Harris says in his foreword: 'After all, it is the medical man who should take the initiative and rouse enthusiasm in those who work with him . . .'. As a practising medical administrator, Russell Barton was not interested in describing institutional conditions; perhaps he knew them too well; and he was not concerned with problems of power relationships. He held the power, and intended to go on doing so, exercising it responsibly and encouraging other staff to do the same. Though the title of the book, and the opening pages, place *Institutional Neurosis* as a text of the 1960s, the purpose is a long-accepted one in the medical and nursing professions: to do the patient no harm, and to help him to recovery.

5   TOWNSEND:
THE REFORMER

Peter Townsend's *The Last Refuge: a survey of residential institutions and Homes for old people* is one of the few major pieces of work on institutions which takes a field of study other than that of the mental hospital or the prison. Published in 1962, it was based on a national survey undertaken in the preceding four years.

Townsend says in the Introduction that he had seen conditions in an ex-workhouse some years earlier which made a deep impression on him:—

> The day-rooms were bleak and uninviting. In one of them sat forty men in high-backed Windsor chairs, staring straight ahead, or down at the floor . . . the sun was shining outside, but no-one was looking that way . . . Watery-eyed and feeble, they looked suspiciously at our troups of observers, and then returned to their self-imposed contemplation. They wore shapeless tweed suits and carpet slippers or boots. Life seemed to have been drained from them, all but the dregs. Their stoic resignation seemed not only attributable to infirmity and old age. They were like people who had taken so much punishment that they had become inured to pain, and robbed of all initiative.[1]

This impression led him to formulate a series of questions: how many other homes for old people in Britain were like the one he had visited? Why did they still exist ten years after the government pledged itself to abolish the workhouse? Why did people enter such places? And was it possible to create a structure of medical and social services which would keep them in the community?

The government pledge had come during the debates on the National Assistance Bill in 1947, when Aneurin Bevan, as Minister of Health, stated categorically 'the workhouse is to go'.[2] The social faith and optimism of the post-war period was such that the promise was to be taken seriously. Yet in ten years, no government committee or commission had investigated the plight of institutionalised old people, and 'the information in official reports was extraordinarily scanty and inept'.

The details of this massive work — the evidence of the continued existence of workhouse-type conditions which most people in Britain thought had been abolished with the coming of the Welfare State — provided an overwhelming indictment. The British contribution to the anti-institutional movement, of which Townsend's work was to be a formative part, was to come largely in the form of such evidence — fact piled on fact, with meticulous attention to the probability and significance of events, and the credibility of those who testified. The facts were amassed with a sense of moral outrage, and intended for practical action rather than for intellectual understanding; and the style was distinctive. Townsend's juxtaposition of statistical material with acutely observed and detailed quotations of individual experience was to set a fashion in social research. For example, a detailed and factual discussion on staffing levels and staff salaries is followed by an account of a small elderly woman sitting by a smouldering fire, who had the temerity to place 'a few knobs of coal on the embers'. An attendant shouted at her in a 'loud, raucous voice' and fetched a charge nurse, who looked at the thermometer on the wall, opened the window, and told the elderly woman that it was warm enough, and she was not to touch the fire. Another resident remarked 'You just have to ignore them, my dear, and keep yourself to yourself.'[3] This counterpointing of statistical and anecdotal evidence to make a point (in this case, the poor quality of underpaid and overworked staff) was to be widely imitated.

'In the institution', writes Townsend in a much-quoted passage,

people live communally, with a minimum of privacy, yet

their relationships with each other are slender. Many subsist in a kind of defensive shell of isolation. Their mobility is restricted, and they have little access to general society. ... They are subtly oriented towards a system in which they submit to orderly routine, lack creative occupation, and cannot exercise much self-determination ... the result for the individual seems fairly often to be a gradual process of depersonalisation.[4]

The evidence of lack of privacy, loss of occupation, isolation, inability to form new relationships and the collapse of self-determination closely parallels Russell Barton's findings in mental hospitals, and need not be repeated at length. Some 88 tables and 438 pages make their case by the sheer hammer-blows of repetition.

What did Townsend make of his evidence? He seems to have been the first British writer to make a distinction between loneliness and isolation — it is possible to have other people within reach, but not to be able to relate to them. In nearly all the institutions, he and his team found people who deliberately withdrew from the group, seeking solitude in odd corners. One said 'It hurts inside of me, but I can think my own thoughts, and dream my own dreams.' He suspected that such a reaction was a kind of passive hostility to the life of the institution: the staff were apt to dismiss it as 'a form of eccentricity or mental infirmity'.[5] In the voluntary homes, where most residents had a room of their own, there was no evidence that their social relationships suffered — indeed, they were sometimes closer than in the large public authority homes where residents shared rooms or slept in dormitories. Townsend comments: 'This seems to be an important finding, because it suggests that the aims of securing privacy for the individual and of creating a residential community are not necessarily in conflict.'[6]

There are many such shafts of insight, sensitively observed and sensitively recorded; but none of them is followed up, because the chosen method of research does not allow for it. Instead, Townsend concentrates on the development of scales for the measurement of the quality of homes and the capacities or incapacities of residents, and on major policy recommendations.

The Quality Scale[7] is of a type now familiar in evaluation studies. It consists of a series of items, ranging from 'age of building' through 'attitude of matron' and 'choice of doctor' to 'special arrangements for birthdays' and 'ratio of TV sets to beds'. The difficulty, as with all such scales, is that it is necessary to defend both the choice of items and the weighting accorded to them; and when this is done, what appears to be an objective and reliable form of measurement often turns out to be both subjective and unreliable. For example, it is important for residents to be able to choose their own doctor if they wish; but the result of this freedom is that there are now many homes where no medical practitioner attends regularly, the staff take no responsibility for the health care of residents, and quite serious health problems can be missed. The simple adoption of 'choice of doctor' as a measure of the quality of care, without qualification, can be misleading. Similarly, it is an excellent arrangement to have special small celebrations for birthdays if this involves some genuine spirit of congratulation; but there are some dreadfully institutional birthday celebrations when it is done to order. A TV set per bed may seem ideal − but not unless they can be placed out of earshot of each other. The problems of institutional care are a good deal more complex than a forty-eight item scale can compass. The scale, which is elaborated on in Townsend's Appendix 3, is described as 'tentative' or 'provisional'. It was to point the way forward for more refined attempts to develop such scales, though the problems of selection of items and weighting remain.

The Incapacity Scale[8] consists of sixteen items, relating to the individual resident's ability to wash, dress, get in or out of bed, see, hear, speak, and such functions as mobility and bladder and bowel control. Again, it is somewhat simplistic by present-day standards, but much of the work which has been done on Incapacity Scales relates back to this early and pioneering example. Notes on the research difficulties involved have been particularly valuable to later scholars.

But Townsend's main achievement, as he intended, was at the political level. Very detailed recommendations include the development of a 'family help service' to provide care for old people in their own homes, the extension of services in the community such as better medical attention and sheltered housing. Townsend has comparatively little time for social workers, who play a very small part in his considerations, preferring the more tangible services of 'domestic help, shopping, laundry, meals, night attendance and occupational therapy'.[9] He also recommends the closing of the old workhouses, and the transfer of public Homes from the local County and County Borough Councils to the National Health Service; the compulsory registration of all private and voluntary Homes, and their periodic inspection; and the expenditure on new and extended services for the elderly of sums of money sufficiently large to 'represent a distinct shift in priorities'.[10]

The pressure-group approach

The book was timely, for the government had embarked on a new community care policy in the previous year (1961), and was shortly afterwards to name the elderly as one of the four main groups to which it applied.[11] *The Last Refuge*, with its assumption that reform was not only possible, but overdue, its fierce defence of the values of family life, and its new techniques of social investigation, was to play an important part in the community care movement. Peter Townsend, a practical reformer as well as an academic, was to work through a variety of pressure groups to put his policy into practice.

More than twenty years later, we can question some of the findings. The jump from evidence to recommendations is over a sizeable theoretical gap, which Townsend makes no attempt to fill: though his methods are statistical, his reactions are intuitive rather than logical. He is a moralist, and a highly political animal, concerned much more with the ways in which social change may be engineered through national politics than with the more detailed work of understanding human reactions and training staff.

Abolish the institution (or, if it cannot be abolished, transfer it to the National Health Service); spend millions on new services; support the family. These were the main recommendations, and while they had an immediate political impact, they have not stood the test of time in the way in which the more tentative and scholarly work on the scales has done. While Goffman and Foucault end their studies with an intellectual shrug of the shoulders — they have said what they had to say, and other people can understand or not — Townsend writes for the politicians and the press, in order to make things happen.

That was his strength, but also his weakness. The masses of detailed fact were to date quickly — while it was fairly easy to demonstrate in 1962 that there were people in old people's homes capable of sustaining an independent life in the community with a little help, that is not the case in a period when we are told that the average age of admission 'is now approaching 82'.[12] The old people's homes are for the most part still there — though the worst of the ex-workhouse accommodation has been taken out of use, some of it is still occupied; and the resident population is now older, more frail, and less able to defend its own rights. Homes were not transferred to the National Health Service — and it is not quite clear why Townsend wanted this to happen, since he provided no evidence on hospital accommodation for the elderly, and remarked in passing that much of it was 'dismally bleak and aseptic' (possibly the potential of the NHS for improvement seemed greater than that of locally administered services). Old people's Homes have continued to be run by local authorities, and the move in the 1960s and 1970s was to be away from rather than into the hospital. Although some are smaller and some more humanely run than in the past, many of the problems of institutionalism remain. As the assumption of continuing economic growth failed, and social priorities came to be sharply questioned, the prescription of 'more money — more services' lost its power.

Behind Townsend's writing, and that of many other British social investigators of the same period, lies the basic assumption that everyone knows what is right and fair, and that it is only necessary to demonstrate a scandal, to expose wrongs, to have them put right; but the demonstration of scandals, the handling of exposés, has now become an industry in its own right, moving from the book trade to the television documentary as the nightly audience of millions sinks back into its armchairs to watch the latest real-life horror story. A simple faith based in the rule of law and the good intentions of government no longer meets the case; and the pressure-group weapon, so promising in the 1960s, has had its edge blunted by constant use. Indignation, even righteous indignation, no longer changes society.

The approach was successful in the nineteenth century: the history books record the success of social reformers who achieved great changes through the revelation of human misery and the passing of appropriate Acts of Parliament; but we have become increasingly aware in the twentieth century that social policy is not determined in Whitehall, nor changed overnight by the magic wand of legislation. Poor Law attitudes survived in the ex-workhouses of 1957; in some places they survive today, and their eradication is slow and difficult. From the point of view of the consumer — patient, resident or Social Security claimant — social policy is an infinitely complex process of national intent mediated through agencies with varying powers and responsibilities, and the competence and attitudes of the nurse, care assistant or counter clerk may be of as great importance as what the law intended.[13]

Against this, it may be argued that law still possesses a denunciatory function. While attitudes and behaviour may not follow changes in the law, an Act of Parliament sets standards, and makes the correction of abuse possible, if not inevitable. Towsend's model of action was successful in its period; but in a very different social climate, we have to subtract the detail and the polemic, and to see what survives in the realm of ideas.

Townsend's theoretical framework

Townsend starts from a fundamental belief in the importance of family life, and of 'three-generation reciprocity' in which grandparents, parents and children provide basic and vital support for one another:—

> Within an organic unit of three generations, largely preserving its identity and independence on the recognition of biological attachment, the individual achieves a large measure of self-fulfilment, and can satisfy many social and psychological needs, first as child, and later as adolescent, husband or wife, parent and grandparent. The family unit

may not be the only unit which can serve these complex functions, but it is the one which does so for the vast majority of the world's population, and, moreoever, it seems particularly difficult to replace.[14]

The clue to this thinking lies in an earlier work, *The Family Life of Old People* (1957) based on a survey undertaken when Townsend was a research officer at the Institute of Community Studies at Bethnal Green in East London. The Institute, founded in the early 1950s with Michael Young (now Lord Young) as its Director, carried out a number of studies[15] of working class life in Bethnal Green, a decaying city area, and the new housing estates to which families were being moved. The seminal *Family and Kinship in East London* by Michael Young and Peter Willmott was published in the same year as *The Family Life of Old People*. The general thesis is that the family life of Bethnal Green was emotionally rich, tenacious and highly supportive, based on the pivotal figure of 'Mum', who held the extended family together and enabled it to survive the storms and stresses of life. This picture was later to be contrasted, in the same authors' *Family and Class in a London Suburb* (1960) with the emotionally impoverished life of nuclear families on a housing estate, where the loss of the extended family was compensated for by the acquisition of consumer goods.

These hypotheses contained some elements of truth, but they were both romanticised and sweeping, clichés of sociological thinking rather than rigorous analysis. From this distinctive perspective, family life was assumed to be natural, normal and desirable, while institutional life was assumed to be unnatural, abnormal and undesirable. The problems of family life were ignored; the problems of institutional life were highlighted by contrast.

In *The Last Refuge*, the analysis of reasons for admission to residential care shows that, by comparison with the elderly in the general population, the institutionalised group had a much higher proportion of the widowed, the divorced and the childless; and that the loss of a close relative, usually a husband, wife or child, often preceded admission. For a substantial proportion of the sample, three-generation reciprocity was not a practical possibility:

The absence of subsidiary or secondary sources of help —
other relatives, friends or social services — is the most
common characteristic of those living with relatives and
afterwards entering Homes. The great majority of these
have no other relatives to go to.[16]

The logic of Townsend's findings is therefore at variance
with his sociological assumptions; and the assumptions remain
untouched, for there is no serious consideration of what is to
be done for old people without families. There are some
references to early child care studies, and there is mention of
'artificial families' and 'quasi-families',[17] but no attempt is
made to work out the differences in the life-situations of
children and old people.

Where institutional care — 'relatively closed and artificial' —
is necessary, small homes are recommended, the maximum
size being 20–25 beds; but the reader is not told where this
figure comes from, nor on what evidence it is based. Are small
homes necessarily better than large homes? Experience suggests that they often have less facilities, and may become
equally institutionalised. One of the problems which has
developed in practice is that small homes cannot support
highly trained or specialised staff. Townsend's recommendations that 'the person in charge of the staff should hold a
Social Science certificate or diploma' and that there should
be a qualified nurse for every four residents[18] were to prove
unrealistic.

In one short chapter on 'The Effects of Institutions'
(chapter 13 — omitted from the paperback edition) Townsend
surveys the existing evidence on institutions. At the time he
wrote, Goffman's early papers were in circulation, and Russell
Barton's *Institutional Neurosis* had been published and widely
reviewed. Neither seems to have made much impression.
Townsend gives Barton five lines, and reduces Goffman to
two footnotes.[19] Much of the evidence on which he relies in
a heavily footnoted section is randomly adduced: the evidence
on children, mentioned above, which is of doubtful relevance
to the situation of old people, and needs much more careful
analysis if it is to be made relevant; evidence on patients in
mental hospitals, sometimes not fully understood. Sommer
and Osmund's 'The Schizophrenic No-Society' is quoted as

evidence that people in institutions 'do not form a community in any accepted or meaningful sense of the word',[20] though the point of that paper is that schizophrenics (in or out of the institution) do not form a community because of the self-isolating nature of their condition. Evidence on the use of institutions as therapeutic communities (a popular theme in the early 1960s) is entirely ignored.

Townsend takes it for granted that the case against institutional living is fully proved, and that the answer is quite simply to abolish institutions. His own evidence in some 150,000 words of documentation must have seemed overwhelming proof of the rightness of this course. He had the capacity to document, the will to find out, and the determination to press for social change. In the long term, however, the detail dates, and the sociological and organisational weaknesses of his work become more obvious. He tells us little about the dynamics of institutions, though his influence on their management may have been greater than that of writers with more analytical power.

6 THE MORRISES: BUILDING ON THEORY

Terence and Pauline Morris, respectively a criminologist and a psychiatric social worker, embarked in 1958 on a depth study of a large London prison. *Pentonville: a sociological study of an English prison* was published in 1963.[1] At that time, the Prison Commissioners were concerned at the 'pathological' features of closed prisons, and looked to social scientists for help in liberalising them. The Home Office Research Unit, which was to finance the study, was in the process of being set up.

Few prison research projects can have been carried out under such auspicious conditions. At the London School of Economics, their academic base, the Morrises had a great criminologist, Professor Hermann Mannheim, as their supervisor. In the Home Office, they had the support of Sir Lionel Fox, a distinguished liberal penologist, and the Prison Commission.[2]

Why did they choose Pentonville? The Morrises state that their task was 'to find a prison which was representative in order that generalisations to be drawn from the study could be tested elsewhere'[3] but the cross-classifications of the prison system (local prisons and training prisons, open and closed, closed prisons with different degrees of security, prisons for men and prisons for women) are such that no one prison can be called 'representative', and Pentonville stood at one end of the range — a local prison with a large, mainly recidivist population.

The Prison Commissioners must have had their own reasons for wanting to site the study in such a prison, which exhibited all the 'pathological' features they deplored. 'The Ville', a highly visible and foreboding paradigm of punishment for the would-be offenders of North London, was not representative of the prison system as a whole; but it was representative of everything that was most deplorable in the prison system.

The Morrises write:

> The facts about Pentonville are incontrovertible. The buildings are archaic and grossly over-crowded. There is not enough work for prisoners to do, the staff are short-handed, 'training' and social work provisions are rudimentary, and in spite of its inhospitable character, familiar faces enter its gates again and again. To some readers, this book will appear no more than an exercise in 'muck-raking' sociology ... but ... [it] is not an indictment, neither of the system nor the people within it. Rather it is an attempt to show that in the maximum security prison, all men are prisoners.[4]

Capital punishment was still in force, and hangings took place in Pentonville. The existence of two condemned cells was another reason why Pentonville was atypical, but worth study as an exercise in pathology.

'In the maximum security prison, all men are prisoners.' The words recall the dedication of Gresham Sykes's *Society of Captives*,[5] published while the Morrises were debating the siting of their research project: 'To the man in prison — both the prisoner and his guard'. Sykes's book is a depth study of Trenton Prison, New Jersey, and the comparison between Trenton and Pentonville showed strong features of similarity. Both prisons were of similar architectural design; both housed a large, male recidivist population — Pentonville 1,000 men, Trenton 1,200 — under maximum security conditions, though sentences at Trenton were generally much longer, and the security much tighter. The Morrises were able to make extensive use of Sykes's findings, and to test them out against their own empirical findings.

Society of Captives is now a classic in prison literature. Despite its timing, it does not, in our judgment, properly belong to the new literature of the 1960s because, although

Sykes showed much understanding of the prison situation, and some compassion, his purpose was primarily managerial: he wrote in the wake of a series of riots in American prisons, and his purpose was to analyse the mechanisms of 'total power' in order to prevent them. His study of the prisoners — the 'rats', 'punks', 'ball busters', 'gorillas', 'hipsters' and the rest — tells us something about prisoners' own stereotypes, but rarely gets beyond them. However, he generated a variety of new hypotheses about the working of maximum security prisons which could be applied in the context of Pentonville.

The focus of the new study was not managerial but organisational — the Morrises set out simply to find out how Pentonville worked, and what went on inside its walls. They noted that 'the maximum security prison, like the mental hospital, has been thrown into relief as a challenging area for the study of organisational problems' to be compared with other structures such as the office, the industrial plant, and the military unit.[6] If this part of their theoretical framework drew on the work of Talcott Parsons, who wrote a well-known paper on 'The Mental Hospital as a Type of Social Organisation',[7] using just those parallels, their analysis was to move well beyond structural-functionalism in other ways.

The problem to be studied was Pentonville — an 'on-going social system' of 1,000 prisoners and 224 staff, interacting in a tightly constricted social situation. The book is written in the British empirical tradition, with a wealth of detail about the daily life of prisoners and staff; but the background in theoretical sociology and criminology is unusually strong for an empirical study, and the ability to combine theoretical and practical insights is of a high order.

A system of 'total power'

Gresham Sykes, in *Society of Captives*, had postulated that a maximum security prison is 'an attempt to create and maintain total or almost total social control', and started with a basic question: is a system of total power 'a juggernaut, capable of crushing all opposition', or does it contain inherent pathologies which cause it to crack?[8] Trenton Prison, New Jersey, was almost an ideal type for the purpose of exploring this problem. The Warden believed in total compliance as a system of management. His aim was not to reform, to rehabilitate, to deter, or even to punish, but simply to exact obedience from prisoners. Sykes comes to the conclusion that this is an impossibility, and that a system based on 'total power' is inherently unstable.[9] Obedience is an internalised compulsion, and cannot be enforced on prisoners, who for the most part feel no compulsion to do as they are told, short of threats of physical force. These are not generally useful, because they have only a short-term effect, and on particular individuals. When the aim is to get 1,200 men moving about in an orderly and co-operative fashion, and working steadily, concentration camp tactics are not only undesirable, but grossly inefficient:—

> A blow with a club may check an immediate revolt, it is true, but it cannot ensure effective performance on a punch-press . . . a straitjacket or a pair of handcuffs may serve to curb one rebellious prisoner in a crisis, but they will be of little use in moving more than 1,200 inmates to the mess hall.[10]

In practice, a comparatively small number of prison staff cannot come to terms with a large number of prisoners without colluding with them in some degree. They work in close proximity with them, and have no rewards to offer them, because full privileges are given to all prisoners on entry. Privileges can be lost (a source of much bitterness and complaint by prisoners) but not added to. Hence prison officers are forced to trade — 'compliance or obedience in certain areas at the cost of tolerating disobedience elsewhere';[11] but power once lost is hard to regain: the slide towards riots and escapes has begun.

The Morrises come to the conclusion that, if this is true for American maximum security prisons, it is not true for their British equivalents:—

> In reality, neither Pentonville nor any British prison even attempts to exercise 'total power' as one of its formal objectives. The activities of prison officials are hedged on every side by restrictions intended to ensure that the rule of law runs inside prison no less than outside it.[12]

The picture is much more complicated than Sykes's outline of the battle for compliance and there are 'important flaws in the Sykes hypothesis'[13]: not all prison officers are involved in the tasks of getting prisoners to work. Those who are can usually find small incentives to offer if they find it advisable, and have no difficulty in withdrawing these if they so decide. Some prisoners have a habit of passive obedience to authority, and co-operate without difficulty. Both prison officers and prisoners vary in their reactions. Though they stereotype each other in conversation — 'All screws are bastards', 'All prisoners are liars and not to be trusted' — in practice they come to a variety of accommodations; and the staff are not really clear what their task is: 'Pentonville . . . is a prison in which reformist, punitive and apathetic attitudes are quite fantastically confused.'[14]

Some are hardworking and reformist, disapproved of by others for 'running their feet off for the sake of the prisoners'. Others are cynical and apathetic — uncaring clock-watchers, indifferent to whether the prisoners are clean or dirty, whether they work or idle their time away. A few are corrupt: as the Morrises point out, Sykes's analysis offers no adequate explanation for the 'bent screw' who traffics in tobacco or assists an escape. Some are harsh; but on the whole, though 'prisoners, by projecting undesirable qualities on to the staff, are able to minimise the degradation of their own captive status', they get along together in a kind of neutrality, helped by the fact that both groups come from the same kind of proletarian sub-culture: both groups swear, both groups roll their own cigarettes, both groups suffer from social alienation.[15] (Of all the Morrises' findings, this one raised the greatest objections from the Pentonville staff.)

The Morrises' description rings true; and the differences between their account and Sykes's account may be partly differences in the perceptions of the research workers rather than differences in the situations observed. On re-reading, Sykes's account of prison officers is as stereotyped as his account of prisoners. Whatever the Warden of Trenton's beliefs about the importance of compliance, his staff cannot have been quite so monochrome.

Another basic theme in Gresham Sykes's work is 'the pains of imprisonment'. He takes the view that all prisoners find prison 'depressing and frustrating'.[16] The Morrises consider that the effects vary enormously from individual to individual — and this is an important finding, because it suggests that equal sentences for equal offences may have very unequal outcomes. For some prisoners: —

> it is not so much being shut in, as being unable to influence the course of events outside. Wives may be unfaithful, children sick, landlords may evict, personal property may be pawned or sold, hire purchase companies may foreclose . . . deprivation of liberty is meaningful, therefore, to the extent that a man is emotionally involved in the outside world, for although family and friends can help him retain his sense of social identity, if they are in trouble they may only emphasise his captive innocence.[17]

But for the homeless offender, on the other hand, 'liberty is, in contrast, often no more than the liberty to trudge from one doss-house to the next. Prison walls for this minority are the comforting if unfeeling girdle of security.'[18]

Sykes emphasised the 'harshly Spartan environment' of prison as 'painfully depriving', 'lacking those subtle symbolic overtones which we invest in the world of possessions'.[19] The Morrises find this a very American point of view, resulting from a much higher standard of living than most of the prisoners in Pentonville had ever known. For some of them, prison even represented an advance in their standard of living — they were clothed, fed, and had a roof over their heads. They complained of the unpleasantness of overcrowding and of 'slopping out' (American prisons, even maximum security prisons, usually have modern plumbing) but they did not complain of the cold, the hardness of the beds, or the difficulties of shaving with a blunt blade and cold water.[20]

The Morrises and Sykes are in substantial agreement about the loss of autonomy which prisoners suffer. It is not the tyranny of official control, but its pettiness and triviality which makes it unbearable. The Morrises comment 'Autonomy, identity, responsibility and sexuality are conceptual areas which are first anaesthetised and eventually paralysed,'[21] and one of the major factors is the nature of the reference group. Sykes quoted a prisoner as saying, 'The worst thing about prison is you have to live with the other prisoners',[22] and this Morrises parallel this with

> In Pentonville, it is not so much the fear of violence or sexual exploitation, though these are ever-present, but the distaste of being compelled to live in close proximity with men who may be degenerate and dirty in their personal habits, socially unpleasant, or guilty of crimes which other prisoners regard as revolting.[23]

Prisonisation

Both *Society of Captives* and *Pentonville* draw on the pioneering work of Donald Clemmer,[24] who developed the concept of 'prisonisation'. Clemmer, who was for many years Director of Corrections in the District of Columbia, USA, used this term to describe 'the taking on, in greater or lesser degree, of the folkways, mores, customs and general culture of the penitentiary'. In prison, a man becomes 'An anonymous figure in a subordinate group. A number replaces a name. He wears the clothes of the other members of the subordinate group. He is questioned and admonished. He soon learns that the warden is all-powerful.'[25]

Prisonisation is assimilation, a swallowing-up process. The prisoner learns how to survive in this tough, deprived and sometimes dangerous society, and picks up prison argot, with its distinctive concepts and built-in assumptions about human behaviour; but where Sykes follows up the linguistic line of approach, showing how prison argot shapes the prisoners' thinking about their own reactions, the Morrises use the much less colourful argot of the English prison casually, without investigating its symbolism. As they say, it is common to prisoners and prison officers alike; and they are more concerned to show that reactions to the phenomenon of 'prisonisation' are not homogeneous.[26] The procedure does not have uniformly destructive effects: much depends on whether the prisoner has had a previous exposure to prison culture – the results may be cumulative over several sentences; whether he is able to maintain his contacts with the outside world; whether he 'consciously accepts the dogmas and codes of the inmate culture'; and the nature of the personal relationships he makes in prison. They add elsewhere that a good deal also depends on whether the prisoner sees himself as a member of a criminal sub-culture extending outside prison.[27]

Both books draw on the work of R. K. Merton[28] in developing a typology of reactions to imprisonment, using his classic typology of patterns of adaptation. Neither appears to have had any contact with Goffman's thought on this subject, which may similarly derive from Merton.[29] (Goffman is not good about acknowledging the derivations of his ideas, which appear to spring fully armed into print.) The four typologies, in the order in which they were published, are set out in Table 6.1.

Table 6.1

Merton (1949)	Goffman (1956)	Sykes (1958)	Morrises (1963)
conformity	conversion	—	conformity
innovation	—	innovation	innovation
ritualism	withdrawal	psychological withdrawal	ritualism retreatism
rebellion	intransigence	rebellion	rebellion
—	colonisation	—	—
—	—	persuasion	manipulation

The Morrises point out that they cannot make a distribution of the Pentonville population between their six categories, because they lacked the resources for interviewing.[30] This suggests that they think it could have been done, and that they would have liked to do it — an attitude very foreign to the three less empirically-based American writers.

As the table above indicates, Goffman is the only one of the four to find 'colonisation', and this seems different in character from 'persuasion' or 'manipulation'. This may be a clue to a real difference between mental hospital and prison populations — mental hospitals rarely contain the people whom Sykes describes as 'gorillas and merchants', who use the system for their own ends. The Morrises approach the problem of comparing mental hospital and prison populations from another angle: is Clemmer's 'prisonisation' the same as Russell Barton's 'institutional neurosis'? The two are often confused, but the Morrises are at pains to distinguish between them. 'Prisonisation' is an adaptation to prison life which involves positive, though pathological, forms of behaviour, 'Institutional neurosis' involves passivity, apathy, loss of interest in personal events. 'Prisonisation' leads to 'a deepening of criminality', not 'a retreat into an apathetic state of a-sociality'.[31]

Sykes ends with the view that 'the prison is an authoritarian community, and it will remain an authoritarian community.'[32] However, some authoritarian communities are preferable to others, and prison need not be harshly repressive. His closing sentences suggest that the problem is in the minds of the authorities rather than in the recalcitrance of the prisoner. The Morrises similarly make no detailed recommendations: the first task is to understand the prison system, and what it does to people. They have an account on one particular liberal experiment which suggests that therapeutic innovation by the authorities is not likely to be easy.

The failure of 'H' Wing[33]

'H' Wing was 'Pentonville's concession to the twentieth century'. In this privileged unit, a development from the Norwich system, prisoners were allowed to wander about at will, play indoor games, watch television, and sit about talking to staff, while the staff were expected to 'assist prisoners by sympathetic listening and advice'. The objective was reform of the most 'hopeful' material, i.e. the men who were not unequivocal 'villains'; but 'H' Wing never quite worked. There were artificial flowers, 'gay murals, television and cage birds, billiards, table-tennis and a music-room, and groups of men in two kinds of blue uniforms discussing the future of Arsenal or Tottenham Hotspur', but these factors were not enough to produce instant rehabilitation. There was considerable confusion over what the Wing was for: objectives were not explicitly stated, and the officers who manned it had no training in social work or group dynamics. The artificial flowers were 'arranged altar-fashion', and the group discussion soon got down to the one common interest — football. 'H' Wing became 'the subject of bitterness, rancour and cynicism' throughout the prison among staff and prisoners. One officer told the Morrises 'the failure rate is 100 per cent', and they point out (fairly mildly) the unwisdom of expecting so low-key and unthought-out a scheme to be anything else. The staff never got the selection procedure right, and it is difficult to see how they could have done so, when there was so much confusion over aims and purposes. Most prisoners were hostile, believing that those who went to 'H' Wing were informers, that the scheme was a way of cutting through a prisoner's defences. Prison officers were equally hostile on the grounds that 'it is merely a place where fiddling is made easy' or that all prisoners should have the same conditions. The outcome seems to have been that the authorities promoted the scheme with less than therapeutic enthusiasm: it was against the tradition, style, ethos and expectations of the prison system as a whole, and the prison system as a whole opposed it.

Pentonville is the work of a husband-and-wife team who were able to share their respective skills in criminological analysis and human relations, and to build up a detailed study which tests out and illuminates the concepts of other writers. This is their strength: writers like Sykes and Goffman create their own compelling frames of reference, and perhaps write with more elegance and originality, but are less prepared to build on existing knowledge. The parallels between Pentonville and Trenton Prison are sufficiently strong to make the Morrises' study a rare and useful exercise in comparative penology.

Terence Morris continued, as Professor of Sociology at the London School of Economics, to be involved in a range of penal research, but has not since attempted this kind of organisational study. Pauline Morris went on to study the prisoners' world outside the prison in *On Licence: a study of parole*[34] and *Prisoners and their Families*[35] before turning her attention to mental handicap hospitals.

'*Put Away*'[36]

Pauline Morris's mental handicap study is subtitled *a socio-logical study of institutions for the mentally retarded*. It has more in common with the methodology of Townsend's *The Last Refuge*[37] than with that of *Pentonville*: a national cover-age, a stratified sample, a pre-structured questionnaire and a team of interviewers. Large-scale research was in fashion, and the research grant, from the National Society for Mentally Handicapped Children, was given to Peter Townsend, who supervised the project and wrote a foreword to the book. Like *The Last Refuge*, it tends to be strong on statistics and comparatively weak on theoretical insight.

There is the same painstaking and detailed study of factual data, the same tabulating of rapidly dating statistics, the same assumption that institutions are inherently unsuitable for long-term living — reflected in the somewhat judgmental title. The aim is administrative reform rather than understanding. There is a cogent summary of the organisational character-istics of mental handicap hospitals — the child-like dependency of the patients, the social and often geographical isolation of the hospitals, the bureaucratic nature of the administration; but the focus is now very firmly on the patients and the possibility of rehabilitation rather than on the hospitals and their problems.

A discussion of the ideology of mental handicap hospitals leads Dr Morris to a belief that their administration has been fundamentally misconceived: though they are called 'hospitals' and largely staffed by doctors and nurses, they are in fact institutions for social care, in which the medical element is relatively slight.[38] There is a good deal of evidence to support this contention: before the creation of the National Health Service, the institutions now called mental handicap hospitals were known as 'colonies' (a somewhat pathetic relic of an imperial heritage, with the patients as 'natives') and were generally administered by local authorities through the Town Clerk's Department, not the Health Department.[39] Their new status as hospitals under the National Health Service Act had advantages in making upgrading in materials provision possible, and in offering better salaries and conditions of service for medical and nursing staff; but it also created a medically dominated form of care which obscured the educational and social elements in the work. The problem is still with us, and has been the subject of recommendations for staff re-training from government committees and other research workers.[40]

Pauline Morris's solution was to cut the Gordian knot by developing (for those patients who were unlikely to be suitable for community care) a 'training arm' of social therapists and other care staff as powerful as the medical and nursing arm, and with a separate director of equal status with the medical director.

> From an organisational point of view, the fact that medical and training staff would be working in parallel might provide greater opportunities for communication and staff involvement in treatment. Clearly, however, such an agreement . . . will not of itself eliminate conflict, nor necessarily reduce it, since the proposal allows for two heads of equal status, a situation in which structurally induced conflict may be endemic. Nevertheless, the presence of two complementary but competing systems may represent productive competition, and to this extent conflict may be functional in so far as it may attack and overcome resistance to change.[41]

The publication date was 1969. Conflict theory was in vogue, and current assumptions about continued economic growth made the massive expenditure which would have been involved in implementing these recommendations seem at least feasible; but even in that very different social context, the proposals were unrealistic. One or two hospitals appointed a 'Director of Training' or 'Director of Rehabilitation',[42] but with something of the same lack of enthusiasm which the authorities at Pentonville had shown to 'H' Wing; such experiments certainly generated conflict, and were generally short-lived.

As Jones and Brown commented:—

> The constraints are simply too great. The hospitals have a staff establishment almost exclusively composed, apart from the administration, of nurses. These staff have contracts. They cannot be arbitrarily dismissed, nor can the

hospitals afford to double their treatment costs by introducing a parallel 'training' staff. Even if they could find
the means for employing the staff, they could not find the
staff. Social workers now have to be seconded from (and
paid by) the local authority Social Services Department.
Their numbers in hospitals are scarcely likely to increase.
Occupational therapists, physiotherapists, speech therapists
and remedial gymnasts are in very short supply.[43]

The scheme fundamentally misunderstood the medical and
nursing politics of mental handicap hospitals, and the man-
power and training problems which would have been involved
in changing it. Though the diagnosis of 'lack of fit' between
the needs of mentally handicapped patients and the resources
available for their care was valuable, *Put Away* did not fulfil
the promise of *Pentonville*. However, it added another dimension to the study of institutions, and Pauline Morris was
able to point out that, like prisons and mental hospitals,
mental handicap hospitals had special characteristics which
set them apart from ordinary living: —

One has only to look at an Ordnance Survey map for the
words 'prison', 'asylum', 'mental defective colony' in order
to see the similarity of their ground plans. Furthermore,
the presence of a building set apart from the rest of human
settlement gives some substance to the vague folk beliefs
concerning the individuals who spend their lives in comparative isolation from their fellows.[44]

7 AEGIS: THE DISAPPEARING PRESSURE GROUP

Sans Everything: a case to answer[1] is a very curious book about the condition of old people in geriatric wards and mental hospitals. The title referred to Jacques's account of the seventh age of Man in *As You Like It* as

> ... second childishness and mere oblivion,
> Sans teeth, sans eyes, sans taste, sans everything.

The book was 'presented by Barbara Robb on behalf of AEGIS', and the acronym, new to the reading public, stood for Aid for the Elderly in Government Institutions.

Sans Everything consists of several different elements: brief contributions from a psychiatrist (Dr Russell Barton) and a geriatrician; depositions made under affidavit by six nurses and two social workers on conditions in particular hospitals: a long account of a particular case by the editor also made under affidavit, and entitled 'The Diary of a Nobody'; and a section headed 'Some Answers' in which a psychiatrist argues for a comprehensive community-oriented geriatric service, the editor and an architect put foward a re-housing scheme, and Professor Brian Abel-Smith makes a persuasive case for the establishment of a Hospital Commissioner. It is not research. The book relies for coherence and effect on the views of people with different professional backgrounds and experience, concentrated on a single theme.

The book jacket sets the tone, referring to

> frightening conditions endured by elderly patients in some

of our Government institutions today. Mercifully, the facts
recorded here happen in a small minority of hospitals . . . .
The sufferers might be *your* parents, your friends or
relatives; might even be you in a few years' time. This
problem cries to heaven for attention.

The material presented by the first-hand witnesses is
pathetic and disquieting, a record of low standards, squalid
conditions and official disinterest. One male nurse writes
that 'Nobody wants to know':—

When you are a student nurse at the beginning of your
career, you want to tell your family and friends about the
exploitation and brutality that you witness every day. But
you soon learn that they don't want to hear about any
such things. In their view, nursing is a special calling, and
they are so pleased that you have accepted it. You find
yourself isolated with your problems. You devote yourself
to your studies, decide to qualify at all costs and as soon as
possible, hoping that you will then be able to try to make
things better. Meanwhile, you do not feel like taking any
risks by reporting the maltreatment of patients by senior
staff to those at the top . . .

Most of us cannot bear too much reality . . . Once you
are qualified you find that attempts to bring about changes
raise problems. If you do not fall in with the rest, you may
find yourself ostracised. It becomes a case of 'Give in — or
get out'.[2]

The evidence of reality is given in full, and the reader is
spared none of the smells, the sights and the sounds of wards
of incontinent and confused old people. Though the disclaimer on the jacket to the effect that situations of cruelty
and neglect happen only in a minority of hospitals is repeated,
the cumulative picture is one of crude and insensitive staff
working under an indifferent or positively hostile administration. Another nurse writes of 'massive corruption and cruelty'
and concludes 'lots of good men are forced to remain silent,
or risk blasting their careers as nurses for ever'.[3]

A highlight of the book is the 'Diary of a Nobody', written
by Barbara Robb.[4] This is the case-history of 'Miss Wills', an

elderly lady who had been a seamstress, but had taken up art and had had 'quite a fair success' with the encouragement of the writer's husband, Brian Robb, himself an artist. According to Mrs Robb, Miss Wills's doctor 'became worried about her' (we are not told why), and prescribed a tranquilliser which made her feel 'muzzy'. She was advised to enter a hospital (presumably a mental hospital) as a voluntary patient. Once there, she was given electric shock treatment, and this frightened her, so that she wanted to go home.

Miss Wills was regularly visited by Mr Eric Buss, a travel agent, who became concerned at the deterioration in her condition. She became partially incontinent. She wanted to draw, but the ward sister could not find her spectacles, and said they were lost. When Mr Buss took her presents, the sister asked him not to do so, because she could not be responsible for them.

Mr Buss saw the social worker, Miss Cloake (a pseudonym of some significance in view of later events) and presented her with a list of Roman Catholic nursing homes which might provide alternative accommodation for Miss Wills. Miss Cloake reported that they all had long waiting lists.

Mr Buss then asked Mrs Robb, a psychotherapist, to visit. Mrs Robb had met Miss Wills some years previously, being introduced by Father Victor White, OP.[5] Mrs Robb was greatly concerned at Miss Wills's deterioration in the fourteen months since she had last seen her. She had become frail, bent and thin, her hair was shorn, and she had neither teeth nor spectacles. She seemed afraid to let Mrs Robb ask for the spectacles, because she said that it would annoy the nurses.

Mr Buss and Mrs Robb both thought that Miss Wills was mentally normal, and were disturbed at the indifferent attitude of the staff. Mrs Robb then visited Miss Wills in the company of Lord Strabolgi, a leading Labour peer, and Lady Strabolgi, and with Audrey Harvey, author of a well-known Fabian pamphlet, *Casualties of the Welfare State*.

By this time, all the visitors were thoroughly alarmed and indignant at the treatment of Miss Wills and the refusal of the staff to take action on her behalf. The visitors thought that Miss Wills was a normal elderly lady who needed only a little support and kindness to be able to enjoy life, and attributed her frailty and incontinence to ward conditions and ECT.

The staff thought that she was mentally confused and incontinent, and that a psychogeriatric ward was the proper place for her, since she would be unacceptable in an old people's home. Lord Strabolgi tried to cheer Miss Wills up by telling her that he had had 'Gyppo tummy' in the Middle East. Mrs Robb bought her a magnifying glass, and bag suspended from a neck-cord to keep it in, together with her spectacles.

Miss Cloake, the social worker, said that Miss Wills was probably dying, and arranged the sale of her flat. When the visitors inquired about Miss Wills's possessions, they were told by Miss Cloake that she had no money, and that the clothes and furniture in the flat were 'terribly musty and horrible'. A man had been paid two pounds to clear everything away, saving only her pictures. Miss Wills's niece, herself an outpatient at the same hospital, and her nearest relative, had given permission for this, though Miss Wills said that she knew nothing of it, and was under the impression that she would be able to return home. She said that she had 'nice pieces' in good condition.

There follows a long story of misunderstandings, accusation and counter-accusation, of defensiveness on the part of the doctor, the sister and the social worker, which ends with Miss Wills's removal to a home run by nuns. Here she again becomes fit and happy in 'the homely, peaceful atmosphere of the convent'. Some money is found in a bank account. Miss Wills is taken out in a wheel-chair on a shopping expedition. Her health improves — about five weeks later, she is 'almost back on her feet' and the problem of incontinence has 'almost disappeared'. A senior official from the National Association for Mental Health visits her, buys one of her pictures, comments on the smiling faces of the nuns, and says 'You could almost cut the kindness with a knife.' This is the happy ending. The lessons are drawn in a memorandum[6] signed by twelve people, including the Robbs, the Strabolgis, Audrey Harvey, her husband, daughter and son-in-law, Mr Buss, and three other friends who had become interested in the case: old people should not be confined in mental hospitals 'merely because they are old'. They should not be given ECT. The voluntary services should be called on to visit. Personal possessions such as spectacles and deaf-aids should be provided. Circumstances in which a lazy or dishonest social worker could collude with a mentally unbalanced relative should be guarded against.

Questions

In medical terms, who was right — the hospital authorities or the visitors? Was Miss Wills mentally ill and incontinent, or was the hospital treatment making her so? Were the staff obstructive and unhelpful, or merely reacting sensibly to a group of persistent busybodies? Should Miss Cloake have kept Miss Wills's flat with her 'nice pieces' ready for her, or was it appropriate to dispose of it because she was never likely to be fit to return to it? Was the niece mentally unbalanced (a fairly stigmatising judgment in view of the repeated insistence that Miss Wills was 'normal')? Or was she within her rights in disposing of her aunt's property as the next of kin?

Clearly there was room for some difference of perception and interpretation on the two sides, but there were matters of fact involved which could be checked. Mrs Robb claimed that the account was 'true, down to the last detail', but it was not to stand up to investigation. A government Committee of Inquiry on the allegations made in *Sans Everything* was set up in the following year.[7] While the evidence of the six nurses and the two social workers was, by its nature, difficult to check, and the verdict in most cases was 'not proven', the details of Miss Wills's case provided a story very different from that given in the book.

Mrs Robb had strongly implied that Miss Wills was perfectly fit until her general practitioner prescribed the tablets which made her 'muzzy' and incontinent. This was not her first period of psychiatric treatment. She had, in fact, previously spent two long periods in mental hospital with a diagnosis of psychotic illness. When seen by Mrs Robb, she was in an advanced senile condition with no possibility of remission or recovery. The Mother Superior and Sister in charge of the nursing home to which she was moved testified that she was practically bed-ridden on arrival. She had a series of mild strokes, and died within a few months.[8]

Mrs Robb refused to give evidence to the Committee of Inquiry — a fact which told against her. The Committee deplored the 'flamboyant and exaggerated way in which she had presented her case in the book', and considered that her account represented a 'serious distortion of the facts'.[9] For instance, though much stress is laid in *Sans Everything* on Miss Wills's status as an artist, this was reduced to 'her hobby was making coloured tinfoil pictures'.[10]

It is possible to dismiss Mrs Robb's case as readily as the Committee of Inquiry did – and certainly the facts they adduced were damaging. It is also possible, starting from another perspective, to suspect that the Committee relied heavily on medical judgments, and shared the hospital staff's view of the AEGIS group as trouble-makers.

It seems likely that Mrs Robb and her friends were actuated by humanitarian motives; that they genuinely cared what happened to Miss Wills, and that they believed that they had uncovered a wrong which ought to be righted. Miss Wills was a Roman Catholic – she prayed with her visitors, was impressed by the views of the lady in the next bed who thought that six patients, including Miss Wills, might be beatified as a result of their trials, and asked to be taken to the Catholic Chapel, which was found to be locked even on a Sunday.[11] Some of the AEGIS group also had Roman Catholic connections: according to the brief biography given on the cover of *Sans Everything*, Mrs Robb was educated at the College of the Assumption in Kensington; Mr Buss produced a list of Roman Catholic nursing homes; and two members of the Dominican Order, Father Victor White and Prior Daniel Woolgar, were involved at various points in the narrative, the latter writing a letter of protest about the Church's failure to care for old people to the *Catholic Herald*.[12] Miss Wills's removal to the convent, where she could be cared for by nuns, was therefore a highly appropriate ending to the story. An inexplicable point is that, according to the Mother Superior's testimony, she died 'within a few months' of her arrival in the convent in June 1965;[13] yet the book, published in 1967, makes no mention of her death, and is dedicated to her as though she were still alive.

The Committee of Inquiry conceded that 'for some obscure reason' Mrs Robb 'had a genuine desire to assist the anonymous patient who was virtually a stranger to her'. The reasons are probably not as obscure as all that. Difficulties may have arisen because Miss Wills was mentally confused (patients are not sent to mental hospitals 'merely because they are old'); but, with little experience of psychogeriatric patients, the visitors took all her statements at face value, and refused to accept the views of the hospital staff. This in turn irritated the staff; and irritation turned to alarm as it became evident that this group of well-connected people was intent on making a test case out of the issue.

The staff evidently considered the visitors to be trouble-makers. They testified before the Committee of Inquiry that Mrs Robb in particular had behaved unpleasantly on a number of occasions, refusing to listen to explanations, and making accusations against the staff.[14] Mrs Robb presumably thought that she had ample provocation for this attitude. The staff clearly thought her over-loud in her protests about one patient, and oblivious to the problems of running a large psychogeriatric ward. Were they in reality callous, secretive and obstructive? Or merely defensive, apprehensive of trouble, and at their wits' end?

There is another strand to be told in the story of *Sans Everything*. Some at least of the protesting group were members of the Fabian Society, and of the Labour Party, to which the Fabian Society is affiliated. Audrey Harvey was editing a Fabian pamphlet, *Social Services for All*, to which Peter Townsend and Brian Abel-Smith were contributors.[15] Sheila Benson, Peter Townsend's research assistant for *The Last Refuge*, gave advice to Lord Strabolgi, who made a speech on the plight of the elderly in institutions to the House of Lords.[16] The Fabians were good at pressure-group tactics, and the *Sans Everything* affair has all the hall-marks of being a skilled pressure-group exercise. It started, in traditional British fashion, with a letter to *The Times*[17] signed by Barbara Robb and a number of well-known public figures, including Lord Strabolgi, Brian Abel-Smith and Prior Daniel Woolgar. We are told that 'three of the signatories' had just formed Aid for the Elderly in Government Institutions, and that the letter 'was its first bow to the public'.[18]

The long-term value of the book is less in the somewhat dubiously supported evidence of abuse than in the fact that it contained well-reasoned proposals for improving conditions, and created enough public pressure to put some of them into effect. Though 'Project 70', a plan for selling off mental hospital land and creating mixed housing estates incorporating sheltered accommodation and small wards and units for geriatric patients,[19] was not implemented, Dr Anthony Whitehead's description of the psycho-geriatric service run from Severalls Hospital[20] (where Dr Russell Barton was Physician Superintendent)[21] and Professor Abel-Smith's closely-reasoned argument for the establishment of a 'Hospital Commissioner'[22] were to be very influential. Professor Frank Stacey traces the origin of the Office of the Health Service Commissioner, set up in 1973, back to *Sans Everything*, though he says that 'the idea might not have got off the ground had it not been for a series of reports into allegations of ill-treatment in psychiatric hospitals at Ely in 1969, and at Farleigh and Whittingham Hospitals in 1971 and 1972'.[23]

These inquiries — and the many others which followed — might themselves not have been held if *Sans Everything* had not set the pattern, and showed that it was possible for staff to protest against the ill-treatment of patients. If the events described in *Sans Everything* were of doubtful accuracy, there were plenty of better-attested cases to follow.[24]

AEGIS remains a mystery. Though Barbara Robb wrote as though it were a well-known and established voluntary organisation, and Lord Strabolgi listed 'President of AEGIS' in his *Who's Who* entry for 1970, it was not heard of again, and subsequent enquiry failed to discover its address (other than Mrs Robb's private address), its membership, or its status. The whole affair was a very skilful exercise in public relations; and despite the flamboyance, the distortions and the inaccuracies, it worked.

PART III
The end or the beginning?

8 ROTHMAN: THE PUZZLED HISTORIAN

David Rothman is of interest in any review or appraisal of the literature on institutions for four main reasons. First, Rothman is one of the very few historians to attempt to chronicle the development of social policy on institutions in the United States of America. Second, within the context of writing about the treatment of different groups of deviants he has attempted to describe the development of different kinds of institutions between 1830 and 1940. In his two major histories, *The Discovery of the Asylum: social order and disorder in the New Republic*[1] and *Conscience and Convenience: the asylum and its alternatives in Progressive America*,[2] Rothman investigates the origins, development, survival and reform of the penitentiary, the mental asylum, the orphanage, the poorhouse and the reformatory — all of which, somewhat confusingly, he subsumes under the general title of 'the asylum'. No other historian has attempted this vast topic in such depth. Third, Rothman is interested in the historical origin of current issues. He has been actively involved in the contemporary review of institutions through his membership (and more recently Directorship) of the New York Civil Liberties Union and the Field Foundation's Committee for the Study of Incarceration. The Committee for the Study of Incarceration has tried to produce a more modern rationale for penal sanctions in the United States.[3] Rothman has also written about contemporary prisons and mental hospitals, introducing material from both historical and civil libertarian perspectives.[4] Finally, his work is of interest because, in addition to his own original contribution to the study of institutions, he has taken up some of the arguments raised by Foucault, and to a lesser extent by Goffman and Szasz.[5]

In his histories of the institution, Rothman is concerned to show how the institution is the consequence of some larger-scale social movement. He argues that institutions have to be seen in the light of the claims made for them by the people in each era who were instrumental in setting them up. The attempt to find social explanations for the existence of 'asylums', leads to the discovery of wider social problems and issues which the 'asylums' were expected to solve. Rothman also uses the claims made on behalf of the institution when it was being set up as the measuring rod against which its later development can be evaluated. He is concerned with comparing the rhetoric and the reality of the institution. In his contemporary writings, Rothman uses a somewhat similar technique as well as introducing civil libertarian considerations.

Rothman on Foucault

Rothman takes issue with Foucault on two separate occasions. He comments on Foucault in the introduction to each of the histories. The main criticism is the same on both occasions — Foucault's method does not provide a history which can describe what actually happened in and to institutions. Rothman also suggests that Foucault's analysis is too condemnatory.

Rothman's view on Foucault changed over time from interest to rejection. In *The Discovery of the Asylum*, Rothman describes *Madness and Civilisation* as an idiosyncratic but fascinating and suggestive attempt to explain the origins of the 'insane asylum'.[6] He then goes on to criticise Foucault for using analytical categories which are too rigid, e.g. the binary division between reason and unreason. Rothman goes on to say

> The explanation here is so caught up with ideas that the base in events is practically forgotten . . . Ultimately . . . the goals of the asylum are purely intellectual . . . Foucault's institutions bear only a slight relationship to the society that built and supported them.[7]

By the time Rothman was writing *Conscience and Convenience*, Foucault had written *Discipline and Punish*. This later book then became the subject of further criticism. Rothman says of Foucault's analysis of the growth of disciplinary institutions in France, Britain and the United States:—

It assumes an inevitability in capitalist societies that makes reform at best foolhardy, at worst deceptive. But this approach is entirely static and thus misleading. As we shall see, prison in particular, and criminal justice procedures in general, do have a history that Foucault's mode of analysis cannot illuminate. The prison did not descend once and for all from some capitalist spirit.[8]

He goes on to say that historical analysis has to take account of the daily activity of the organisation of being studied in order to explain these activities. Foucault is attacked for confusing the theory of surveillance with practice. The historian, Rothman argues, parts company with the ideologue in order to provide complex analyses of complex events. Rothman sees his task, and that of the historian in general, as getting the story straight, of looking precisely for the gap between theory and practice. Rothman's model and account of history permit possibilities which Foucault's could neither imagine nor allow.

The Jacksonian asylum

Rothman's history of the asylum falls into two distinct parts. First, there is the early stage, Jacksonian America, the period of the 1820s and 1830s. This period saw the 'discovery of the asylum' to use the title of the first book. The later period, the Progressive era, covers the years from 1880 to 1900. During this period, the old asylums were subject to considerable criticism and attempts were made to introduce reforms. These reforms provide the background against which contemporary criticisms are raised.

In *The Discovery of the Asylum*, Rothman sets himself the task of answering a basic question: 'Why, in the decades after 1820, did Americans begin to construct and support institutions for the deviant and dependent members of the community? In a short space of time, public authorities constructed penitentiaries for the criminal, asylums for the insane, almshouses for the poor and reformatories for the delinquent. Rothman provides examples of how social problems were dealt with in the earlier colonial period: the criminal was held in jail until his trial and was then fined, whipped or executed. The jail closely resembled the ordinary household in structure and routine. There was no distinctive architecture, and there were no special procedures. The poor and the insane were seen as a normal part of the community, and were not treated in any special way. Charitable endowments provided alms for the poor, whilst families looked after their own mentally ill members.

After the War of Independence, with the gradual expansion of the New Republic, social problems came to be seen in a different way and new fears gripped the established citizenry. Crime, in particular, began to concern Americans. The newly opening frontier, the breakdown of traditional social control and the arrival of new immigrants led to a search for new ways of solving this social problem. The traditional colonial-style punishments were abandoned because of their links with Britain but new methods were difficult to find. This new society was frightened by its own characteristics of rapid social and geographical mobility: the whole of society was at risk of dissolving into chaos. Fluidity and instability seemed to be on all sides. Studies were made of the backgrounds of prisoners, and the cause of crime was found almost invariably to be a failure of upbringing; the old pattern of rigorous training in discipline and obedience had disappeared.

A connection was made between social instability and the failure of parents to instill discipline in their children. Discipline and obedience would have to be taught to adults. The general social view was that people could be changed for the better — the problem was simply one of finding the most effective method. The obvious solution was through the design and organisation of institutional environment, which would discipline the disorder within the individual. The new Republic would be brought back under control as the effects of the institution were felt in the wider community.

Since the convict was not inherently depraved, but the victim of an upbringing that had failed to provide protection against the vices at loose in society, a well ordered institution could successfully re-educate and rehabilitate him. The penitentiary, free of corruptions and dedicated to the proper training of the inmate would inculcate the discipline that negligent parents, evil companions, taverns . . . had destroyed. Just as the criminal's environment had led him into crime, the institutional environment would lead him out of it.[9]

The environment of the penitentiary was the most complete example of the principle. The individual offender was to be isolated from the sources of corruption both within and without the walls; habits of industry and obedience were to be substituted for individual chaos. The regularity of the regime would lead to self-control. In Sing-Sing penitentiary, all official activity resolved around inmates' duties 'To labour diligently, to obey all orders and preserve an unbroken silence'.[10] Silence was of particular importance in preventing contacts which might corrupt the prisoner. Officers had to establish a total routine in order to bring about this state of affairs. A quasi-military model was chosen both to control the activities of the staff and to demonstrate to society outside the right principles of organisation. Not only did the régime follow a military-style model, but the cell and the equipment given to the inmate followed the same principles. Prisoners wore uniforms of coarse material and had their hair cut, to increase unformity.

Rothman argues that the prison was designed to train the most notable victims of social disorder in the ways of discipline, teaching them to resist temptation. The institution would become the laboratory for social reform and improvement. The penitentiary would create a new respect for order and authority.

The other important new institution being developed was the mental asylum. The Jacksonians believed that the apparent rise in the incidence of insanity could be traced to the increasing materialism of society. The asylum would offer a place of security, a sanctuary from the mad rush of the outside world. The environment of the asylum 'would re-create fixity and stability to compensate for the irregularities of the society. Thus, it would rehabilitate 'the casualties of the system'.[11] The organisation of the regime showed strong similarities to that of the penitentiary, and Rothman writes of the preparation of manuals specifying the size and location of rooms, the width of rooms and height of ceilings. Details were provided on such intricate matters as the type of plaster to be used on the walls. But these manuals also dealt with the more difficult questions of how to group patients together and how to staff the organisation.

> But the most important element in the new program, the core of moral treatment, lay in the daily government of the mentally ill. Here was the institution's most difficult and critical task. It had to control the patient without irritating him, to impose order but in a humane fashion. It had to bring discipline to bear but not harshly, to introduce regularity into chaotic lives without exciting frenetic reactions . . . To this end it had to isolate itself and its members from chaotic conditions. Behind the asylum walls medical superintendents would create and administer a calm, steady, and rehabilitative routine. It would be, in a phrase that they and their lay supporters repeated endlessly, 'a well-ordered institution'.[12]

Rothman says that in the 1830s and 1840s more and more asylums were built on very similar lines throughout the USA. Europeans such as de Tocqueville and Charles Dickens visited the new institutions and returned home with this new American model of social organisation impressed upon their minds. The paradox was that while these institutions were becoming increasingly central to the thinking of Americans, the régimes were also being undermined. Costs soon began to increase and penitentiary labour was contracted out to commercial interests. Productive work became increasingly important, replacing work originally seen as being for rehabilitation. The nature of the tasks involved changed little, but the inmates were brought together to work, thus defeating the practice of silence and segregation.

The Civil War produced a severe pressure on financial resources; funds were needed to finance the war between the states and less was available for the asylums. While the funding became more restricted, state legislators had a considerable investment in bricks and mortar, and made sure that the penitentiaries and asylums continued to be used. Slowly but inexorably, these institutions became overcrowded and understaffed. The ethos shifted from rehabilitation to simple custody. If the system was challenged, it was possible to demonstrate to the naïve observer that incarceration was really improvement.

At the same time, the nature of the institutional population began to change. The number and proportion of foreign-born inmates increased because of influxes of new immigrants into the country. Gradually the poor standards became known outside, and this meant that every effort was made to keep the less ill or less deviant out of these places for fear of making them worse. The penitentiary populations began to feature a more violent type of prisoner. As the quality of populations and régimes declined, reform and rehabilitation were replaced by the considerations of custody. The asylums which began as places to accomplish change were now available to keep the violent and the chronically insane out of society.

The 'Progressives' and the asylum

Rothman's second historical book, *Conscience and Convenience: the asylum and its alternatives in Progressive America*, is concerned with the period in the late nineteenth and early twentieth centuries when a new generation began to reform the asylums. In this book, Rothman tries to answer the questions of why and how the Jacksonian institutions had to be reformed. In the years after the Civil War, there were exposures of scandals and excesses through state commissions, newspapers and personal accounts of the conditions in the institutions. It became clear that the survival of the staff was now the main goal of most of the asylums. The treatment of the inmate was secondary. The various reports catalogued the exploitation of inmates, hard labour and barbaric punishments to exact control.

The explanation Rothman gives is that in the last decades

of the nineteenth century there occurred groups of benevolent and philanthropic people who made it their business to reform the institutions. He says that he had at first thought that these people were against incarceration in much the same way as many contemporary critics, but soon recognised his mistake.

The Progressives were anti-institutional in a very special way. Their quarrel was not so much with the institution per se, as with uniformity and rigidity. They were not so much struggling to return the offender to the community (although the theme does appear in one form or another) as attempting to individualise treatment.[13]

The scope of this study is slightly less wide than *The Discovery of the Asylum* in that Rothman concentrates on the criminal justice system, juvenile justice and the mental hospital. The Progressives did not want a complete change in the way that institutional populations were dealt with: there was some degree of continuity of thought about the causes of crimes and delinquency, but the solutions did need to be changed dramatically. Deviance was still seen as being environmental in origin, resulting from poor child-rearing practices, lack of commitment to the American way of life, or through poverty.

The Progressives of the sub-title had two guiding principles when confronting these problems. First, they believed that social problems could be solved by bringing the power of the state to bear, and second, that the response to each individual case should be individualised. Public officials should exercise whatever discretion was necessary. Rothman argues that these principles allowed the Progressives to bring about considerable change to the prisons, courts and reformatories. They were less successful when they came to the mental hospital for a number of reasons which will be referred to later. The Progressives also recognised that institutions were difficult to control, as the reports of scandals had shown. Boards appointed to check abuses were generally ineffectual and often helped to provide legitimacy for senior staff. What was needed was the blast of fresh air that the community could provide. While the Jacksonians believed that the institution

could revitalise and re-affirm society, the Progressives believed
the reverse — society would normalise the institutional populations.

In the criminal justice system this meant that ideas of
personal culpability would no longer be held in the light of
what was known about the environmental causes of crime. It
was believed that it was sensible and effective to deal with
each individual according to his needs, and also just to do so.
Elementary fairness meant that each offender had to be
treated as an individual. The power of the state had to be
brought effectively to the aid of the offender. In practice this
meant a process of helping the offender through the preparation of a pre-sentence report which would describe his problems to the court. The judge would operate a system of
scientific sentencing, choosing between probation and prison
in accordance with information provided in the pre-sentence
report. If the judge decided that the offender needed a prison
sentence, then the sentence would be an indeterminate one,
so that the prison authorities could decide the most appropriate time for his release in the light of his behaviour. Each
prisoner would be released on parole, and after-care would be
available. In some reformed prisons, systems of inmate self-
government were discussed, though rarely introduced.
Psychiatrists were appointed to allow a continuation of the
process of treatment begun in the diagnosis presented to the
court.

As an alternative to custody, probation was set up in some
of the larger towns and cities. Judges were responsible for
selecting and appointing the new probation officers. Unfortunately, the new service was patchy, and found rarely in
rural areas. Probation officers were usually untrained, poorly
paid and over-worked. Probation caseloads were often in
excess of two hundred and fifty, and individual attention was
rare in the early days.

While probation became better organised, and staff training improved, other aspects of the criminal justice system
remained untouched until the 1960s. The prison riots of the
1930s led to the abolition of many privileges which went with
some early reforms. Inmate self-government disappeared
at about the same time. The courts assumed the prison
administrators were experts in their field, and refrained from

interfering on the few occasions when prisoners contested the constitutionality of either their indeterminate sentences or the conditions in which they were held. Prisoners were held to be 'slaves of the state'; any relaxation of the prisoners' régime, including parole, was regarded not as a right, but as a privilege which might be arbitrarily withdrawn.

The Progressives invented the concept of juvenile justice as a system separate from the adult courts. The Chicago courts in 1900 rediscovered the English idea of the power of the Chancery Court which allowed the individual welfare of the child to be considered. Protecting the unfortunate child was more important and vital than dealing with questions of guilt. The use of chancery powers meant that the adversarial principle of the criminal courts would be dispensed with since the interests of society could be assumed to coincide with those of the child. The needs of the child were paramount and the state could act *in loco parentis.*

The juvenile courts moved to their own premises to stress their independence. Lawyers slowly opted out of appearing in juvenile courts as they were ignored or excluded from discussion when they did attend.

The reformatories invented by the Jacksonians to cope with delinquent youths were criticised as strongly as other institutions. Indeed reformatories were if anything worse than other institutions because they were now being compared with the family home and the 'worst home was better than the best of institutions'. A more suitable model or image was available, with more positive connotations, that of the school. The school combined with cottage living in family units provided the solution and this was adopted rapidly throughout the United States. Later the juvenile correctional institutions adopted practices from the Child Guidance Clinics of the 1920s and the 1930s with diagnostic interviews on admission and case conferences throughout the child's stay.

The Progressives saw mental hospitals as institutions that were inefficient at providing custody, and also unsuccessful in providing treatment. They completely rejected the argument that the hospital routine could be rehabilitative of itself. At first the critics had little to offer by way of improvement beyond saying that the Medical Superintendents should behave more like doctors than administrators and custodians.

An alternative model was provided by Adolf Meyer: the old asylum would become back-up for the new mental hospital, which would deal with acute cases and provide out-patient services, allowing psychiatry to become involved in 'civic medicine'. The old asylums would still have to deal with long-stay, chronic patients, but possibly their numbers would be less.

After this historical account, Rothman also produces a number of criticisms of each of the newly reformed services. He catalogues the failure of this system of discretionary justice to respect the rights of convicted persons. The probation system extended surveillance and supervision into the community without providing skilled support to probationers. Parole and the indeterminate sentence increased control both within prisons and in the community. Parole conditions often went beyond the content of the criminal code. The juvenile courts brought to official notice the poor and the immigrant. Juvenile court judges developed their own idiosyncratic styles while their courts dealt increasingly with cases on an unofficial basis. The system was at once powerful and unpredictable. A discretionary system could easily turn into an arbitrary system. The schools reverted quickly to military drill to instill discipline, and 'training', degenerated into unskilled farm labour for children who would be returning to urban centres. The asylums did not change, the new mental hospitals that were built were used almost exclusively as diagnostic centres processing large numbers of patients on their way to the state hospitals. The few new mental hospitals to operate as intended were privately funded and dealt entirely with voluntary admissions.

Simple questions and complex answers

Rothman's distinctive method is one in which he poses questions, and then unravels history to find the answers to them. For instance, the questions in *The Discovery of the Asylum* are 'Why did Americans in the Jacksonian era suddenly begin to construct and support institutions for deviant members of the community? Why, in the decade after 1820, did they all at once erect penitentiaries for criminals, homeless children, and reformatories for delinquents?'[14] In *Conscience and Convenience*, he asks 'How does each generation arrive at its reform program? What elements come together to earn a proposed innovation the title of reform? Who makes up the cadre of reformers? . . . where do they find their constituents? How do their programs win enactment?'[15]

The difficulty is that such a method is heavily dependent on the quality of the questions asked; and it is a good deal easier to ask a question than to find a satisfying answer to it. Rothman starts as a grand theorist, in the expectation that such questions can be answered; but he is also an honest historian, and he finds history complicated. In *The Discovery of the Asylum*, he notes: 'a curious ambivalence toward the entire movement . . . the story of the origin of the asylum is too complex to lend itself to simple moral judgements'.[16]

He is prepared to admit that the insane were probably more comfortable in 'a custodial hospital than in a filthy cellar, prisoners better off in a crowded cell than on the gallows or whipping post, and the poor happier eating the miserable fare of the almshouse than starving on the streets'. On the other hand, the evidence of the mechanical application of discipline in the Puritan mould is overwhelming – and the acceptance of this mould discouraged the search for solutions less susceptible to abuse.

Rothman ends with 'an acute nervousness about all social panaceas'. The clear-cut questions with which he started had fragmented, and proved more complicated than he expected. Despite his own personal revulsion – 'we instinctively shudder when passing a building surviving from a nineteenth century institution, or a building of the twentieth century designed in this tradition' – he has come to see that conspiracy theory does not really account for the development of institutions. There was a genuine will to reform, and yet it somehow went wrong: 'Proposals that promise the most grandiose consequences often legitimate the most unsatisfactory developments . . . arrangements designed for the best of motives may have disastrous results. The difficult problem is to review these events without falling into a deep cynicism.'[17] Searching for a hopeful end to this tale of mixed motives and unintended consequences, he finds comfort in the reflection that 'we need not remain trapped in inherited answers' and that we can gradually escape from institutional responses.

The Discovery of the Asylum is a very interesting exercise in historical analysis — the work of an author who starts from Marxist assumptions, sets out to validate them, and finds the facts too complicated to support them in their entirety. In *Conscience and Convenience*, he is concerned with the problems he has uncovered — the curious nature of reform movements, and the gap between the reformers' ambitions and what they achieve; but here another aspect of his method creates further problems.

Rothman juxtaposes detailed historical material with comments about how and why the events he describes came about. Statements from contemporary reports are pieced together to chronicle the history of the asylum, and then the level changes to an assessment of why these events occurred. The explanation given for the reforms of the Jacksonian era is that a frightened society saw the asylum as a means of reforming the whole society and saving itself from disorder and chaos. In the later period under investigation, the Progressives are described as being concerned with social equality and turning the newly arrived immigrants into middle-class Americans. The problem with this method of writing about and analysing historical trends is that the writer is making all the connections between the two levels. There is always the risk that while the description may be scrupulously accurate, the analysis may be more tenuous and difficult to sustain. An associated problem is that of ascribing a social philosophy to the whole community or society. In each book one is told 'the Jacksonians believed . . .' or 'the Progressives believed . . .', but who were the Jacksonians and the Progressives? How many of them were there? Rothman is concerned to demonstrate how the demands for reform coincided with the interests of administrators, legislators, and judges, but we discover little of the detailed politics of achieving large-scale change. What positions in the political systems in America did these people hold?

The national level of analysis jars somewhat by comparison with other detailed historical inquiries into some of the same events. For instance, Rothman makes a reference to the work of Anthony Platt on the invention of juvenile delinquency in

Chicago and the state of Illinois.[18] Platt concentrates on one relatively small locality where it is possible to show in detail how alliances came together to bring about changes in the way children were to be treated. Rothman does not produce anything remotely like this, tending to operate at a more general level. Questions remain concerning the practical politics of these changes. The reader is told how interests which might have been expected to conflict actually coincided. It is not clear whether the coincidence if it really occurred, was fortuitous, or whether Rothman is saying that in the nineteenth century, American politics was dominated by small and very powerful groups who would almost invariably achieve whatever ends they set out to achieve.

Rothman is concerned with the problem of evaluating historical change. He says that he wants to compare rhetoric and reality, and uses the statements made by reformers as the baseline against which comparisons can be made. The comparison is between intentions and historical events. Almost invariably there is an enormous gap between the two: historical fact rarely if ever approaches the intentions. Penitentiaries which should reform offenders concentrate on custody. Rothman argues that this is evidence of failure. He then goes on to raise the question in *Conscience and Convenience* of whether reforms can have the consequence of causing cruelty, commenting that historians rarely confront questions of this kind. The question is not followed up in the narrative at this point or later.

Rothman's method of evaluating the success or failure of institutions is somewhat dubious. The problem is that the two items being compared may not be strictly comparable. The claims being made for institutions may be cultural entities in the sense that they relate to ideal ends rather than practical objectives, and hence are not capable of realisation. Historical events are of a different order. If this is the case, then history will always reveal a failure to live up to our ideals. The question is whether the method of analysis will always produce the same stereotyped and predictable results. A further, related problem is that while it is possible to demonstrate what failure looks like, it may not be so easy to recognise what the evidence for success might look like.

The technique of comparing cultural ends with historical

fact may conceal another process. Statements of cultural
ends are statements of moral principles. This kind of statement may be important not so much as a plan for action but
as a guide to the way a problem should be seen. An example
is provided by the American anti-poverty programmes in the
1960s, which did not greatly affect the income levels of the
poor but had a considerable influence in ensuring that poverty
was seen officially as a structural problem rather than one of
individual pathology.

Rothman gives the impression that his analysis accounts
for the development of the asylum in the United States. The
discussion of foreign contact is largely one way: the Europeans were impressed by what they had seen in the United
States, and rushed home to practise American institutional
methods. Rothman does not comment on the traffic in the
other direction, either of people or ideas.[19] Prisons had
existed in Europe while America was still a colony and some
penal ideas were already well developed before the Jacksonian
period. Prisons and penitentiaries were constructed in both
Europe and America at more or less the same time, but
Britain and Europe were not confronted by the sorts of
problems facing the Jacksonians. The question of who
imitated whom cannot be answered easily, as there is no
starting date for prison planning and building, only eras can
be described. Ideas sped back and forwards across the Atlantic
and the English Channel, and there must have been a common
stock of ideas available to people in public life. If a number
of countries with different histories adopted the same sort of
institutional methods within a few years, was this in response
to some deeper social problem which all countries were facing
at this period? The other possibility is that the discovery of
the asylum was in reality independent of particular social
movements. By concentrating on the United States, Rothman
excludes evidence which might produce an international
explanation. He has treated Jacksonian America largely as a
closed system.

Despite the limitations of Rothman's method — the simplistic nature of some of his questions, the tendency to
generalised analysis, the somewhat harsh judgment of the
reformers, and the American-centred approach, his achievement is considerable. In two scholarly books, he has attempted

to describe the dynamics of a wide range of institutional provision and management over a period of two centuries. In his carefully researched and detailed documentation of the movements he describes, he is quite exceptional. Other writers may have produced work with greater detail, or more breadth, but not both. If he has raised more questions than he can answer, this need not lead to cynicism. As with the reformers he describes, his vision has a power of its own.

9 KITTRIE:
THE ADVOCATE

In *The Right to be Different* (1971), N. N. Kittrie develops the lawyers' case against 'the therapeutic state' — the kind of society in which people may be treated against their will on the decisions of experts such as psychiatrists or social workers, without the opportunity to have their case heard in accordance with full legal procedures. Kittrie regards this as a human rights issue, and his book marks an important stage in the development of the literature on institutions, reviving some very old debates about the liberty of the subject, and giving a distinctly new twist to the anti-institutional movement which, by the early 1970s, threatened to run out of steam.

Kittrie's legal backgound is impressive. He is a professor of law at the American University of Washington. His work for the study was supported by the Council on Education in Professional Responsibility of the Association of American Law Schools, and the National Defender Project of the American Bar Association. He had previously directed a national research project on the rights of the mentally ill; he acknowledges the advice and assistance of a number of leading American experts in jurisprudence; and while preparing the material for *The Right to be Different*, he also prepared *amicus curiae* briefs dealing with the treatment of drug addicts and procedural safeguards for juvenile offenders in cases of national and constitutional importance, one of them in the US Supreme Court.[1]

The book consists of two kinds of material: a preface and an introductory chapter set out the main argument, which is taken up in the two final chapters. In between are six specialist chapters on the mentally ill, juvenile delinquents, psychopaths, drug addicts, alcoholics and the sterilisation of the mentally and physically unfit. Kittrie also acknowledges the assistance of six of his own students and other colleagues in 'painstaking and able research'.[2] It is a reasonable inference that this forms the bulk of the six specialist chapters, and that these may be taken as illustrative of the main argument. The middle part of the book is therefore more like an intensive departmental research project than the work of an individual writer, but the case presented in the opening and closing sections is argued with an individual force and brilliance.

Kittrie's basic plea is contained in the book's title: there is a 'right to be different', at least for the six groups under discussion. Provided that people do not break the criminal law, their behaviour should be tolerated in a civilised society. The chief philosophical grounds for this plea are contained in John Stuart Mill's celebrated definition of liberty, which is quoted twice — once in full, and once in part. The full version runs:-

> The principle is, that the sole end for which mankind are warranted, individually or collectively, in interfering with the liberty of action of any of their number is self-protection. That the only purpose for which power can be rightfully exercised over any member of a civilised community, against his will, is to prevent harm to others. His own good, either physical or moral, is not a sufficient warrant. He cannot rightfully be compelled to forbear because it will be better for him to do so, because it will make him happier, because, in the opinions of others, to do so would be wise, or even right. These are good reasons for remonstrating with him, but not for compelling him, or visiting him with an evil in case he does otherwise. To justify that, the conduct from which it is desired to deter him must be calculated to produce evil in someone else.[3]

Mill's principle, which has been widely utilised on both sides of the Atlantic in defining the boundary between the rights of the individual and the rights of the society to which he belongs, provides a clear-cut measure which can be applied either to the framing of legal enactment or to judgment in individual cases. The American Civil Liberties Union, which has published a series of handbooks on the rights of mental patients, juvenile offenders and other groups reviewed by Kittrie, frequently uses it as a fundamental statement of human rights. Kittrie's conclusion, and the ACLU's conclusion, is that intervention in the rights of the individual sufficient to curtail personal liberty (whether in the form of physical intervention, such as brain surgery or sterilisation, or in the form of compulsory commitment to an institution) must be limited to those cases where there is a 'clear social danger' provable in terms of the commission of an overt act;[4] and in those cases, the operation of the criminal law is sufficient protection for the public.

Further, Kittrie states that therapeutic intervention without 'due process' is unconstitutional.[5] 'Due process', a phrase more common in American legal circles than in Britain, is shorthand for procedures followed in the criminal courts of both countries and endorsed by the international Human Rights Conventions to which both countries subscribe: the defendant should have a right to a fair trial, an opportunity to be heard and a right to confront his accusers; he should have time to prepare his case; he should be legally represented; trial should be by his peers (i.e. by a jury, not by 'experts'); and the procedure should be adversarial, involving the making and rebuttal of allegations.[6] Dicey's *Law of the Constitution* provides a strong case for this method of approach, in contrast to the French 'droit administratif', where a single judge or other official conducts his own search for the facts of the case without safeguards.[7] These safeguards are specifically guaranteed by the Fifth and Fourteenth Amendments to the US constitution, which provide that US citizens may not be deprived of life, liberty or property without due process. The Fifth Amendment refers to the action of the federal government, and the Fourteenth Amendment to state governments.

Kittrie finds the origin of the 'therapeutic state' in legal enactments which refer to the absolutist powers of English medieval kings. He sees a possible basis in common law, which goes back to Roman law in giving the head of a household power and supervision over any member of the household, including adult sons and daughters; but the transfer of this power to the state is traced to the role of the sovereign as *parens patriae*:—

> the English sovereign also assumed the function of protect-
> ing certain incompetent subjects. Suggestions of the
> sovereign's role as *parens patriae* are evident in the eleventh
> century enactments of the Anglo-Saxon King Aethelred II
> (nicknamed 'the Unready'), a prolific law-giver though a
> weak king. . . . Another early manifestation of the *parens
> patriae* role in English law was the recognition by Edward II
> in the fourteenth century of the sovereign's responsibility
> towards the property and later the person of the insane.[8]

The exercise of this kind of protective power by the state
is 'unconstitutional' according to reasoning which Kittrie
does not need to explain in full for an American readership:
the US constitution was framed in order to protect American
citizens from the evils of absolutist government and royal
tyranny. A fundamental part of that process was the decision
to separate legislature, executive and judiciary. The result is
that there are today very great differences in American and
British constitutional practice: neither the president nor the
members of his cabinet sit in the legislature; the president's
term of office is strictly limited; and the judiciary, which has
the task of interpreting the constitution, is independent of
both the presidency and Congress. Kittrie's statement that he
is developing 'the lawyer's traditional concern with the evils
of unchecked power' therefore has a weight of American
constitutional experience and practice behind it. *Parens
patriae* powers, which enable decisions about life, liberty and
property to be made by officials who are members of the
executive are unconstitutional, placing the executive above
the law.

But the extension of *parens patriae* powers is not only unconstitutional: Kittrie holds that it is also morally wrong.
Lawyers are concerned with the issues of good and evil, with
personal responsibility, with a system in which the innocent
are upheld and the guilty punished. For this system, the
therapeutic state is substituting one which blurs the important
distinctions, substituting the descriptive vocabulary of the
social sciences for moral judgment by the use of such terms

as 'mentally ill', 'socially delinquent', and 'psychopathic'. It is deterministic, finding explanations for human conduct in circumstances over which offenders have no responsibility rather than in their own decisions.

> The implications of the therapeutic state for the treatment of crime and criminals are dramatic, representing a departure from the moral-religious concept that crime and other antisocial behaviour are manifestations of 'evil', and should therefore be suppressed and punished as a means of purging the evil-doer as well as society.[9]

At the root of this critique is 'the fear of therapeutic tyranny', of the power of therapists to mould and change human behaviour. Kittrie believes that 'the pressure for yet more comprehensive therapeutic controls has not yet diminished'.

At times, he equates the therapeutic state not only with the *parens patriae* state, but with the Welfare State, and it is clear that he regards the development of welfarism as a threat to liberty. Early in his argument, he quotes Charles Reich as pointing out that an extension in public welfare must, for reasons of public accountability, include an extension of power over the recipients:—

> The law of social welfare grew up on the theory that welfare is a 'gratuity' furnished by the state, and thus may be made subject to whatever conditions the state sees fit to impose. A corollary legal theory holds that, since all forms of welfare represent the expenditure of public funds, the public may properly interest itself in these funds . . . the poor are all too easily regulated . . . They are subject to social workers' urges to prescribe 'what is best'. And they are necessarily caught up in the workings of large organisations which by their nature are rigid and dehumanising.[10]

His target is clearly the development of social welfare in the United States in the Kennedy–Johnson era, and in particular, the growth in the activities of the National Institute of Mental Health, one of the Government's National Institutes of Health at Washington, DC, which at that time included in its scope of operation the treatment of homosexuals, drug abusers and alcoholics. Subsequent decisions by the US government to exclude homosexual practices from the mental health laws, and to transfer the administration of services for drug abusers and alcoholic patients to other auspices owe much to the kind of reasoning which Kittrie employed.

Kittrie's final exercise is the construction of a 'Therapeutic Bill of Rights' designed to safeguard the rights of individuals in defence against the threat of unconstitutional intervention. This forms an excellent basis for discussion of the rights of patients, and is therefore quoted in full:—

1. No person shall be compelled to undergo treatment except for the defense of society.

2. Man's innate right to remain free of excessive forms of human modification shall be inviolable.

3. No social sanctions may be invoked unless the person subjected to treatment has demonstrated a clear and present danger through truly harmful behaviour which is immediately forthcoming or has already occurred.

4. No person shall be subjected to involuntary incarceration or treatment on the basis of a finding of a general condition or status alone. Nor shall the mere conviction of a crime or a finding of not guilty by reason of insanity suffice to have a person automatically committed or treated.

5. No social sanctions, whether designated criminal, civil or therapeutic, may be invoked in the absence of the previous right to a judicial or other independent hearing, appointed counsel, and an opportunity to confront those testifying about one's past conduct or therapeutic needs.

6. Dual interference by both the criminal and the therapeutic process is prohibited.

7. An involuntary patient shall have the right to receive treatment.

8. Any compulsory treatment must be the least required reasonably to protect society.

9. All committed persons should have direct access to appointed counsel and the right, without any interference, to petition the courts for relief.

10. Those submitting to voluntary treatment should be

guaranteed that they will not be subsequently transferred to a compulsory program through administrative action.[11]

In item 4, the reference to 'a finding of a general condition or status alone' refers to such diagnoses as 'mentally ill' or 'psychopathic' without detailed supporting evidence. Item 5 and item 9 are a spelling out of the requirements of 'due process' and a claim to the right of legal intervention in therapeutic decision-making. Item 6 refers to the principle of 'double jeopardy' — a person should not be 'tried' twice for the same offence. Item 7 arises from legal cases in the United States on 'The Right to Treatment' in the case of the mentally ill, where, as Kittrie wrote, judicial decisions were 'reaching into the dark corners of the institutions'. Item 8 is an expression of the principle of 'the least restrictive requirement' necessary to meet the circumstances of the case: a principle which appears to go back to Ockham's Razor.[12]

Kittrie's conclusion is that what has occurred is a process of 'divestment' in which the law has lost authority and power to protect fundamental liberties.

In its formative years, the therapeutic state has heavily and uncritically relied upon what appeared to be scientific criteria and discretion. Often it has been satisfied to relinquish control over the need and type of therapeutic sanction to the experts and administrators. Slowly, the trend is changing. It is in fact a sign of maturity for the therapeutic experiment that we finally dare test its precepts in our judicial forums..... Ill-defined, multi-purposed and expert-reliant throughout much of its history, the therapeutic state is slowly being fitted into more carefully delineated molds . . . legal scrutiny is the tool which is increasingly being utilized both for the preservation of individual liberty and for the necessary audit of societal fulfillment vis-à-vis the therapeutic promise.[13]

As the right of individuals not to be incarcerated in institutions without judicial consent declines, the therapists may find a proper outlet for their services in the provision of community-based models of care to which people in need of assistance may go on a voluntary basis.

The style of the advocate

In this, as in other chapters of the present study, we have attempted to follow the normal rules of fair argument, which are also the rules of the courts: one allows a full statement of a case before challenging it, examining its allegations and pointing out its possible deficiencies. In the case of *The Right to be Different*, this has been particularly difficult, because Kittrie is an advocate, and does not himself follow these rules. His book is not a complete statement of a case, with the pros and cons fairly argued and the judgment at the end: it is a prosecuting counsel's speech, the written equivalent of a good courtroom performance. There is much detailed legal quotation, involving lengthy footnotes — one with thirty-eight citations. Lawyers can also blind people with science. Strong assertions are made with all the authority which the law (and in the American context, the Constitution) can command. Legal phraseology, sometimes concealing arguable premises, is used to make an effect by sheer repetition. History is raided in a search for precedent; and sudden vivid emotional appeals are introduced to sway the jury — in this case, the readers. For instance, the book begins with five examples of non-judicial activities[14] of a kind calculated to alarm:

(i) an unnamed group of black Assemblymen from the Bronx and Harlem are quoted as considering 'setting up health camps for narcotics addicts'. No details of this proposal are given.

(ii) A report from the National Institute of Mental Health is quoted as stating that racism is a health hazard. This somewhat loose phraseology leads, without discussion, to the posing of the question 'if racism is a contagious health hazard, should its most dominant carriers be isolated for individual treatment so as to stop the spread of the epidemic?'. There is no evidence that the NIMH report mentioned contagion, or advocated the incarceration of racists.

(iii) An attorney is instanced as stating that some of his clients would rather be called alcoholics that 'put in the looney businesss'.

(iv) A lesbian reports that she is happy as she is, and does not want to be 'cured'.

(v) 'Recent interviews of 100 persons' (we are not told how

selected or interviewed) 'disclosed the overwhelming opinion that the New York State programmes for narcotics addicts were more like prison than rehabilitation'.

These disparate examples are linked together by the familiar device of the story about five blind men who tried to describe an elephant: one grasped its tail, one its hoof, one its trunk, and so on, and each described a different beast. One might wonder in Kittrie's examples whether they are all grasping part of the same beast; but the elephant is the therapeutic state which could lead to 'the kingdom of therapy' and 'the demise of criminal justice'.

Lest the reader should miss the point, the five examples are headlined with such titles as 'The Vision of the Irrepressible Therapist' and 'The Vision of the Apprehensive Patient'. Later, Kittrie tells a story which is calculated to win over any reader who doubts the importance of freeing mental patients from involuntary commitment:—

In 1907, a fragile but determined old lady, who claimed to have founded a new religion, was battling for her liberty from commitment to a mental institution in Pleasant View. Her proclamation of new religious tenets in the modern scientific age was asserted as proof of her derangement. Yet Mary Baker Eddy won her battle, and the Christian Science Church now occupies a respectable place among America's more traditional creeds.[15]

Of course everybody is on the side of fragile but determined old ladies, particularly if they turn out to be Mary Baker Eddy; but this is special pleading; and in fact much of the book is special pleading, since reference is made only to material which supports the argument, and not to material which does not. The book title assumes a right which has not been examined or discussed. If individuals have a 'right to be different', in what way may they be different, and from whom? To what extent, and under what circumstances? The chapter titles assume the existence of the therapeutic state: the preface is entitled 'The Dynamics of the Therapeutic State'; chapter 1 is 'The Divestment of Criminal Justice and the Coming of the Therapeutic State'; and the two final chapters are headed 'The Therapeutic Ideal: the Evils of Unchecked Power' and 'Liberty in the Therapeutic State: Reducing the Dominance of the Savers'. These titles reveal the basis of the discussion, but they are assertions, not reasoned arguments.

With this in mind, it may be useful to look again at the five basic concepts: Mill's definition of liberty, *parens patriae*, 'due process', 'divestment' and 'the therapeutic state'. These issues are not as clear-cut as Kittrie encourages us to believe.

Mill on liberty

Kittrie is selective in his use of Mill, who qualified his celebrated statement quite carefully:—

> It is perhaps hardly necessary to say that this doctrine is meant only to apply to human beings in the maturity of their faculties. We are not speaking of children, or of young persons below the age which the law may fix as that of manhood or womanhood. Those who are still in a state to require being taken care of by others must be protected against their own actions as well as against external injury. For the same reason, we may leave out of consideration those backward states of society in which the race itself may be considered in its nonage . . . a ruler full of the spirit of improvement is warranted in the use of any expedients that will attain an end perhaps otherwise unattainable.[16]

Mill therefore specifically excludes juveniles and 'persons who are in a state to require being taken care of by others', and his analysis could be used equally well to justify therapeutic intervention as to deny it. He does argue that man ought not to be punished simply for being drunk; but he goes on to argue that a soldier or a policeman ought to be punished for being drunk on duty. This is no indication that he is thinking here of chronic alcoholism; but he states quite categorically: 'Whenever there is a definite damage, or a definite risk of damage, either to an individual or to the public, the case is taken out of the province of liberty, and placed in that of morality or law.'[17] The question this passage raises is what Mill meant by 'a definite risk of damage'. In this respect, Kittrie does not rely on Mill alone, but adds his own premise to Mill's: —

> If we accept Mill's criterion for the exercise of societal intervention — the prevention of harm to others — *and further agree* that an overt act is necessary before the state can interfere with individual liberty, there remains the question of what type of harm must be suffered by society before the state is justified to impose therapeutic controls for its defense.[18]

But Mill would not 'further agree'. He makes it clear that in his view 'It is one of the undisputed functions of government to take precautions against crime, before it has been committed, as well as to detect and punish it afterwards.'[19] Mill's splendid argument in favour of free speech and religious toleration is thus twisted to purposes which its author would not have supported.

It can, of course, be argued that Mill was writing before the development of 'the therapeutic state' and could not have foreseen its dangers; but that argument also is double-sided. Mill was writing in England in the late 1850s. He accepted colonialism (the care of 'backward states of society') and benevolent despots (rulers 'full of the spirit of improvement'), neither of which are congenial to Kittrie. Mill was expressing a very English and liberal nineteenth-century doctrine of non-interventionism; if he could not have foreseen the dangers of therapeutic interventionism, he could not have foreseen the dangers of legal interventionism either. If Mill is to be quoted, let it be in the context of his own period; and let us have Mill, the whole Mill, and nothing but Mill.

Parens patriae

It will be recalled that, in searching for the legal sources of the state's power over individuals, Kittrie makes reference to Roman law as a source of English common law, to Aethelred II, and to a statute of the reign of Edward II. All three references are of dubious validity. Lawyers tend to use historical evidence rather differently from historians, to establish a legal precedent almost irrespective of meaning and context; but in these instances, meaning and context do not suggest that there was a continuous process at work.

Roman law in the time of Gaius and Justinian did, as Kittrie suggests, place a good deal of power in the hands of the head of the household (and Kittrie seems to approve of this concept, since in his introduction to *The Right to be Different*, he thanks his own wife and children for their forbearance in passing 'too many evenings without the family head'); but it also makes specific reference to the power of the state in relation to *furiosi* or madmen. Jurisdiction over a *furiosus* came through the magistrates (who were executive officials as well as legal officials). There was provision for the appointment of a *curator*, who would have the care, or *cura* of the property; and of a *tutela*, or tutor, who would have the care of the person. Neither needed to be the head of the household; and indeed the provisions were probably most clearly invoked when the *furiosus* was the head of the household himself.[20]

VIII Aethelred 33 states: 'if an attempt is made to deprive any wise man in orders or a stranger of either his goods or his life, the king shall act as his kinsman and protector . . . unless he has some other'. This section, which is the passage quoted by Kittrie, refers fairly clearly to the general protection of the clergy and of foreigners, who would travel from place to place and therefore lack the protection of any lord of the manor. It has nothing to do with the kinds of cases which Kittrie is reviewing.

Most English historians of jurisprudence follow Dicey in tracing the development of English law (including common law) back to the reign of Henry II, but not beyond it.[21] Anglo-Saxon legal history is too remote and too specialised a study to form part of the main stream of development.

The *De Praerogativa Regis* of Edward II (17 Edw. II c.9 and 10, 1324) is well-known, but is usually quoted either as the origin of Chancery powers (those powers relating to the property of the mentally ill or the mentally handicapped) or as evidence that a distinction was made between mental illness and mental handicap as early as the fourteenth century. No historian seems to have seen it as the origin of state power over the person, for two good reasons: the act refers quite clearly to property; and the medieval world had no doctrine of statehood as now understood in nation-states. The full text of the passage is as follows:—

> The King shall have custody of the lands of natural fools, taking the profits of them without waste or destruction, and shall find them their necessaries, of whose fee soever the lands be holden. And after the death of such idiots, he shall render them to the right heirs; so that by such idiots no alienation be made, nor shall their heirs be disinherited.
>
> The King shall provide, when any happen to fail of his wit, as there are many having lucid intervals, that their lands and tenements shall be safely kept without waste or destruction, and that they and their households shall live and be maintained completely from the issues of the same; and the residue beyond their reasonable sustention shall be kept to their use, to be delivered unto them when they recover their right mind; so that such lands and tenements shall in no wise within the time aforesaid be aliened.

The intention was probably to protect the estates of feudal lords from the depredations of their neighbours. Kittrie claims that this kingly power was applicable 'to the property and later the person' of the mentally disordered: 'From this modest beginning, followed by the slow process of welfare functions shifting from the feudal lords, the mediaeval guilds, and the Church to the State in the seventeenth, eighteenth and nineteenth centuries, the *parens patriae* state of the present day came into full bloom.'[22]

This headlong dash through the centuries omits two important stages: the development of the idea that a person is his own most inalienable property, which seems to have come to the fore in the late seventeenth century, and the history of the *parens patriae* theory in juvenile justice.

Throughout most recorded history in the western world, the law has been much more preoccupied with property than with personal liberty. Ideas on liberty, which form part of the modern movement for Human Rights, are commonly traced back to the writings of John Locke at the end of the seventeenth century. Locke wrote: 'Though the earth and all inferior creatures be common to all men, yet every man has a "property" in his own "person". This nobody has any right to but himself.'[23] This was new thinking, part of the forward surge in ideas which was to make the American and French Revolutions possible. It would have been quite out of place in the fourteenth century, and for long after.

The doctrine of *parens patriae* in juvenile justice does appear to have longer roots. It has been traced back to the system of wardship (involving the lack of a natural guardian, not the commission of offences) in Roman law, and recognised in medieval England. Bracton, writing in the thirteenth century, mentions this in relation to the administration of property: 'Si quis fundum habuerit in manu sua ratione custodiae in quo quia non habet nec proprietatis nec ius possessionis nisi tantum nudum dominum cum possessione.' '[where] one has an estate in his hand by reason of wardship in which because he has neither proprietary nor possessory right, [he has] nothing except bare *dominium* without possession.'[24]

But again this did not apply to the person; and Bracton, who writes in detail about many medieval legal practices, such as mortdancestor, manumission, advowson, essoin of bedsickness and villeinage, does not mention *parens patriae*.

Blackstone, whose authoritative *Commentaries on the Laws of England* were published in 1783, does refer to the *parens patriae* power in relation to the administration of charities, as Kittrie suggests;[25] but he also makes it clear that the administration of property and the care of the person were separated in respect of lunatics and idiots in his day.[26]

Professor Phyllida Parsloe, who writes on juvenile justice in America and England, takes the view that the doctrine of *parens patriae* grew up through common law and Chancery (property) cases, but that it was not until 1847 that an English court held that 'the cases in which this Court interferes on behalf of juveniles are not confined to those in which there is property'. She concludes that 'the question of property raises some doubts about the juvenile court's claims to an ancestry in Chancery . . . on the whole, it seems that early writers . . . were much more concerned with acquiring prestige for their juvenile courts than with historical accuracy'.[27] Kittrie's search for precedent therefore involves at least four jumps in logic: from Roman Law on the household to the feudal control of property; from the feudal control of property to the control of the person; from medieval wardship to the juvenile court; and from the juvenile court to the complexities of modern therapeutic policies.

The use of the term *parens patriae* is not confined to Kittrie: Phyllida Parsloe mentions its use in American jurisprudence to refer to protective provisions relating to 'children, the senile, the retarded and the insane'; but it involves a very inaccurate piece of historical attribution. Its use in the United States is largely pejorative, and conceals an emotive reference to the tyranny of English kings; but whatever the shortcomings of George III and his predecessors, the invention of the therapeutic state was hardly one of them.

The phase is often mistranslated. Though Kittrie does not fall into this particular error, it should perhaps be pointed out that *parens patriae* literally means 'the father of the country', and cannot be construed to mean 'the state as parent', a phrase used by Rothman[28] and other writers.

'Due process'

The citing of 'due process' as the only proper procedure for the infringement of life, liberty or property rights is an American legal appeal to the US Constitution which has no parallel in English law. Because Britain has no written constitution, judgments on the legality of particular procedures depend on the citation of public general statutes (i.e. Acts of Parliament), case-law, and ultimately, if the case is referred to the House of Lords, on principles of natural justice. There is still some doubt as to whether Parliament's ratification of international conventions overrides statute law, and Lord Denning's judgment that it does not (though he hoped that the two would never conflict) has been widely quoted.[29] In the United States, the provisions of the Constitution may be held by the judiciary to override both statute law and case-law; and the requirement of the Fifth and Fourteenth Amendments to the Constitution that life, liberty and property rights should be protected by 'due process' therefore may be held to take precedence over both federal and state law which provides to the contrary. According to Kittrie:—

Due process is a guarantee offered to the American citizen by the Constitution, a safeguard against arbitrary government and officialdom. Historically, due process was derived from the colonists' experience with oppressive European governments, in whose hands the citizen was a helpless pawn. The requirement of due process assures the citizen protection in his efforts to defend himself against the overwhelming government apparatus. It requires that the fate of the citizen's life, liberty or property not be decided in closed chambers, that he be advised of the specific charges against him, and have an opportunity to challenge adverse evidence, that he be permitted to introduce his own witnesses, and that the necessary assistance of Counsel be afforded for his defense.[30]

Kittrie points out that the Fifth and Fourteenth Amendments do not place any limitations on the application of 'due process'. It can be held to apply not only to the criminal law, but to all kinds of law or administrative procedure limiting the constitutional rights of mental patients, juveniles, or the other categories covered by his analysis. He goes on to attack administrative law in general:—

What is administrative law? This expression refers to a system of settling social problems by means that have little to do with law in the Anglo-American sense of the term. In such a system, public officials, called administrators, bureaucrats or civil servants, settle certain disputes in accordance with rules made not by legislators, but by the administrators themselves. No less a person than the Right Honourable Hewart of Bury, Lord Chief Justice of England (1929) asserted that this was not a system of law but of lawlessness.[31]

Lord Chief Justice Hewart (who wrote a rather contentious book called *The New Despotism* on the subject, and published it in New York) clearly shared Kittrie's forthright views. Attacks by legal luminaries on administrative law (which

Dicey also regarded with horror) are not uncommon. The growth of administrative law, and the setting up of quasi-legal systems of tribunals, has occurred largely because of the slowness, the cumbersome nature and the expense of court proceedings. The claim that only the model provided by the courts represents the true process of justice, and that this is freely available to any citizen, is somewhat disingenuous. As Abel-Smith and Stevens comment, for the citizen to go to law is virtually equivalent to writing out a blank cheque to the legal profession, since he cannot with any confidence predict either the costs to his own pocket or the outcome — and the latter may have more to do with the persuasive power of counsel or with legal technicalities than with the true course of justice.[32]

Further, the adoption of the procedures of the criminal courts involves the concept of an offence, and the question of guilt or innocence. Counsel frequently ask such expert witnesses as psychiatrists or pathologists, questions which require simple answers: is this defendant sane or insane? Did he know what he was doing at the time: Is he guilty or not guilty? The establishment of *mens rea*, or guilty intent, requires 'Yes' or 'No' as an answer, and the structure of the legal discourse is such that expert witnesses' attempts to answer such questions honestly, within the understanding of their own professions of the complexities of human hehaviour, often leads to confusion and apparent contradiction. The question as asked may seem either unanswerable or irrelevant.[33] Expert witnesses frequently make a poor showing in court, and this accounts for some of the contempt which Kittrie manages to attach to the word 'expert'.

Kittrie mentions the English Mental Health Act of 1959 as evidence of

> an accelerated trend in Anglo-American society away from a strict judicial process to a more informal administrative procedure . . . widely endorsed by social reformers who argue that anachronistic legal formalism needlessly imposes requirements and sanctions on people who require psychiatric assistance, not legal aid.[34]

That Act has now been amended in a more legalistic

direction; but the problems which Kittrie mentions only briefly remain: psychiatrists argue that legal procedures are stigmatising and traumatic for patients, that they involve 'a resultant taint of criminality', and that they 'represent the last ditch stand of archaic legal prerogatives'.[35] If there are dangers in discretion, there are also dangers in legal formalism; and these have in the past been seen more clearly in Britain than in the United States.

Against such views, Kittrie is prepared to contend that only a system maintained by lawyers and controlled by lawyers is constitutional. The difficulty with this argument is that, while the Fifth and Fourteenth Amendments to the US constitution do not limit the operation of due process to criminal cases, and it may therefore be held to be applicable to mental patients, juvenile offenders and others now dealt with by more discretionary procedures, those admirably clear and brief statements of constitutional intent do not define 'due process' either. There is nothing in the US Constitution to indicate that the lawyers' definition of 'due process' is the right or the only definition.

'Divestment'

Kittrie writes: 'The criminal law in the United States has been undergoing a process of divestment — a relinquishing of its jurisdiction over many of its traditional subjects and areas.'[36]

Some rather curious arithmetic follows to support his contention that only 46 out of every 100 American citizens are subject to the sanctions of the criminal law — the other 54 per cent consisting of children under the age of eighteen, mental patients, chronic alcoholics and psychopaths. This brief statistical exercise appears to be based on fairly slender evidence — US population estimates, a brief paper from the National Committee Against Mental Illness Inc., a memorandum to a senator, and a telephone call to the National Association of Retarded Children. It appears that Kittrie is only making a debating point: it occupies a single paragraph, and a footnote indicates that the calculation is based on the assumption that the conditions described as characteristic of the 54 per cent would be sufficient in any individual instance to exempt the person concerned from criminal charges in all circumstances. A professor of law must know that this is not the case, and that the figures are not to be taken seriously.

Kittrie maintains that the general public is not growing more tolerant, but merely substituting non-legal forms of social control for judicial control:—

> Divestment, carried out in the name of the new social emphasis upon therapy, rehabilitation and prevention — as contrasted with criminal law's emphasis upon retribution, incapacitation and deterrence — has produced new types of borderland proceedings and sanctions, lodged between the civil and the criminal law.[37]

It could be argued that therapy, rehabilitation and prevention are more civilised forms of social action than retribution, incapacitation and deterrence; but by describing the 'new social emphasis' as 'non-legal', Kittrie strongly implies that it is *illegal* — a very different matter. The reader is left to associate 'divestment' with the sinister 'borderland proceedings'. Kittrie's basic claim is that the model of the criminal courts should be employed, whatever the taint and whatever the trauma, to any case involving the limitation of individual rights, and that only this model is legal, constitutional and moral. One may wonder whether the special pleading is on behalf of human rights, or on behalf of the legal profession.

The therapeutic state

This phrase seems to have originated in the work of Thomas Szasz, who has a chapter in *Law, Liberty and Psychiatry* entitled 'Towards the Therapeutic State' in which he writes: 'Although we may not know it, we have, in our day, witnessed the birth of the Therapeutic State. This is perhaps the major implication of psychiatry as an institution of social control.'[38]

It is, of course, a loaded term — not a description, but an allegation. All the weight of Szasz's arguments about the nature of liberty, the dangers of social control and the persecutory potential of 'institutional psychiatry' is summed up in it. Kittrie describes *Law, Liberty and Psychiatry* as 'a colourful but alarmist account of the Therapeutic State', but commends Szasz for his manifestation of 'conservative concern' and for being 'a pronounced critic of his own psychiatric fraternity'.[39] Kittrie's own references to 'the Therapeutic State' in his index include the following:—

'abuses resulting from conglomerate nature of'
'critics of the unlimited'
'dangers of'
'erosion of personal responsibility in'
'judicial review as limitation of'
'unchecked by legal institutions'

Index references to 'Therapy' begin with 'failure of' and end with 'See also Lobotomy; Rehabilitation; Shock Treatment; Sterilisation'.

Both Szasz and Kittrie argue for a return to a straightforward and unqualified judgmentalism if the 'deviant' breaks the criminal law, and an equally unqualified tolerance if he does not. The simple dichotomies of the legal profession are to be applied without exception — to children, to the mentally handicapped, to the deluded or confused, to those in the grip of alcohol or drug addiction. All are to be 'suppressed and punished' in the name of justice.

But Kittrie and Szasz do not always see eye to eye. While Szasz thunders against the development of the Community Health Center Movement on the grounds that it infringes contractual (fee-paying) psychiatry, Kittrie commends it as offering a way for patients out of their 'custodial storehouses'.[40] While Szasz fears that the substitution of health values for social and political values may be used to justify coercion, Kittrie thinks that he 'undervalues the importance of the Therapeutic State's humanizing effects';[41] and while Szasz sees psychotherapy as the arch-enemy, and most psychotherapists as claiming technical skills they do not possess, Kittrie is concerned with behaviour modification in its more extreme forms, and fears that psychiatrists already have 'a disturbing number of skills for the modification of man'.[42]

When Kittrie writes about the therapeutic state, he is more

concerned with the diminution of legal powers than with psychiatrists' fees, and he is careful to distinguish between compulsory welfare and voluntary welfare:—

The therapeutic state differs from its more established sister, the public welfare state, in that the latter offers its services to the voluntary recipient, whilst the former seeks to impose its 'beneficial' services compulsorily (since the recipient is held to be incompetent) . . . the state's therapeutic function is often authoritarian, and may be exercised on a deviant individual for the asserted public interest with little or no consideration of his own choice.[43]

Kittrie states that 'the study of human deviation and deviants has increasingly become popular in the psychological and sociological circles' and claims that his aim is 'to fill the existing gap by synthesising diverse interdisciplinary approaches and subjecting them to the scrutiny of current legal and constitutional standards'. He complains that, in their campaign against 'the tyranny of health and welfare', the new critics, of whom he is one, 'find themselves cast, in some eyes, not in the role of libertarians, but in the role of archconservatives'.[44] Much of his writing is indeed of a very conservative nature; but there are some surprising departures from rightwing orthodoxy in the evidence of the six specialist chapters, which juxtapose accounts of the dangers of social control with evidence that they are already disappearing; in comments at the end of some of these chapters, which recommend widespread and sweeping social reforms; and in the Therapeutic Bill of Rights, which is well thought-out and in most respects progressive.

Though Kittrie contends that 'the operations of the therapeutic state are on a condition of constant growth', the specialist chapters contain brief acknowledgments of evidence to the contrary. The chapter on the mentally ill contains a short account of the development of the Community Mental Health movement;[45] the chapter on delinquent youths acknowledges 'a drastic departure from primary reliance on institutional treatment facilities'.[46] Though Kittrie (in 1971) thought that this would largely take place 'in the coming years', Andrew Scull records that a massive reduction in institutional treatment for juveniles had been taking place since the mid-1950s.[47] Kittrie also notes that the use of sterilisation is declining — and unexpectedly argues that it may sometimes be justified.[48]

In this respect, Kittrie is perhaps merely behaving like an advocate. He occasionally acknowledges evidence which is against the case he is making — but he does so in a few words, and only after rousing considerable public apprehension about the topic under discussion, making a strong emotional case first.

The reformist comments at the end of the specialist chapters require a different explanation, since some of them are totally at variance with the main line of attack. For instance, there is the view that the answer to the problems of juvenile justice is not severer penalties but a major move against 'poverty, unfit parents, broken homes, inadequate schools, improper vocational training and lack of opportunities';[49] or the contention that the real answer to drug addiction is 'the removal of urban poverty and racial ghettoes which breed a sense of inadequacy and worthlessness'.[50] These comments suggest the need for a 'public welfare state' of considerable dimensions. If such statements are merely rhetorical, they employ a very different rhetoric from that of the attack on the therapeutic state; and Kittrie is a sufficiently meticulous writer not to say what he does not mean. We might suspect that such comments came in his students' reports and escaped the editor's notice if it were not for that final balanced and humane section on the Therapeutic Bill of Rights.

Kittrie remains an enigma. Perhaps, inside the flamboyant and highly orthodox representative of the American Bar Association, there is a social reformer quietly struggling to get out.

10 COHEN AND TAYLOR: THE INFILTRATORS

Pictures of 'E' Wing at Durham Prison in Cohen and Taylor's *Psychological Survival: the experience of long-term imprisonment* show a standard prison block: cells on four floors, iron staircases, a cat-walk on each floor, a central well with wire mesh across the upper floors to prevent suicides. Uniformed officers stand to attention. The paintwork is monochrome, bright and clean. All is orderly and clinical — except that some twenty long-term prisoners had to live out their disordered and frustrated lives in this setting, in close and abrasive contact. The contrast between the extreme orderliness of the setting and the chaos of personal experience which occurs within it is acute.

Psychological Survival was published in 1972, and represents some four years' work by two young social psychologists in Britain who organised a class for prisoners under the auspices of the Extra-Mural Department of the University of Durham. The governor was 'nervous'[1] about the prospect of the class according to the authors (though a representative of the Extra-Mural Department at Durham subsequently wrote to *New Society* to say that a similar class had been running successfully for a year already[2]). If the governor was nervous, he might have been more so if he had realised that he was admitting to his maximum security wing two of the leading exponents of the new school of deviancy theory. We are told that he 'cautiously suggested' that the lecturers might talk on any subject provided that it was not connected with the men's lives. In fact, the classes developed into an unorthodox research project organised precisely around that theme. There

149

is mention later in the narrative of an application to the Home Office for research funding, with the governor's support, but the situation must have involved some anxieties for the prison administration.

Some of the prison officers expressed strong doubts, suspecting that the new lecturers were 'in league' with the men. One senior officer was curiously reassured to find that they were being paid for the classes, and 'not going to talk to those animals for nothing'.[3]

It seems that the research project grew naturally out of the situation. The subject of the effects of long-term imprisonment was a matter of considerable discussion among the sociologists and criminologists in November 1967, when Stanley Cohen and Laurie Taylor first walked into 'E' Wing, for the Mountbatten Report on *Prison Escapes and Security*[4] (following the celebrated escape of the spy, George Blake, two of the Great Train Robbers and Frank Mitchell, dubbed by the press 'the Mad Axeman') was only two years old; and the Radzinowicz Committee's Report on *The Regime for Long-Term Prisoners in Conditions of Maximum Security*[5] was newly-published. Radzinowicz had been asked to recommend a type of régime suitable for Category 'A' prisoners. Instead he recommended, among other things, that the policy of concentrating Category 'A' prisoners should be replaced, in the interests of both security and humanity, by a policy of dispersal; but when the classes began, 'E' Wing was still housing a concentration of the most well-known criminal names in Britain — while it is difficult to tell from *Psychological Survival* exactly who was in the wing at what time, we are certainly told that in the period 1966–8, the inhabitants included three Train Robbers, one of the Kray twins, and two other well-known figures of the criminal world, Walter Probyn and John McVicar.

'E' Wing was heavily guarded in the belief that (as the popular press was frequently apt to tell the public) there was a new type of criminal to be dealt with — highly intelligent, ruthless, and backed by powerful organisations likely to attempt to engineer their escape. After the escape of Ronald Biggs from Wandsworth Prison, there was, according to Cohen and Taylor, a 'paranoid escalation' in precautions, which included electronic surveillance, guard dogs, possibly a machine gun nest, and for a time the presence of troops.[6] The Chief Constable of Durham spoke of the dangers of full-scale military attack on the prison, with tanks, bombs, and even limited atomic weapons. (He was later to claim that this speech was intended to create a diversion while three prisoners were transferred to Parkhurst, the maximum security prison in the Isle of Wight.)

Inside, the Wing seems to have provided a scrupulous avoidance of any conditions which might have been construed as constituting cruelty or abuse with an equally scrupulous avoidance of those less tangible factors — freedom of movement, privacy, choice, variety, stimulus — which make human life bearable. The food was good, there was medical attention, the building was clean, and there are no recorded complaints about the plumbing or the heating. In that sense, the prisoners were better off than many badly housed families outside. The press made much of these conditions, calling the prisoners 'a pampered élite'; but closed circuit television, monitored by an officer in a bullet-proof cage, destroyed any illusion of privacy. The block was 'a lifeless cavern of railings and landings and pipes'. and it had no external windows, so there was no view of the outside world, or even of that small patch of sky which meant so much to Oscar Wilde in Reading Gaol. One prisoner called it 'like living in a submarine'. The atmosphere was claustrophobic, the neon lighting uniform, and there was no variation in colour. There were only about twenty prisoners at any one time, but it was impossible for them to get more than twenty feet away from one another, or from the prison officers on duty. There were often twice as many officers as prisoners, 'peering through the glass windows in doors, leaning over the landing rails, chatting through the anti-suicide netting'.[7]

The only relief from the cell block was a small, bare exercise yard, approached through a concrete corridor, and heavily fortified with barbed wire.

The Radzinowicz Committtee, commenting on conditions of this kind, which were not unique in the British Prison Service, drew the contrast between the good physical health of prisoners ('probably . . . better than that of many of their friends outside') and their deteriorating mental health, leading in some cases to irreversible personality damage.

This 'deadening of aspects of a prisoner's personality' was a subject on which 'a multiplicity of opinions have been expressed, but on which there are virtually no hard facts, and on which very little research has been carried out'.[8]

After the public outcry concerning the escapes of two of the Train Robbers and the Mountbatten Report had endorsed the concept of strong perimeter security combined with relatively humane conditions inside the perimeter, there were attempts to improve the conditions of the Category 'A' prisoners. The lights were put out at night, television and radio were introduced, the men were allowed their own cooking facilities, there was new floor covering and fresh paint, and educational classes were extended.

For some time, Cohen and Taylor took their own class in a room with no door. The prisoners dragged a blackboard across the opening. A prison officer sat outside for some sessions, but after that, the instructors and their students were left to their own devices.

Cohen and Taylor had no prepared scripts to deliver. They were teaching live, picking up ideas from the minds of their students and trying to relate book-knowledge to their immediate needs and understanding, relying on their existing knowledge of criminological and other literature to illuminate the perceptions of their class. It is a stimulating, if sometimes rather unsystematic, form of adult teaching, and was evidently the only method possible in the circumstances. If they had never written *Psychological Survival*, the exercise would still have been worthwhile within the context of the Radzinowicz Committee's comments on deterioration. It might have been a total failure; but they caught the interest of the prisoners, some of whom at least co-operated willingly, writing essays, stories and poems on their experiences.

The discussion was about crime and punishment, deprivation and alienation, and the problems of survival in extreme conditions. The texts included Dostoievsky's *Crime and Punishment*, Camus's *Outsider*, Genet's *Our Lady of the Flowers* and Roth's *Portnoy's Complaint*, as well as accounts of prison life and other kinds of institutional life. In their account of 'E' Wing, Cohen and Taylor rely fairly heavily on Sykes's *Society of Captives*, John Irwin's *The Felon,* Victor Serge's *Men in Prison*, and Goffman's *Asylums*.

If the teaching was unsystematic, so was the student participation. As is common in prison and mental hospital classes, the audience, deprived of greater liberty, would walk in and out of the class, going off to make tea, coming back to pick up an argument. The class 'varied in size from two to twelve', starting at six o'clock in the evening and ending some time before lights out at nine. It may not have been the only class of its kind. Other 'E' Wing teachers at this time included Ian Taylor and Paul Walton, two of the authors of *The New Criminology* (1973), who may have been working on rather similar lines.

How many men attended, and for how long, is obscure. Cohen and Taylor write 'As we walked into the Wing each week for three years'. They also note that 'some fifty men' passed through the classes 'in the early months of 1968', which suggests that many of the men in 'E' Wing did not stay there long (since the total capacity was about twenty) and many only had a brief acquaintance with the classes; but they got to know ten 'intimately' and an equal number 'fairly well'. They talked to the ten 'more intimately than to any other people we knew'.[9] The play had a small cast of stars, with a large number of walk-on parts.

'Whose side are we on?'[10]

The aim was to discover 'how, under extreme circumstances, people cope with universes changing, machineries being sabotaged, and pictures being blurred or obilterated'.[11] The basic perspective corresponded to that of Berger and Luckmann's *The Social Construction of Reality*, an important sociological text published in 1971, and used in the final analysis.

Cohen and Taylor refer to their book as 'a somewhat journalistic exercise', and so it is. The scholarship and the personal concern are undeniable, but they are mediated through the exaggerated (and now rather dated) views of the early deviancy theorists. There are many references to the drug sub-culture, to homosexuals, to hippies and to freedom fighters as representing groups with whom the prisoners ought to feel some kind of identity. One of the outstanding weaknesses of deviancy theory was its tendency to create new forms of social stereotyping, lumping all 'deviants' together as suffering a common experience. This approach does not seem to have corresponded with the experience of the prisoners, who were 'mostly from London', had 'a metropolitan smartness' and possessed 'a strong awareness of their public image'.[12] Most of them probably preferred the life-style being lived by Ronald Biggs the escaped Train Robber in South America, to that of Timothy Leary, the prophet of LSD, or George Jackson, the Soledad Brother. We are told that the prisoners were 'against the contemporary hippie form of drop-out', that they had no sympathy with black radicals, and that they soon tired of R. D. Laing.[13]

In the symbiotic relationship which grew up between Cohen and Taylor and their class (they write of 'our bond to the prisoners: there are certain trusts we cannot betray, certain information we cannot now give') there was a strong element of snobbery. They note 'an odd reciprocal granting of status between us and them. We are university teachers, they are Category 'A' prisoners. Outside on the landing sit the plebs.'[14] To get the full force of this comment, one has to recall that university teachers enjoyed a very much higher social status in the expansionist period of the late 1960s than they have in the anti-intellectual and straitened 1980s.

Later, they note of the prisoners: 'It would not be going too far to say that they felt in some danger of being contaminated by what they regard as the dull, prejudiced lumpenproletarian nature of their guards.'[15] The smart, metropolitan prisoners did not find it too difficult, with the aid of their lecturers, to score off the dull northern peasants. We are told of one officer who displayed 'cheery satisfaction' when told that he was an authoritarian psychopath.

References to the lumpenproletariat jar when the reader realises that, so far from welcoming a Marxist ideology, the prisoners were for the most part high-class entrepreneurs who needed the capitalist system to operate within. The language becomes more believable when we read of 'screws, who, they claimed, were "thick" and insensitive'.[16]

'Whose side are we on?' Towards the end of the book, the authors face up to this question, and make it clear that they were not offering 'blanket moral approval' for the offences which the prisoners had committed; and it seems that the prisoners neither expected nor wanted this. They seem to have oscillated between trying to convert Cohen and Taylor to their own 'smart, metropolitan' styles and attitudes, and expecting them to retain 'some conventional notion of morality'.[17] The authors were evidently aware of the problems, and attempted to keep to the 'appreciative' stance proposed by David Matza in *Becoming Deviant*[18] — trying to understand without becoming judgmental, and to refrain from challenging their subjects' ideologies without losing their own. However, Matza's argument also entails appreciating the world of the prison officer or policeman as well as that of the prisoner. Cohen and Taylor use the argument to justify their study of the prisoners, but ignore it in relation to the staff.

The two lecturers 'found it difficult not to feel sympathy for the prisoners' situation', and became friends as well as teachers; but they are aware of Howard Becker's point that defining the deviant as anti-hero can lead to sentimentality.[19] They say that it would 'be facile to talk about anything like full identification with the prisoners'. There is clearly considerable ambivalence in their attitudes: at times they write like responsible social scientists with a strong, if unorthodox, moral sense; at other times they are very celebrity-conscious, highly impressed by their own success with criminals who have made the headlines, and well aware of the media value of what they are writing.

In this second vein, they note 'We were rarely conscious of any danger' and mention the possibility that they might have been taken hostage (which cannot have been much more real than the threat of the use of atomic weapons); and they compare the prisoners not only to the anti-heroes of the late 1960s, but to figures more generally regarded as heroic: Captain Scott of the Antarctic, Anthony Grey (the Reuter correspondent imprisoned for some years in Pekin), Sir Geoffrey Jackson (the British ambassador held captive by the Tupamaros), and 'monks, hermits and ascetics'.[20] This comparison has the excuse of trying to find parallels to the prisoners' experience of deprivation, but in most cases the resemblance is extremely slight, and the main purpose appears to be the attribution of prestige by association. There is a reference to J. R. L. Anderson's *The Ulysses Factor* which attributes to the heroes of 'great individual exploits in

exploration and adventure' such qualities as 'courage, selfish-
ness, physical strength, ability to lead, self-discipline, endur-
ance, cunning, unscrupulousness and even strong sexual
attraction'.[21]

Again it is implied, though not explicitly stated, that the
prisoners share these qualities. The worlds of heroes, anti-
heroes and non-heroes are confused in the predilection for
notoriety. One does not have to share the prison staff's habit
of referring to long-term prisoners as 'villains' to find this
moral confusion unattractive.

Surviving and fighting back

These are serious flaws in a book which has much fresh
research material on the experience of long-term imprisonment. The main analysis, based on Berger and Luckmann's
theoretical framework, is concerned with the way in which
imprisonment causes a massive disruption in normal living
patterns. Such experiences are 'literally and metaphorically
shattering — they break the web of meaning we have built
up around ourselves, and at the same time show how fragile
this web is'.[22]

It is argued that the fact of imprisonment is analogous to
other shattering experiences — a serious car accident, a prolonged illness, a bereavement; but while people in the outside
world can compensate and form fresh webs of meaning
through such recourses as forming new relationships, becoming workaholics or drowning their sorrow in drink, prisoners
do not have access to any of these forms of relief. The
prisoner's family life, his working life, his social life are all
taken away from him, and they are not 'held in cold storage
till his return'. Year by year, as he serves his sentence, they
slip away. Family and friends cease to visit, skills rust, contacts atrophy. 'He has been given "life" — a prison life — and
somehow he must learn to live it'.[23]

In such a situation, the prisoner has to find ways of main-
taining his own identity, and Cohen and Taylor argue that
for their group, this means 'fighting back'. Though they
adopt Goffman's concept of 'the collapse of domains' (family,
work and leisure) in the institutional setting,[24] they reject

most of his analysis as irrelevant to their group of celebrities. The mortification of the self simply does not occur — institutional degradation ceremonies 'long ago ceased to be disconcerting'. Secondary adjustments to prison life are not rated as worth examination: they can be taken for granted; and the four-fold classification of adaptation to the institutional environment is dismissed on the grounds that these men do not adapt, and that they have little in common with mental patients. While Goffman lists 'intransigence' as one mode of adaptation (the other three being 'withdrawal', 'colonisation' and 'conversion') Cohen and Taylor are insistent that this is not the same as 'fighting back', because the intransigent is merely fighting the institution, not the wider system which it represents: 'Given that the fight is defined in these terms, and that the institution from which Goffman's main evidence is derived is a mental hospital, it is not surprising that the struggle is not of a very disruptive kind.'[25]

This insistence requires some explanation, because the internal evidence of *Psychological Survival* is that Goffman's analysis fits more closely than the authors are willing to admit. A closer acquaintance with the patients of St Elizabeth's Hospital, Washington DC, where Goffman undertook his research, might have suggested that the 'intransigent' were fighting the whole world, not merely the staff of 'St. E's'. And the sex deviants on the top floor of 'E' Wing (separated from the other prisoners by a locked door, and treated as pariahs by the other prisoners) are described as following solitary hobbies, and characterised by 'inner-worldliness' and 'mystical retreatism',[26] which sound remarkably like 'colonisation' or 'withdrawal'. Why then, do Cohen and Taylor refuse to accept a useful and evidently relevant form of classification? Part of the answer seems to lie in their own characterisation of their group as romantic and news-worthy heroes or anti-heroes: all the attributes of machismo are necessary to sustain this interpretation. Part may also lie in the attitudes of the prisoners, perhaps communicated unconsciously to their lecturers. The fear of mental deterioration was evidently very strong, and that involved a rejection of any comparison with the mentally ill. It is interesting that, when Paul Harrison of *New Society* commented that some 30 per cent of long-term prisoners were likely to be suffering from mental disturbance, Stanley Cohen wrote to reject the proposition, and to challenge the writer to substantiate it. Paul Harrison provided the evidence.[27]

Cohen and Taylor provide their own classification of the mechanisms of 'fighting back'[28]:

(i) *'self-protection'*: refusing to accept images of their own identity which show them as vicious or depraved, as a 'pampered élite' or as 'paying a debt to society'. Their chosen self-image, based on the celebrity status accorded to them by press and television, involves the denigration of prison staff as a functional identity-preserving technique, and is carefully fostered by such outside contacts as they can maintain with Members of Parliament, journalists and other influential figures.

(ii) *'campaigning'*: making contact with organisations sympathetic to prisoners, such as the National Council for Civil Liberties and Radical Alternatives to Prison (RAP). This activity, somewhat surprisingly described by the authors as 'moaning, niggling, complaining and making a nuisance of oneself', comes close to Mathiesen's use of the term 'censoriousness' in *The Defences of the Weak*.[29] The prisoner uses the standards of fairness and justice which he has been sentenced for breaking, and then accuses the authorities of breaking those same standards. He 'points a finger at them, and accuses them of being unfair and unjust by their own rules'. The record in 'campaigning' among Cohen and Taylor's group of prisoners was held by 'Robert', whose correspondence over ten years included 63 petitions to the Home Office and 543 letters, including 130 to MPs, 67 to Lord Longford and 44 to Lady Wootton. There is no record of the responses.

(iii) *'escaping'*: while escapes from the extreme conditions of confinement in 'E' Wing proved impossible, the *idea* of escaping played an important part of the prisoners' life, just as the idea of preventing escapes formed an important part of the working life of the prison staff. Even if there was no prospect of getting out of 'E' Wing, getting out of 'E' Wing was the first step in making any other plans for the future. Cohen and Taylor touch on the complex reaction which the escape plans of individuals can touch off in the group: the would-be escaper is acting out the aspirations of the whole group; but he is at the same time endangering its precarious working arrangements with authority, and betraying it by proposing to leave it. Similar reactions are well-documented in the prisoner-of-war literature.

(iv) *'striking'*: industrial strikes, or the takeover of part of the prison, were impossible in the close confinement of 'E' Wing. The only available strike weapon was the hunger-strike, which, in the late 1960s, still carried a kind of moral respect in the outside world. The subsequent experience of the H-block prisoners in the Maze, who were allowed to starve to death, has probably destroyed this weapon for all time.

(v) *'confronting'*: this involved direct confrontation with the authorities in the prison — 'mutiny, rebellion, insurrection' — but does not seem to have been much employed in 'E' Wing. Cohen and Taylor note somewhat regretfully that the prisoners did not have 'an articulated revolutionary ideology'. It seems likely that they did not have an unarticulated revolutionary ideology either — as noted earlier, their main aim was not to destroy capitalist society, but to profit from it. The very limited instances of the 'football mutiny' and the 'Chapel barricade' (both of which occurred before Cohen and Taylor entered the prison) were expressions of frustration rather than deliberate attempts to overthrow the system, 'intransigence' perhaps, but hardly revolution.

Cohen and Taylor's classification is a useful descriptive device, because it can be applied to other prison populations. Prisoners in the Maze, for example, fought for special category status partly because it reinforced their own view that they were soldiers and heroes, not terrorists and criminals. Prisoners in many prisons have tried to use Human Rights organisations to establish their claims — and the Human Rights organisations have become somewhat belatedly aware of how they may be used in this respect for purposes not in accord with their own liberal reformist ideals. Confrontation frequently occurs in prisons where the prisoners have sufficient freedom of movement to take over part of the accommodation, or to sit on the roof waving banners at the television cameras; but the most interesting part of the classification concerns 'self-protection', a somewhat unmemorable phrase for an important phenomenon which the authors might have explored in greater depth. It refers to the ways in which the prisoners preserve their personal identities in the face of institutional attack.

Goffman's concept of 'role-stripping' is summarily dismissed on the grounds that 'the men are constantly being reminded of other identities'[30] through letters from friends and outsiders who regard them as 'experts'; but this does not accord with the detailed description of restrictions on correspondence. As in the rejection of the analogy with mental patients, it may be that this judgment came from the prisoners' own anxiety to cling to their outside identities rather than from objective observation of what was actually occurring. The 'E' Wing prisoners had lost most of their outside roles, virtually ceasing to be husbands, sons, fathers, workers, citizens and neighbours; and while they rejected the role of 'criminals' imposed on them by authority, and the role of revolutionary heroes offered by their instructors, they clearly appreciated and fostered their own concept of their role as public figures. They were not Goldfingers or Che Guevaras, but it helped to be regarded as latter-day versions of Jesse James.

Cohen and Taylor quickly came to the conclusion that the prisoners did not form a homogeneous group. The mass media lumped them together as 'super-criminals', and the Radzinowicz Report characterised them as 'young or fairly young violent professional criminals who are both dangerous and persistent in their criminal activities',[31] but on closer acquaintance, predictably, they turned out to be as mixed a group as any other logical class of men. The only common denominator was the use of physical violence.

This suggests that they were not highly educated. On the whole, those who can do so fight their battles with words rather than with guns, knives or fists; but the authors are frequently at pains to tell us that the prisoners were, if not intellectuals, at least capable of profiting from a highly intellectual level of discussion. The classes moved 'from formal sociology to unprogrammed discussion . . . away from the night-school syndrome'; but there was Genet and Camus and Dostoievsky and Freud and R. D. Laing, and much more. We are told that several of them were capable of taking university degrees (at least one of them — John McVicar — subsequently did so), and that they had an understanding of the technical limitations of existing academic literature on their problems: 'They pointed out to us the inadequacies of the literature, the psychologists' concern with sensory rather

than general psychological problems, the sociologists' reliance upon large-scale surveys of medium-term prisoners .'[32]
There may have been times when the instructors were putting words into the students' mouths; but even if this process sometimes gets in the way of finding out what the prisoners' own experiences were, enough comes through to form a basis for further research.

Following Maurice Farber and John Irwin,[33] Cohen and Taylor sketch out a typology designed to link outside criminal characteristics (the type and duration of the offence) with the prisoner's subsequent reaction to imprisonment.[34] This leads to some tentative hypotheses, which may be summarised as follows:—

(i) those who confront authority outside (through bank raids, or armed hold-ups or robberies) will tend to confront authority inside.

(ii) those who circumvent authority outside (through business frauds or protection rackets) will tend to continue the contest of wits through 'campaigning'.

(iii) those who were 'traditional professional career thieves' with specialist skills will tend to keep the rules in prison, and have some respect for authority.

(iv) sexual deviants (curiously described as 'private sinners') will tend to develop solitary habits. It is not clear whether this is by choice, or because they are shunned by others, or because they are segregated for their own protection.

(v) 'situational criminals' (the term used by Farber to describe people without major criminal intent who commit crime through being caught in a web of adverse circumstances) display no common characteristics.

This may be somewhat facile: Cohen and Taylor do not enter into the considerable debate about the nature of free will and personal responsibility which underlies the fifth category[35]; moreover, many personality factors and experiences may affect the ways in which a particular prisoner comes to terms with prison life. At the same time, the categorisation provides some testable hypotheses, and it takes us further than the previous literature or the official generalizations.

Evaluating the findings

What really happened during those sporadically attended classes in 'E' Wing? Two bright young university lecturers formed a genuine bond with a small group of long-term prisoners, and found in it an unusual and fascinating research opportunity. A few long-term prisoners, fighting against the loss of identity, found support and stimulus in the weekly visits of instructors who respected them as individuals, took them at their own valuation as celebrities — 'How does it feel to be talking to people you've read so much about?' one prisoner asked — and appeared to join in their denigration of the 'lumpenproletariat' prison staff outside the door. There was an educational element in this process, and a psychotherapeutic element; but there was also an element of collusion. It may be that the prisoners were prepared to put up with Camus and Genet and the comparisons with the situation of blacks, homosexuals and hippies in order to have their own role reinforced as the VIPs who still made the headlines; while Cohen and Taylor were prepared to ignore a good deal of the evidence that their students did not fit into their concept of deviancy as a phenomenon of the poor and oppressed, in order to get their research material.

Was it research, or a mutually beneficial ego-trip? If Cohen and Taylor were part of the 'self-protection' process for the prisoners, it could be argued that they were not the objective observers they claimed to be. Their identification with the prisoners made it difficult for them to claim objectivity, though there was some justice in their argument that too much prison research in the past had been undertaken from the official viewpoint, and that they were merely redressing the balance. The Home Office, perhaps predictably, refused to support a further research project on the grounds that the approach was not 'scientific' — the sample was too small, there was no control group, and there was no intention of using standard personality inventories, such as introversion-extroversion scales or intelligence tests. Yet Cohen and Taylor's very deadpan reportage in the Appendix of another, officially-approved research project into 'psychological changes associated with long-term imprisonment' shows only too clearly the limitations of orthodox methods of investigation.[36]

'E' Wing closed in June 1971, the prisoners being dispersed to other prisons. Cohen and Taylor's battle with the Home Office continued for seven years, and the story of this stuggle is known only from their account in *New Society*.[37] By that time, they had become professors of sociology in their respective universities (Essex and York), and their standing was high among their professional colleagues. They say that they write

> not out of any sense of personal pique, or a desire to attack particular individuals, but to draw attention to the highly selective notion of 'proper' research held by the Home Office; to the techniques — effective, if not self-conscious — by which 'improper' research proposals may be frustrated; and to the ways in which . . . concerns about secrecy and censorship are used to preserve the impenetrability of the penal system.

Technique no. 1 was 'This is not proper research.' Technique no. 2 was 'Things are changing anyway.' Separate security wings, condemned by Mountbatten and Radzinowicz, were being phased out. Yet in 1975, Cohen and Taylor were able to point out that at least half of their original Durham sample were still being 'shunted around from one wing to another' (a phrase to which the Home Office had apparently taken exception) in conditions very similar to those they had described; that the introduction of the new control units for intransigent prisoners introduced 'a punitive and isolated regime undreamed of even at the peak of the security tightening-up in the middle sixties'; and that 'E' Wing at Durham was to be reopened to hold 'high-risk' women prisoners.

Psychological Survival was, in the authors' view, 'inevitably weakened by the fact that it only covered four years of the prisoners' lives. The theoretical edifice was too heavy for the empirical material. There were many questions left in the air.' The situations they wished to study had continued to exist, and the Home Office had continued to refuse them access to prisoners. At one point, in 1973, they obtained agreement in principle to a research proposal, re-drafted to meet Home Office objections, and a Social Science Research Council grant to cover a five-year investigation; but when it came to 'what were typically referred to as the "nuts and bolts" of the project' they suffered 'restricted access, intolerable delays [and] censorship of basic material'. Eventually, following a meeting with SSRC representatives and the Prison Department, the grant was returned and the project abandoned.

Subsequent correspondence in *New Society* included some critical letters from other social scientists, most of whom took the view that it was hardly reasonable to expect the Home Office to support unorthodox research methods allied to anti-official views. 'It was rather like an anti-blood sports group expecting assistance from fox-hunting enthusiasts,' wrote one correspondent.[38]

Though the dust has long since settled on this controversy, the authors have never subsequently been allowed access to long-term prisoners, and it may be that the interests of other research workers have been somewhat prejudiced by the media publicity accorded to the Cohen and Taylor project. The awkward fact remains that officially approved methods of prison research are limited in their capacity to get at the truth of the experience of imprisonment, and that some of the issues raised by the authors of *Psychological Survival* need further investigation. In particular, they give insights into problems touched on in the Radzinowicz Report: 'the need to preserve self-respect, to give the prisoner some choice and autonomy, to allow him variety and some movement, to give him privacy.'[39]

Cohen and Taylor tell us that 'the ideology of liberal penal management is . . . virtually bankrupt'. They are not concerned to suggest either a new ideology or a better system of management because they are basically abolitionists. In a conference organised by the Howard League for Penal Reform in 1977 at Canterbury, Laurie Taylor was to argue: 'we have become seduced into a way of regarding prison which forever compounds the ethical-expedient distinction. The only way to get out of the trap is to make a few changes in organisation.'[40] These included calling a halt to all new prison building 'so that we could allow the present structures to rot away'; cutting prison staff; and announcing 'the resignation of at least twenty criminologists and the closures of two research institutes'.

Such proposals may be born out of exasperation. They are hardly likely to help with the task of finding ways of preventing personality deterioration in the abrasive and destructive conditions of long-term imprisonment. The examination of prisoners' perceptions, of the possibilities of stimulus, of the breakdown of the normal capacity to handle time and to have some control over privacy and association, may be of vital importance if prisoners are not to be turned into human vegetables; but the operationalising of such findings will depend on the co-operation of prison officers and Governor grades. It cannot be carried out in the full glare of publicity, or from an abolitionist platform.

Despite selective perceptions and somewhat biased conclusions, *Psychological Survival* stands as the most relevant testimony to date to the central dilemma of long-term incarceration: society has a right to contain the violent and persistent offender, to prevent him from doing further harm; but if it is to retain any legitimate moral sanction, it must find ways of doing so without destroying him from within.

11 HANEY, BANKS AND ZIMBARDO: THE EXPERIMENTALISTS

Three academic psychologists from Stanford University, California, carried out an elaborately-designed study on 'Interpersonal Dynamics in a Simulated Prison',[1] reported in 1973. While the study is usually quoted in the field of social psychology, with reference to the formation of the authoritarian personality, it has also been quoted as evidence of the effect of institutional life on individuals. Larry Gostin, in *A Human Condition*, cites it in some detail, and comes to the conclusion that

> something in the character of a secure institution itself
> impedes the process of rehabilitation. The typical inmate
> becomes passive, dependent, depressed, helpless and self-
> deprecatory . . . the Haney study . . . clearly illustrates that
> it is the secure institution itself, and not the professional
> staff, which causes many of the problems.[2]

Later, Gostin cites the study again as evidence that 'Where staff and patients both live under closed, high-security conditions, tensions are bound to develop.'[3]

Since this is the main reference to institutional conditions, in what is primarily a treatise on the need for reform in mental health law, and the argument about the unsuitability of institutions largely depends upon it, it is worth looking at the Haney, Banks and Zimbardo study in the context of its relevance to institutional life.

A 'simulated prison'

The study was an empirical one, carried out under laboratory conditions. The 'prison' was constructed in a section of a basement corridor, thirty-five feet long, to provide three small cells, six feet by nine, in each of which three men were detained. A newspaper advertisement secured 75 volunteers, all college students, who were given intensive medical, psychological and social tests to enable the investigators to select 'the most stable . . . most mature, and least involved in anti-social behaviour'. Twenty-four students were selected by these rigorous criteria, and then randomly allocated to the roles of guard and prisoner. The experiment actually took place with ten prisoners[4] and eleven guards: two stand-by prisoners were not called upon, and one stand-by guard decided not to participate. The participants were all strangers to one another: there were no existing relationships to complicate the observations.

All the participants were told that they were to take part in a psychological study of prison life, and were paid fifteen dollars a day for their part in the experiment, which was to last two weeks. The conditions of the experiment were that the prisoners would remain in their cells for twenty-four hours a day, and the guards would work a three-man, eight-hour shift, being allowed to return to their normal lives when off duty. The contract guaranteed the prisoners minimally adequate food, shelter, clothing and medical care. They were told that they could expect to be under surveillance, that they would have little or no privacy, and that some of their basic civil rights would be suspended, short of physical abuse. The guards were instructed that they must not use physical punishment or physical aggression against the prisoners.

The experiment was closely monitored by the investigators by means of a one-way screen, video-taping and audio-recording. A variety of rating scales were used, including mood adjective checklists, personality tests and sociometric measures. There were daily reports from the guards, the experimenters kept detailed diaries, and all the subjects completed questionnaires after the experiment. Few experiments can have been carried out with such care for the scientific accuracy of the findings.

The findings were that the prison guards behaved like prison guards, and the prisoners behaved like prisoners. 'Despite the fact that guards and prisoners were . . . free to engage in any form of interaction, the characteristic nature of their encounters tended to be negative, hostile, affrontive and dehumanising.' The prisoners were largely passive, while the guards were 'active and initiating'. Exchanges between the two groups were 'strikingly impersonal', but 'verbal affronts were used as one of the most frequent forms of interpersonal contact'.

The evidence of the impact of this situation was dramatic: five prisoners had to be released early, four because they suffered from 'extreme emotional depression, crying, rage and acute anxiety' and one because he developed a psycho-somatic rash. Of the others, only two said that they would not be willing to forfeit the money they had earned in order to secure their release. The experiment was terminated early, after six days, because of their reactions, and 'all the remaining prisoners were delighted by their unexpected good fortune'. The guards, on the other hand, did not want the experiment to end: 'it appeared to us that they had become sufficiently involved in their roles so that they now enjoyed the extreme control and power which they exercised, and were reluctant to give it up'. One guard did report being personally upset at the suffering of the prisoners, and offered to change places with one of them. Some guards were 'tough but fair', but others 'went far beyond their roles to engage in creative cruelty and harassment', and some remained on duty for extra hours without extra pay.

Conclusions from the experiment

Haney, Banks and Zimbardo report the variety of reactions scrupulously, and come to the conclusion that 'the extremely pathological reactions which emerged in both groups of subjects testify to the power of the social forces operating'. Normal college students, randomly allocated to roles, had in a very short space of time, replicated the reactions of prison guards and prisoners with remarkable accuracy.

Most dramatic and distressing to us was the observation of the ease with which sadistic behaviour could be elicited in individuals who were not 'sadistic types' and the frequency with which acute emotional breakdowns could occur in men selected precisely for their emotional stability.

Comments made by both groups were revealing. A guard said afterwards (presumably in a de-briefing session) 'Looking back, I am impressed by how little I felt for them', and another said 'Acting authoritatively can be fun. Power can be a great pleasure.' One was disgusted by the sight and sound of the prisoners 'in their rags, and smelling the strong odour of their bodies'. Prisoners afterwards spoke of the fear of losing their identity, and of feelings of degradation. For the few days of their confinement, the 'Stanford County Prison' was apparently intensely real to them. The harassment of prisoners by guards escalated over time, and 90 per cent of all conversations between prisoners related to prison topics — they had effectively forgotten their outside roles. Prisoners perceived guards as physically bigger than they were, though in fact there was no difference in the mean height of the two groups.

The conclusion is that 'the abnormality resided in the psychological situation, and not in those who passed through it'. In the real world, 'prisoners and guards are locked into a dynamic, symbiotic relationship which is destructive to their human nature'.

Haney, Banks and Zimbardo are aware that simulated research of this kind is always open to the objection that the situation is artifical, and that subjects' reactions are not fully 'real'. Certainly when the experiment was over, the guards explained away their behaviour by saying that they were 'just playing the role', but the authors indicate that this does not entirely explain their behaviour — and may not condone it. The prisoners' reactions seem real enough. After four days, one of the investigators asked the remaining five if they would forfeit their pay for freedom, and three agreed; but when told that a decision could not be made immediately, they allowed the guards to take them back to their cells — though there was in fact nothing to prevent them from simply walking out. This is very convincing evidence. In addition, there were three external observers to the experiment — a consultant with sixteen years' prison experience, a priest who had been a prison chaplain, and a 'public defender' — all attested to the reality of what they had observed, and its relevance to the prison situation.

The experiment has an obvious parallel in Stanley Milgram's experiments[5] in including subjects to administer painful, and possibly fatal, electric shocks to strangers when ordered to do so. That chilling piece of evidence on human suggestibility and the power of authority to compel obedience is quoted as a further demonstration of the proposition that 'evil deeds are not necessarily the deed of evil men, but may be attributed to the operation of powerful social forces'. The difference is that Milgram's experiment took place in an ordinary social psychology laboratory, without the additional factor of a simulated institutional environment; and in Haney, Banks and Zimbardo's study, it is the environment which is blamed for the reactions. The 'situational attribution' takes precedence over the 'dispositional attribution' — their conclusion is that it was not the nature of the subjects but the prison situation which caused pathological reactions.

The report, despite its comparative brevity, gives statistical results for the Personality Inventory and other tests in some detail. There was no statistical significance in the mean scores of guards and prisoners on the Comfrey Scales, though the Comfrey definition of masculinity — 'people who are not bothered by crawling creatures, the sight of blood, vulgarity, who do not cry easily and are not interested in love stories' might raise a few eyebrows in both sexes. On the F-scale, designed to measure rigid adherence to conventional values and a submissive, uncritical attitude to authority, the prisoners who stayed scored significantly higher than those who left; but since they also scored higher on 'masculinity' empathy and extroversion, we are left uncertain whether their motives in staying on in their mock prison were due to submissiveness, or an ability to stick it out.

But it is not necessary to puzzle over the confusion of the statistical results to find reasons why the study is, on closer examination, less than satisfactory. Haney, Banks and Zimbardo describe their methods at length; and the situation which developed was heavily structured to produce the results they found.

Sources of bias

Though they took care over the random allocation of their subjects, the sample was hardly 'representative'. The subjects were all white apart from one 'oriental', while a large proportion of the American prison population is black. They were all college students; most prisoners have a much lower standard of educational attainment. They were all volunteers for a prison study — which meant that either they had an interest in prisons (and pre-formed ideas, probably culled from films and television, of what prison life was like) or they needed the money. There appear to have been no inquiries on their motives for participating in the study, since the tests were designed only to measure their 'normality'. Whatever this meant, it does not appear to have borne much relation to the norms of real prisoners.

Those subjects who had agreed to become prisoners were prepared to take part in the study, but they were not informed of either the time or the mode of arrival. They were unexpectedly 'arrested' at their homes by a real police officer, who charged each in turn with suspicion of armed robbery or burglary, cautioned him, handcuffed him, searched him while the neighbours watched, and took him to the police station. There each prisoner (still in isolation) was fingerprinted, had an identification file prepared on him, and was placed in a detention cell and blindfolded. 'Subsequently' (we are not told how long after) he was driven to the mock prison. 'Throughout the entire arrest procedure, the police officers involved maintained a formal, serious attitude, avoiding answering any questions of clarification as to the relation of this "arrest" to the mock prison study.' There is no comment on the ethics of the participation of the police in this exercise.

On arrival at the mock prison, each prisoner was stripped, sprayed with a delousing spray (in fact a deodorant) and 'made to stand naked for a while in the cell yard'. Eventually, he was given his uniform, had an identity picture taken (a 'mug shot'), and was taken to his cell, where he encountered other prisoners for the first time, but was ordered to remain silent.

The 'uniform' in which they were photographed, and which they had to wear throughout their stay, was specially designed by the psychologists to emphasise the degradation of their position. It consisted of a 'loosely fitting muslin smock' with a prison number on the front and back, worn without trousers or underclothes; a chain and lock round one ankle; rubber sandals; and a cap made out of a nylon stocking. The smock-dress, the authors explain, 'made the prisoners feel awkward in their movements, since these dresses were worn without undergarments, the uniforms forced them to assume unfamiliar postures, more like those of a woman than a man — another part of the emasculating process of becoming a prisoner'. This enabled the guards to insult them as 'sissies' or 'girls'. The chain and lock were 'a constant reminder of the oppressiveness of the environment' — when a prisoner was asleep, the chain would hit his free ankle as he turned. The stocking cap was designed to eliminate personality by concealing hair colour, length and style.

Real prisoners, even in the more punitive penitentiaries of the American south, do not have this grotesque appearance. Though the prison may (and usually will) insist on a short haircut, which the stocking cap was allegedly designed to replicate, the usual dress is the uniform of the American college student — sweat-shirt and jeans.

The guards, by contrast, were equipped with all the symbols of authority: khaki shirts and trousers, to give them a military appearance; night sticks, whistles and reflecting sunglasses 'which made eye contact impossible'. They must have looked like the Tontons Macoute.

Though the prisoners had 'movie rights' (not yet included in the Human Rights Conventions) this must have meant the provision of a television screen in or within sight of their cells, since they were locked up in the cells for twenty-four hours a day, apart from exercise periods. Two factors which must have greatly affected their conditions during their stay are only briefly mentioned: they were under constant and detailed supervision in a situation where they were being paid for acting 'like prisoners'; and they were allowed only three 'supervised toilet visits' a day. There was a single toilet, outside in the corridor, for all ten prisoners; and the detailed listing of provision in the cells (only a bed, mattress and pillow, no personal belongings) does not include that basic need of the prisoner, the chamber pot. There may therefore have been very good reasons why the guards found the prisoners malodorous. If there was 'creative cruelty and harassment', the experimenters may have played their part in providing the circumstances for it.

In a real prison, as Haney, Banks and Zimbardo point out, there would have been other causes for fear and distress: the threat of violence from guards and other prisoners, the threat of homosexual attack; but the prisoners' extreme responses may owe more to the inventiveness of psychologists than to any situation to be found in real prison life.

The denial of any human interaction was particularly artifical. Prisoners do interact with prison staff (and not always in the form of bullying commands and cringeing submission) and also with other prisoners. The structuring of the experiment was designed to make both forms of interaction impossible.

Confusion, degradation and loss of identity on the part of the prisoners and bullying authoritarian behaviour by the guards were therefore built into the study by the research team. These factors may also arise from institutional situations, but there is ample evidence that Haney, Banks and Zimbardo engineered the creation and reinforcement of stereotypes.

Despite the careful objectivity of their tests, the subjective judgments involved in the construction of the study are pronounced. This is regrettable, because there are undesirable features in institutional life, and it is important to clarify them; but this kind of experiment is not the way to do it.

12 KING AND ELLIOTT: THE ANALYSTS OF FAILURE

H.M. Prison Albany, on the Isle of Wight, was opened in 1967 as a new and hopeful departure in the prison system. At the much-publicised opening ceremony, it was hailed as a 'breakthrough', 'a new concept in prison administration' which would provide 'dynamic and personal training' for medium-security recidivists.[1] In *Albany: birth of a prison — end of an era*, Roy King and Kenneth Elliott tell the story of how this innovation, described by its first governor as 'about as safe as a caravan in a meadow' turned within five years into 'an electronic coffin'; how experiments were frustrated, order disintegrated, and both prisoners and prison officers became alienated.

The story is sufficiently dramatic. It is told soberly and without histrionics. Those who believe that institutional systems are inherently pathological may read it as a sort of Greek tragedy — story of failure in which liberal hopes reap their inevitable harvest of repression. Those who believe that, pathological or not, prisons are likely to continue will read it differently. If the prison system cannot be abolished entirely, because there are some prisoners who must be contained at least for a time for the safety of the rest of society, was the Albany experiment on the right lines? And what went wrong?

Like the Morrises, King and Elliott were funded by the Home Office in their research, and had the support of the Prison Department. The new régime planned for Albany required monitoring and evaluation. Neither the Home Office Research Unit nor the Prison Department can have expected that the outcome would be as disastrous as it proved to be. To their credit, they continued to give the research workers access to the prison even at the time when Albany was 'becoming the focus of adverse publicity', and made no attempt to place constraints on publication. The result is an exceptionally useful case-study of penal policy in action. While *Pentonville* shows a static picture of the prison system in operation, *Albany* shows the prison system trying to change, and failing. Whether that failure was inevitable (in the sense that no experiment of this kind could possible have succeeded), purposeful (in the sense that certain groups of interests did not want it to succeed) or accidental (in the sense that it might have succeeded in different circumstances) is the point of the story.

The original plan

H.M. Prison Albany was meant to give meaning to Rule 1 of the Prison Rules: 'The purpose of the training and treatment of convicted prisoners shall be to encourage and assist them to lead a good and useful life.'

This was translated by the first governor as involving the objectives of 'humane custody' and 'behaviour changing from criminal to non-criminal' by means of two programmes — an industrial training programme and a social training programme. The first involved a scheme of production workshops in textiles and tailoring, with a two-shift system, each prisoner working about thirty hours a week. Social training was defined as: —

(a) involving the prisoner with the staff in running the prison
(b) giving the prisoner opportunities to talk with staff both in groups and especially individually
(c) letting the prisoner take as many decisions for himself as possible
(d) using careful reports on the prisoner's response to make reports to parole boards, hostel boards and working out boards.[2]

The two-shift system in the workshops was 'the keystone

which held the twin pillars of Albany's commitment together'. It meant that work experience could be provided for all prisoners without excessive cost, since two men could share one work-bench; and there would be time in the working day for other activities while the prisoners were off-duty.

The governor told his staff that 'the new prison has to progress by trial and error':—

It is important that staff should feel and know that their participation is necessary and wanted. There is no magic formula for running our prison. We must all intelligently work out the best way to do our tasks, and to collaborate with others. It is hard but interesting work. Ideas do not only come from the governor or from Head Office. It is the governor's pleasure to harvest ideas from anywhere, and to consult staff both formally and informally whenever he can.[3]

Staff were 'to consult prisoners, but not be put off by them. Sound ideas put forward by prisoners should be respected, and used if they take us towards our ends'.

This statement of intent involved consensus management — the small 'g' for 'governor' is significant. Prisons were inherently centralised, militaristic, hierarchical. Was it possible for any prison to be run on Popperian lines of trial and error, experience and insight? Such a system had never been tried; and it was not to be tried now. The implementation of the principles of the White Paper, *Penal Practice in a Changing Society*,[4] was made difficult by a number of factors: the staff of this new and experimental prison were not specially selected, but allowed to apply for posts on the vaguest of specifications. The prison was not ready for occupation; and the consensus-minded governor lasted only eighteen months, being promoted to an assistant directorship in the Prison Department five weeks after the research team began work.

The early period had been one of continued teething troubles. The governor was designated only four months before the official opening in April 1967. The advance party arrived only two months before the arrival of the prisoners, and the main body of staff only ten days before. There was thus little time for staff induction and training. There was 'a rather loosely formed committee for the co-ordination of the opening of new establishments', but it confined its infrequent meetings to the consideration of 'the co-ordination of dates for the arrival of staff, stores, and prisoners with the dates of completion of prison buildings and staff quarters, and eventually with the convenience of the minister for the opening ceremony'.[5] The minister arrived, and was photographed, smiling broadly, in a 'typical Albany cell' of somewhat bleak aspect.[6] The publicity was excellent; but behind the official congratulations lay a story of desperate improvisation.

Problems in practice

The governor had arrived to find

> no chairs or desks, no paper or pens, just uncompleted work and mud. . . . There was nothing to wipe or scrape off the mud, no soap or towels, so we went home, to wade through more mud and sort out our furniture, and meet again the next day. We met, our domestic bases a little more secure, and resolved to lick this muddy bloody mess into passable working order.[7]

There were basic design problems: security was inadequate, and even before the prison opened, extra work was commissioned to provide a new security fence and electronic devices to allow prisoners to request access to the toilets. Inexplicably, even in this new prison, the practice of 'slopping out' was retained. Since 'slopping out' remains one of the most degrading and unpalatable aspects of prison life, it is hard to resist the conclusion that punitiveness played a part in this decision.[8] King and Elliott seem to take this for granted, noting that there was 'of course' no sanitation in the cells.

The five 'halls' or association areas were connected with the five dining halls by a single corridor, providing a movement pattern for prisoners which was 'almost unsupervisable'. Quality control on building had been defective: kitchen cupboards and Venetian blinds fell suddenly from position, 'causing grievous bodily harm'. Drains would not empty, ventilators would not close. The site and the gymnasium flooded. A baker's oven exploded, 'mercifully in the middle of the night'.[9]

At this point, it was discovered that there was no accommodation for the Works Department. In these circumstances, the governor's comment that 'We think more planning is required, not less, to open a new prison' has all the hallmarks of a temperate and restrained nature.

Anxieties began to rise. As King and Elliott note, 'staff, no less than prisoners, have a vested interest in "knowing where they stand in a quiet nick" ',[10] and Albany was proving to be anything but a quiet nick. As a medium-security prison, it was designed for Category 'C' prisoners, who presented comparatively low security risks; but, though the majority were classified as Category 'C', they consisted of two groups who presented distinct problems. The majority were young (under thirty), London-based, and had committed property offences with violence. Most of them came on transfer from Wandsworth Prison, the London prison for longer-term men serving a second or subsequent prison sentence, and with a reputation for violence. They were no strangers to prison life — many had graduated through approved schools, detention centres and Borstal training, and had served several prison sentences. To this young recidivist population, serving relatively short sentences, was added a group of older prisoners with longer sentences from Parkhurst, including one life sentence prisoner:—

They arrived on 26th April and quickly decided that they did not like what they saw, nor what was expected of them. The following morning, they demanded to see the governor to make their complaints.. . . They objected to having to live with young prisoners from Wandsworth; and they objected to what they saw as a young and inexperienced staff who had an excessive concern with smartness and who tried to impose unnecessarily petty or restrictive rules. They pointed out that the screws did not have to live there twenty-four hours a day, and that all these regulations might be suitable for the young cons from Wandsworth, but not for seasoned prisoners like themselves who had been used to some comforts and privileges.[11]

Appealing to the governor was the prisoners' right under

Rule 8 of the Prison Rules, but it was a denial of the new system of consensus management. The governor saw the prisoners' representatives, listened to their complaints – and referred the matter back to the hall principal officers for decision. 'This only reinforced the belief of the prisoners that the prison was being run by the screws.' They began to petition the Board of Visitors and the Secretary of State.

Rules were enforced, relaxed and enforced again. Prison staff were uncertain and inconsistent. Gambling and baroning increased among the prisoners, and there were violent assaults. When the new governor took over in July 1968, after an interregnum of six weeks, the system changed in important ways. The Central Management Meeting, originally designed as a forum where staff might share 'therapeutic anxiety', had already undergone some restriction. Now it became a briefing meeting for senior staff (excluding the tutor-organiser, the medical officer and the chaplain, but including the industrial manager). The frequency of meetings was reduced. There was an agenda, and a shorthand writer took formal minutes. A Principal Officers' Meeting, for middle management, was intended as a training forum, but quickly became preoccupied with the details of domestic routine rather than with policy issues. 'The minutes reveal the constant pressure towards greater consistency in the control and management of prisoners.'[12]

As the reconstitution of the central management group suggests, 'social training', never very well formulated or supported, gradually became abandoned. 'Deep meaningful human relationships' and 'officer involvement' degenerated into a formal framework of recording and file inspection, and about the only real innovations were the purchase of 'games such as Monopoly and Scrabble . . . a record-player . . . and . . . communal birdcages and fish tanks'.[13] Industrial training became of greater importance; and the Prison Department decided that industrial training should be organised on profit-making lines. By October 1968, the decision had been taken to move to a single-shift pattern of production, which meant that the work of the psychology, welfare, education and physical education departments were effectively shifted to being a spare-time activity, out of normal working hours, or seen as an interruption to normal work-patterns. A rearguard action by the senior staff to protest about the demise of 'social training' failed; and staff morale suffered badly. The Prison Officers' Association became involved in the dispute, and the scene was set for a continual battle over staff pay and conditions.

Meanwhile, arrangements were going ahead for the introduction of Category 'B' and forty Category 'A' (high security risk) prisoners into Albany. The first intimation of this change, a consequence of the Radzinowicz Committee's recommendations for the dispersal of such prisoners, had arrived during the period of six weeks between the leaving of the first governor and the arrival of the second. Plans went ahead steadily, and the upgrading of security was more extensive than had at first been expected. A separate segregation unit was set aside, and the cells strengthened. More electronic devices were installed. Officers were sent on a dog-handling course, and Alsatian dogs added to the security precautions. A second security fence was constructed. Floodlights and television cameras were added. The gate staff were protected by bullet-proof glass, and a new telephonic communications system was provided. To some of the prisoners, as to the research workers, 'the element of overkill in the mounting security arrangements seemed, at times, little short of paranoia'.[14] Albany was turning, as they watched, into something very close to Lord Mountbatten's plan for Vectis, the ultimate secure establishment.

Category 'B' prisoners arrived during 1969, and the first Category 'A' prisoners arrived in October 1970. The second governor was promoted to headquarters in April 1971, and left behind some notes for his successor in which he predicted 'a definite bid for power' by some prisoners.[15] The third governor did not have long to wait. In June, a letter was smuggled out of Albany alleging that about a fifth of the long-term prisoners were being held in the segregation unit, in solitary confinement: 'A Home Office spokesman played down the allegations, but they had been close enough to the truth — except that by the time the letter was published, the governor had succeeded in transferring the "subversives" back to their own halls.'[16]

In September, there were numerous incidents, and 'two notorious prisoners were removed, struggling, to the segregation unit'. In the resulting disturbances, several staff and one prisoner were seriously injured. The Press began to report stories of gang warfare and Mafia-type activities in Albany.

In May 1972, PROP (Preservation of the Rights of Prisoners) held a conference which indicated that its activities were extending to a number of prisons. There were prisoners' strikes in Albany — one attracted 100 per cent support, but 'passed off peacefully and with good humour'; but confront-ation by prisoners led to confrontation by staff. When the governor returned from his summer holiday, it was to find that the Prison Officers' Association threatened a work to rule unless action was taken to deal with subversive prisoners.

Some escape equipment was found, and a two-day security search took place. Prisoners rioted, and the headline in the *Daily Mirror* was 'Siege in the jail of fear'. Albany was no longer a liberal success: it was a notorious and punitive failure.

There were two more riots, causing extensive damage. The perimeter fence was solidified into a wall. A prisoner was burned to death in his cell. A officer was taken hostage at gun-point. Prison staff worked to rule, and their wives picketed the prison, calling on the governor to take action against the subversives; and in November 1973, shortly before he was due for transfer, the third governor died. The story of the 'electronic coffin' was complete.

King and Elliott left Albany in 1969 to carry out compara-tive studies in other prisons. Before the deterioration in con-ditions,

> the prison represented nothing so much as a secure labour camp, in which the main activity appeared to be digging trenches. Apart from a small number of prisoners and a substantial minority of basic grade officers, the overwhelm-ing verdict of the participants was that, if you had to do or spend your time in prison, Albany was the best, or better than most places to do it in.[17]

Not long after, the *Good Jail Guide* gave Albany four stars — the highest rating.

When the authors went back in 1971, it was to find 'a pro-gressively deteriorating situation'. One of the main problems was the use of Rule 43, by which the governor was able to remove any prisoner from association (not only the Category 'A' prisoners) and place him in the segregation unit in the interests of good order and discipline, or for the prisoner's protection. The use of Rule 43 requires the approval of a member of the Board of Visitors or of the Secretary of State if it is more than 24 hours' duration, but in practice, this is almost automatic. It does not require more than the prisoner be charged with a specific offence, and it can be used for the ringleaders — those who 'make the bullets for others to fire'. The increasing use of Rule 43 and the segregation unit was indication of how far conditions had deteriorated. There were constant outbreaks of violence among prisoners, and stories (uncorroborated) of violence by prison staff.

What went wrong?

Almost everything went wrong, both inside and outside the prison. There was the failure in physical planning — the defects in the design of the building, the poor timing which resulted in the staff taking over and the prisoners arriving before the prison was ready for occupation, the poor quality control which resulted in unsuitable or broken fixtures. Some of this is inexplicable — whatever the difficulties of the Prison Department, and the problems in defining the goals of the penal system, it should at least have known how to have a prison constructed.

There was the failure in administrative planning: the first governor, full of enthusiasm for a new and therapeutic system, had very little in the way of support from the Prison Service. For a time, two members of the Prison Staff Training College acted as consultants, but the governor never had the professional advice and guidance which an experiment of these dimensions rated.

There was the failure in management: above all, the fact that Albany, basically a hierarchical system like any other prison, had four governors in just over five years. King and Elliott note: —

Prison Department appears to take the view that no governor

is indispensable, and that there is no place in a prison system for programmes that cannot be replicated by persons other than their originators. Such a view would be quite acceptable if the problems concerning organisation and management in prisons had been solved. But they have not. It would be a tolerable view in institutions where even an unsatisfactory structure had been passed from one generation to another over the years. But in Albany, where the management structure had been made problematic from the outset, such a view seems to us untenable.[18]

Security was a problem from the beginning. It is probable that when David Gould described Albany as 'about as safe as a caravan in a meadow' he was not commending a relaxed and unthreatening setting, but pointing to the impossibility of running a prison properly in those conditions. Some of the problems were built in, a matter of architectural design, and the electronics experts were called in straight away. The laudable intention of making it possible for the prisoners to go out of their cells to the toilets somehow got translated into increased means of surveillance, and these escalated as the fences rose and the perimeter security assumed symbolic and massive proportions.

When the transfer of Category 'B' and Category 'A' prisoners was approved, Albany was already very far from its original ideals. The development of the segregation unit was the *coup de grâce*. Again, the original purpose was comparatively limited — the provision of some forty cells for high-risk prisoners. In practice, the unit became a means of disciplining any prisoner, and its use during the period of the riots in 1971 and 1972 seems to have been a clear exercise in 'total power'.

King and Elliott end by casting doubt on the usefulness of Rule 1 of the Prison Rules. Nothing which was done in Albany encouraged them to think that 'training and treatment' had been a success, or that Albany was encouraging and assisting prisoners to lead 'a good and useful life'.

'Social training' never stood a real chance of success. When the research team first entered the prison in May 1968, there was an industrial manager with twelve civilian instructors plus seven officer instructors. The single tutor-organiser had only five part-time teachers, while there were three psychologists and two welfare officers.[19] The structure was heavily weighted against the development of 'social training' from the outset.

It is not surprising that the two-shift system, which was to accord equal weight to the two aims of the prison régime, was never operated. The Central Management Team was re-organised to reduce the representation of the 'training' staff (who made constant representations about the difficulties of their position), and 'social training' died quietly even before the arrival of the Category 'A' prisoners. The second governor, Brian Howden, had views very different from those of his predecessor. 'Therapeutic anxiety' and 'Delphic ambiguity' were out. Firmness and certainty were in.

> In so far as he was concerned with such matters it is prob-
> able that Brian Howden believed that behaviour changing
> was as likely to be brought about through the carrot and
> the stick as by talk and introspection. If confidence in
> such a system was to be upheld, it would be necessary for
> everyone to know what the carrots and sticks were, and
> who wielded them under what circumstances.. . . Howden
> praised the achievements of his predecessor, and insisted
> that he would do his utmost to keep the prison on the
> course that Gould had charted. Those achievements would
> be best consolidated, he argued, by bringing them within a
> more consistent framework of routine administration. And
> in the name of consolidation and consistency, Albany
> moved into a very different phase of development.[20]

What appears to be a failure in a therapeutic experiment was therefore deliberately brought about within eighteen months of its opening. The prison, though in appearance the most total of total institutions, is not an autonomously-operating organisation. Individual prisons are subject to policy decisions and constraints which arise in the prison system as a whole, and a series of changes in Prison Depart-ment policy lay behind the development of the 'electronic coffin'.

In a somewhat uncharacteristically florid passage, King and Elliott describe the loss of faith in 'social training': 'The delicate, undernourished twins of social and industrial training had been conceived in the bed of optimism left by the Prison Commission, and they were allowed to be born without regard to the rigours of bringing them up in the same household.'[21]

Changes in penal policy

The Prison Commission, merged into the Home Office to become the Prison Department in 1963, had been concerned to leave a legacy of optimism and a change of further innovation. The Prison Department, more bureaucratic and more directly susceptible to political influences, was not to prove the ideal guardian of the 'delicate, undernourished twins'. Industrial training was to flourish, while social training was quietly killed off.

The contrast can be seen in two key documents: the Prison Commission's *Penal Practice in a Changing Society* (1959) and the Prison Department's *People in Prison* (1969). In *Penal Practice in a Changing Society*, Rule 1 of the Prison Rules is specifically quoted, and it is stated that 'much progress has been achieved' in training and treatment:—

Methods of training have been progressively extended and improved, notably in the application of psychiatry and psychology . . .

At Wormwood Scrubs, the method of group therapy is fully employed, including the technique of psychodrama . . .

A psychiatrically experienced doctor can do much to help disturbed prisoners not only to adjust themselves to prison life, but also to change their general attitudes so that they make a better adjustment to society after their release.[22]

Though the Prison Commission noted that it was difficult to quantify what was being achieved, they had no doubt that the achievements were real, and that this was the humane and civilised way forward in penal policy for the future.

There was a specific disavowal of an isolated industrial training policy: 'Offenders do not come to prison because they have failed as workmen . . . a prison is not therefore, and should not be, first and foremost a factory.'

King and Elliott do not take the view, made famous by Sir Alexander Paterson, that 'it is impossible to train men for freedom in a condition of capitivity'. As they point out, 'it is in the nature of training that it takes place in one setting while preparing the recipient for another of which he has yet to gain experience' — a factor which holds good from the kindergarten to the military academy. They conclude:—

> There is no reason to suppose that one could not train a
> man for freedom in conditions of captivity if one *really*
> wanted to.. . . But the truth is that prisons have never
> *really* been about training at all. They have always *really*
> been about, and continue to be about, captivity: that is,
> safe custody. And there is nothing on earth to be gained
> from pretending otherwise . . . what endures and is common
> to them all is their custodial function for the duration of
> the sentence of the court; and therein lies the reason for
> their existence.[23]

By the time *People in Prison* was published, the policy changes were marked. There was a commendation of the regime at the new Coldingley Prison, a training prison geared to industry, with light engineering workshops and a commercial laundry. Coldingley was expected to have a turnover of £400,000 a year, and it was noted 'This project is designed to be a commercial success.'[24] A rather thin paragraph on social training was mainly concerned with encouraging prisoners to help other people by such activities as making toys for handicapped children, and two paragraphs on social work in prisons (by that time being carried out by probation officers) noted that research on its efficiency or otherwise was being carried out by the Home Office Research Unit.

J. E. Hall Williams, in *Changing Prisons*, comments that the ideas of treatment and training derived from the liberal ideas of the Prison Commission, notably from Sir Alexander Paterson and Sir Lionel Fox. In the 1950s and 1960s much effort was expended on the development of group counselling, which 'achieved quite a wide-spread degree of acceptance at one time. But counselling was one of the first casualties of the new emphasis on security which followed the Mountbatten Report, and it had practically disappeared by 1973.'[25]

Similarly, the group approach was used, following American experiments (particularly in California) to give prisoners some degree of participation in decisions about their daily lives; but such experiments were short-lived on both sides of the Atlantic. By the early 1970s, participation was confined to membership of industrial committees or recreational committees, or prisoners were 'reduced to the status of suppliants making requests'.[26]

This is a sobering conclusion, emphasising 'the essential vacuity of the concept of social training'. The fact that the prison system pays lip-service to this idea may be harmful, encouraging judges and magistrates to commit offenders to prison in the hope that they will be provided with treatment and training. If this is appropriate, and can be provided, then it should be provided outside prison: it will not succeed inside the prison system, and there is no justification for the designation of half our adult prisons for men as 'training prisons'.

The claim that prisons do provide treatment and training leads to an 'awesome burden' on staff which they cannot possibly fulfil — 'an endless charade of data collection, categorisation and the development of "treatment plans" ' which merely make staff feel guilty, inadequate or contemptuous of the system, and give prisoners scope for endless complaint.

King and Elliott do not wish to see the kinds of activities which are subsumed under 'training' abolished entirely: there is no reason why prisoners should not take educational classes, learn a trade, join Alcoholics Anonymous or receive psychotherapy. What is wrong is that the Prison Service should make exaggerated claims to change behaviour which it cannot possibly fulfil, and which it is evidently unwilling to attempt to fulfil.

> We view with some alarm the possibility, however remote, that prison industry, based on a captive labour force paid at preposterously low rates might become such an important investment that the prospect of closing down prisons in favour of alternative methods of dealing with offenders could become problematic on economic grounds.[27]

Prisoners should have a right to work if they wish. This idea is not elaborated, and it would have been interesting to have it operationalised. If the main aim is custody, on what grounds does a prisoner have a 'right to work'? And how is this to be organised in the prison setting — are men to be allowed to volunteer? Under what circumstances? For how much work, or what sort, at what rates of pay?

The end of an era

The cost of building Albany, at 1967 prices, was £1.2 millions. The cost of installing security arrangements to 1976 was a further £2 millions. It is unlikely that another prison will be set up on the lines of the original Albany scheme, and the reader is left with the impression that the Prison Department has got what it wanted — which was not at all what the old Prison Commission intended. All the major decisions were made outside Albany — the architectural design, the failure to plan ahead, the transfer of the governors, the decision to introduce high-risk prisoners, the organisation of RAP and PROP; and if Albany now looks like a total institution, despite the energies, the enthusiasm and the dedication of many staff in the early days, it is because that is what society (in the form of judges, magistrates, higher civil servants, politicians and the popular Press) wants it to be; and what the prisoners made it.

The study raises important issues in prison policy. The policy issues are thoroughly discussed, and King and Elliott come out in their conclusions with some proposals on the future of the Radzinowicz dispersal policy. They make the very basic point that the classification of prisoners as 'high-risk' or 'low-risk' derives from the Mountbatten Report, and that Mountbatten was concerned with the prisoners' potential for escape, not with their potential for causing disruption within the prison. 'Symptoms of unrest' were regarded as often being a preliminary to escape.[28] The Radzinowicz Report similarly accepted that Category 'A' prisoners would be primarily escape risks, though they widened the definition specifically to include prisoners who, if they escaped, would be a danger to the public and/or 'lead to a national scandal and gravely damage the repute of the prison service'.[29] Mount-batten was concerned with the fact of escape. Radzinowicz was concerned with the consequences of escape; but neither was concerned with the problem of keeping order within the prison. King and Elliott therefore propose that a more useful form of classification would be in terms of the prisoner's 'sub-versive enforcement potential' — how likely he was to take subversive action, and how likely he would be to intimidate or manipulate other prisoners. These two assessments would be different, but a balance might be struck between them.

King and Elliott are aware that their proposals are not likely to command the support of the radical lobby:

> Before we are taken to task by radical reformers, or by our professional colleagues, for prostituting the name of soci-ology in the interests of maintaining a docile and subser-vient prison population, we should say at once that we think our proposals would command the support of the great majority of prisoners we spoke to in Albany.[30]

As Cohen and Taylor discovered, prisoners were not always radical in their views of what should happen in the prison system, and how it should be organised. If the overwhelming desire is for 'a quiet nick' in which the prisoner can serve his time without fuss or argument or intimidation, then this proposal, which would remove the greatest trouble-makers, has something to commend it.

There is no suggestion that prisoners with a high 'subversive enforcement potential' should be kept under conditions more punitive than those of other prisoners: control units, and the increasing use of Rule 43 for the purposes of segregation, are explicitly discounted; but King and Elliott are working their way towards the view that Radzinowicz was wrong, and Mountbatten was right: there are a few prisoners who cause trouble, and 'a relaxed régime within a secure perimeter' might meet their needs. There would need to be a high staffing ratio, and some very experienced officers, to deal with them. The policy of dispersal has recruited additional prisoners to the ranks of the subversive, and resulted in the application to large numbers of prisoners of the maximum security con-ditions which Mountbatten proposed only for the few:

When we returned to Albany in 1971, the paraphernalia of security were ever and obviously present: electronic locks operating on virtually all doors with a system of double gates at strategic points, a perimeter bounded by two high security fences topped with barbed wire and fringed with geophonic alarms, high-mast floodlights, television cameras, dog patrols and UHF radio communications. Only the underground corridors and anti-vehicle concrete blocks were missing.[31]

In the kind of system which King and Elliott envisage, trouble-makers would be separated out; and if there were still prison disturbances, these would be dealt with on the quarantine principle — by breaking up small groups, and sending them to different prisons for a time. For most prisoners, prison would be 'humane, but unambiguously custodial'. They would have opportunities to work, to take recreation, to attend courses and programmes if they wished; but no great claims would be made to change their behaviour. Under such a system, perhaps fewer people would be sent to prison, as judges and magistrates lost the belief that treatment or training would result from a sentence.

The prospect, as they say, is 'not an inspiring one to behold'. King and Elliott, respectively Director of the Prison Régimes Project set up by the Home Office and an ex-Chief Inspector of Police who graduated in law and criminology are very far removed from the wilder shores of sociological criticism. Perhaps this makes their disillusionment with the shattered hopes of Albany the more telling.

However, other interpretations of what happened at Albany may be developed from their carefully recorded data. We can ask whether the conditions were such that a psychodynamic regime of the type proposed by David Gould ever had any chance of success; alternatively, we can ask whether the Prison Department at that time had any serious interest in the régimes of individual prisons.

Was a psychodynamic approach possible?

It is unlikely that the full operation of the therapeutic

community system, which was then showing signs of spreading from the mental hospital service to the prison service, could ever have been fully implemented in Albany, given the circumstances. The system, as described by Dr Maxwell Jones, its chief proponent, involves such principles as shared decision-making, permissiveness, free communication, group consensus and the 'flattening of the authority pyramid' which are alien to the prison system. Decision-making cannot be shared in any important respect; the system cannot be permissive; group consensus cannot be achieved, because the interests of prisoners and prison staff are essentially opposed – one group wants to get out of prison, while the other group is there to keep it in; the authority pyramid cannot be flattened; and while free communication (from prisoners to prison staff, not in the other direction) would be advantageous to staff, prisoners are less enthusiastic. Even Maxwell Jones, who worked with the Correctional Service in California during the brief period of enthusiasm for the movement, foresaw difficulties, writing that it was doubtful whether a fully psychotherapeutic régime could be applied in a prison 'unless some of the antitherapeutic factors which are typical of the social organisation of most prisons could at the same time be modified'.[32]

A comparison of the conditions which Maxwell Jones lays down as necessary for such an experiment with the conditions which King and Elliott report at Albany indicates the gap between the psychodynamic view and Prison Department practice.

Conditions necessary for a therapeutic community in the prison setting (Maxwell Jones)[33]	*Actual conditions at Albany* (King and Elliott)
1. a pilot project	no pilot project – prison went straight into full use
2. maximum number of participants 80–100	313 in May 1968 : 480 in 1969
3. a core staff with a particular interest	staff not selected – applied for transfer on vague specification. Senior staff in some cases arrived months later

4. special staff training — six months' preparation	officers arrived ten days before opening
5. support from psychiatrist — coping with staff difficulties	left to governor (no training or support
6. prisoners selected by careful assessment	prisoners sent in groups on general (and conflicting) criteria
7. first offenders.	recidivists

If the Prison Department had been trying to show that the new methods would not work, they could hardly have structured the situation more negatively. Albany was also simply overtaken by events: the switch to industrial training, the impact of the Mountbatten and Radzinowicz Reports, and the prison riots. Whether David Gould's work could have survived in more favourable circumstances must be a matter for conjecture; but the social training programme at Albany was virtually doomed before it began.

The reality of the prison service

Those familiar with the prison system may find an explanation on rather different lines. Prison staff are regarded by the Prison Department as interchangeable employees who can be moved around the system at relatively short notice. Some grades of staff, such as the governors, are moved on average every two or three years. The basic grade custodial staff have greater stability and are usually the culture-carriers. Further, few prison staff have any specialist training. Often the only specialists are the trade officers, who are skilled craftsmen. The governor grades are essentially managers rather than therapists, and their expertise is seen as managerial in character.

Prison governors have traditionally had a high degree of autonomy when organising their prisons. Governors who wish to innovate have been able to do so, provided they could persuade their staff to follow. This autonomy has also meant that a newly appointed governor has not been under any obligation to follow policies laid down by his predecessors.

Indeed, it is highly questionable whether much thought would be given by Prison Department staff to the question of finding a successor who would be sympathetic to any established régime design.

This situation is changing. The idea of the 'accountable régime' developed as part of Home Office policy in the early 1980s. This means that a plan for the régime of each prison has to be agreed by the governor and the Regional Director. Any subsequent departure from the plan has to be negotiated and agreed by both parties.

Many of the problems which beset Albany in its early days have their roots in the wider crisis which shook the prison system in the late 1960s and 1970s. There was a radical change of direction in policy to greater physical security, and Albany was simply changed to serve a new purpose. It is highly probable that no thought was given to the destruction of an innovation in prison organisation: a more important problem had arisen and the new problem took precedence. The Prison Department's view of any prison régime is essentially pragmatic.

CONCLUSION: REFORMULATING THE PROBLEMS

A fundamental question raised by our study is whether the material we have presented has any unity of approach other than the unity we have imposed upon it. It is certainly a heterogeneous collection. Are we right in thinking that it is possible to study 'institutions' as a generic category, or are the similarities merely superficial? Though the same message about the evils of institutions apparently comes from many quarters, are the differences in the scope of the studies and the writers' intentions so great that the category fragments on examination? How can we tackle the problem of similarities and differences?

Foucault gave us the answer. Alan Sheridan records that he faced a similar problem when writing *The Archaeology of Knowledge*:

> Reviewing his previous work . . . Foucault concludes that the apparent unity on which such large groups of statements . . . were based was in fact illusory. What he found was rather 'series full of gaps, intertwined with one another, interplays of differences, distances, substitutions, transformations'. The types of statements found were much too heterogeneous to be linked together in a single figure . . . So he was led to describe these discontinuities, these dispersions, themselves, and to see whether, nevertheless, one cannot find certain regularities.[1]

We shall adopt Foucault's methodology in describing the 'discontinuities' and 'dispersions' in the literature about institutions in search of 'regularities'.

Different contexts

Ideas cross seas and frontiers, and are in some sense international: yet it was surprising to find how often the ideas we examined bore the marks of their national origin. Foucault's own predilection for French dates and western European events has already been noted: his focus spans the area from Paris to the Rhine Valley. He has read the English Gothic novels of the eighteenth century, Samuel Tuke on the York Retreat, Bentham's *Panopticon*, and much more; but he still thinks like a Frenchman, and a Parisian at that. When he writes of liberty, it is the 'liberté' of 1789, not the very different cluster of ideas which comes from the writing of John Stuart Mill and Dicey, still less from the lady with a torch in New York harbour. When he writes 'We need to cut off the King's head', the king is a Capet. Behind his writing lies a distinctive weight of political experience, and an intellectual experience rooted in European philosophy.

Goffman, Szasz, Rothman and Kittrie write as Americans — with, so to speak, less background and more foreground. They write from a context which produced in the 1960s such major sociological movements as ethnomethodology, phenomenology and deviancy theory. Goffman writes about mental hospitals of a size and a degree of depersonalisation unknown in western Europe. Before the 'deinstitutionalization' policy took effect, some US mental hospitals had as many as 15,000 patients. Rothman sets himself specifically American questions, treating the British heritage of the United States as merely a matter of colonialism, and ignoring the many continuities from British origins in the laws and practices he studies. Szasz and Kittrie write within the context of the American judicial system, with its ultimate appeal to the US Constitution, and with a typically American distrust of federal government intervention in the affairs of the states.

The British writers come from an island with its own traditions of social reform and social investigation. They believe in the importance of revealing abuses, and in the ability of quite small pressure-groups to influence social policy by a direct appeal to moral standards. They are highly pragmatic, and acutely aware of the importance of timing and publicity.

Most of the British work has not travelled well. It was too

closely tied to the nuts and bolts of factual data, too much written for its own time, and with specific policy ends in view. The ideas which have crossed seas and frontiers, and which continue to generate fresh questions, have been those of Goffman and Foucault, the theoreticians who wrote about the human condition and the mechanisms of power. Their work has proved relevant to the study of institutional care and custody in many countries. The work of Szasz and Kittrie has encouraged movements for patients' rights and prisoners' rights, but has proved awkward to adapt to different constitutional and legal systems.

Different administrative frameworks

Goffman argued that establishments with different titles and apparently different purposes in fact served the same purpose: that of isolating certain categories of people from the rest of society. He thought that these establishments had common features, but he was wary of defining them, writing only of clusters of attributes which might or might not be found in particular cases. All his first-hand evidence comes from one very atypical mental hospital. Evidence about other institutions comes from secondary sources, chosen from a wide range of reading, but chosen selectively to illustrate the points he wants to make.

Kittrie, with legal precision, explores six sets of circumstances, but deals with them separately. They are drawn together only in the abstract generalisations about 'The Therapeutic State'. Foucault writes about mental hospitals and prisons — but with a fourteen-year gap between the two studies, and treating them within different 'discourses'. Rothman writes historically about a range of institutions, but calls them all 'asylums', switching from one sub-type to another in a fairly ragged analysis. The rest limit their field to a particular sub-type as administratively defined. Szasz and Russell Barton are concerned only with mental hospitals; the Morrises, Cohen and Taylor, Haney, Banks and Zimbardo and King and Elliott and concerned only with prisons; Pauline Morris studies mental handicap hospitals; Townsend and AEGIS focus on different kinds of accommodation for old people.

There is very little which deserves the name of comparative analysis. At the end of it all, we still know very little about how prisons and mental hospitals are alike or unlike, about how either relate to mental handicap hospitals or accommodation for old people. We do not know what differences arise from different forms of administration, or in what respects people categorised as 'offenders', 'mental patients', 'mentally handicapped' or 'old people' may be said to share common problems. Nor is there any serious attempt at a theoretical level to look at differences and similarities within a single administrative category. All prisons are not alike in all respects, nor are all mental hospitals. Only Townsend and Pauline Morris, by taking a national sample, indicate something of the range and variety to be found in their areas of study.

Different intellectual disciplines

Contributions to this literature have come predominantly from social scientists, but they profess and practise very different kinds of social science. Goffman is primarily an ethnographer, with much of the basic strength of his work coming from his training in anthropology. Townsend, the Morrises and King and Elliott work on the borderlands of sociology and social policy. Cohen and Taylor, like Haney, Banks and Zimbardo, are primarily psychologists, but their writings are a world apart: Cohen and Taylor are social psychologists moving into sociology. Haney, Banks and Zimbardo are strictly experimental psychologists.

For the rest, Foucault develops his own discipline – the Archaeology of Knowledge. Szasz is a practising psychotherapist. Russell Barton is a practising 'institutional psychiatrist'. Kittrie is an academic lawyer. Rothman is a social historian; and the AEGIS group are public figures with some unexpected connecting links.

Intellectual training and tradition condition the questions writers ask, and the methods they use. So, of course, do factors of finance, opportunity and access. Goffman, with the freedom of a US National Institute of Mental Health fellowship, could work more or less as he pleased. Foucault wrote the *Histoire de la Folie* in self-imposed exile, working out his alienation from Parisian psychology and philosophy, but *Surveiller et Punir* was written years later from the much greater freedom of a Chair of his own designation in the Collège de France. Townsend, the Morrises and King and Elliott had research funds for particular projects, which implied official approval, but may have meant a more limited scope for their enquiries, since they had to specify a research design in advance. Haney, Banks and Zimbardo were able to set up their own experimental unit, and evidently had the funds to do so. Kittrie set his law students to work looking up cases. Cohen and Taylor began by taking cover as extramural teachers, and ended up, by their own account, working in the teeth of official opposition (which they may have done something to stimulate).

The methodologies employed range from the highly orthodox to the highly unorthodox, from the would-be objective to the frankly subjective, from grand theory to remorseless fact-gathering, from the work of solitary thinkers to that of organised research teams, from those with generous financial support to those with none.

It would be extremely surprising if this body of work possessed a coherent quality, each piece of research building on what had gone before; but there is more traffic in ideas than one might expect. Though the professional disciplines, the methodologies and the opportunities for research are so disparate, the later writers do draw considerably on the work of the earlier ones. Again, Goffman and Foucault are the main sources quoted. Both were unorthodox, subjective, theoretical, and had a considerable degree of freedom of thought and action. Perhaps this is fortuitous. Perhaps such conditions of work are only suitable for research workers of very good intellectual qualities; but the facts of the situation are sufficient to raise doubts about systems of research funding which put a premium on orthodoxy, objectivity, empirical investigation, tightly organised research design and official specification of what should be studied.

Different interests

As we have indicated at various points in the study, not all the writers were interested in institutions as such, and those who were had different kinds of interest. Russell Barton wants to motivate medical and nursing staff to help patients. Townsend, the Morrises and King and Elliott are interested in the functioning of different kinds of institutions as social systems — but Townsend is interested in all old people's Homes (or at least, a national sample), while the Morrises and King and Elliott study individual prisons as socio-political systems.

Goffman is frankly consumerist, concerned with the rituals to which inmates are subjected. Staff only impinge as an alien group exercising power. Cohen and Taylor follow him in this respect. The question raised by the deviancy theorists — 'Whose side are we on?' implies the inevitability of a binary split between the interests of staff and inmates, and the necessity of taking the inmates' side because all previous research has adopted the official perspective.

Foucault, Szasz, Kittrie and Rothman are not involved in this controversy. Their concern is with the dangers of social control at the national level, and with institutional popula-tions as special cases in which these dangers can be demon-strated. All imply that the danger is widespread: the forces of sovereignty/Institutional Psychiatry/the Therapeutic State/Jacksonian repression threaten all their readers.

Haney, Banks and Zimbardo want to demonstrate a theory about human personality. Next to Russell Barton, the AEGIS group has the simplest and most direct aims — a housing scheme, better hospital practice, a Hospital Commissioner.

Yet despite these very considerable differences, there is one fundamental similarity between all the writers. They are all, in different ways and to different degrees, on the side of the inmate.

Different conclusions

All the writers agree that the institutions they study exhibit many undesirable features, but they are not in agreement as to the causes of these problems, the possibilities of remedying them, or the means of doing so. Russell Barton is the most optimistic. He believes that a training programme for nurses can revitalise mental hospitals, and create genuine processes of rehabilitation. Townsend believes that reform is possible, and sets out to achieve it, partly in the development of scales of measurement, and partly by political pressure. AEGIS aims directly at media publicity to help in the implementation of its chosen solutions. Kittrie advances a code of Human Rights practice (with incidental benefits for the legal profession). King and Elliott are still hopeful about training prisons, taking the view that Albany was defeated by a particularly unpropitious set of circumstances. Pauline Morris advocates a massive change in staff skills.

Some offer no solutions. The Morrises, working at Pentonville, are concerned with understanding the system, but seem to regard prison pathology as inevitable. Rothman is past-oriented rather than future-oriented, concerned with understanding the origins of societal attitudes rather than how they can be changed.

Then there are the pessimists. Goffman thinks that society is to blame, and sees no hope of changing the attitudes of relatives, policemen and judges, the 'true clients' of the system. Cohen and Taylor find the situation of the prisoners in 'E' Wing intolerable, but have no solution apart from the total abolition of prisons. As they say, even the prisoners are not agreed about what they want. Foucault thinks that the enemy is the absolutist power of kings, generals and capitalists, and implies that there is no hope of change this side of the Revolution. Szasz, at the other end of the political spectrum, thinks that the enemy is state power, and the solution is full-blooded entrepreneurialism.

It is all very confusing.

Are there any 'regularities'?

We have come to the conclusion that there is a basic theme to these very disparate works. It has five aspects:
  (i) loss of liberty
  (ii) social stigma
  (iii) loss of autonomy
  (iv) depersonalisation
  (v) low material standards.
Talk of 'total institutions' is misleading, because no

institution is entirely cut off from the outside world. The community shapes its architecture, determines the nature, number and quality of its staff, frames its policies and creates its inmate population. The story of Albany indicates very clearly how the internal affairs even of a closed prison may be affected by direction from above. In 'E' Wing at Durham and on the geriatric ward at Cossett Hospital, the pressures of the outside world had strong and very different effects on what went on inside.

However, when Goffman used the term 'total institutions', his central interest was not the nature of the social system, nor the experience of staff, but the inmate experience. An institution may be experienced as 'total' or 'encompassing' if one cannot leave it, for conditions, however intolerable, must simply be suffered. Those who can do so vote with their feet. Those who cannot include prisoners, even in open prisons, mental patients and mental handicap patients under compulsory or involuntary detention (a small proportion in Britain) but also anyone who for reasons of sickness, infirmity, age, fear of the consequences or lack of a viable alternative cannot leave. In that sense, long-stay patients in general hospitals or residents in old people's Homes may be as surely institutionalised as those confined by lock and key.

Any concept of liberty is subjective. Some people rate their liberty of movement more highly than others, and some are able to retain a mental and spiritual freedom in conditions of close confinement. The literature of prisoner-of-war camps is a good guide to the wide range of human reactions possible, though it is almost entirely confined to accounts by officers; but if stone walls do not a prison make, the converse is also true: a prison-like deprivation of liberty may be experienced in the absence of walls and bars. While French, American and British writers have different images of liberty, and their own distinctive historical experiences in mind, all share the same fear of social control arbitrarily enforced and freedom arbitrarily denied. If this comes through most clearly in the case of Dr Szasz, the reason may be that he comes from a society where both threats have been only too real.

Goffman was to write about stigma and 'spoiled identity' in another book.[2] Though he had much that was useful to say about the mechanisms of stigma, he did not return to the major problem of people in institutions: that admission means identifying oneself with an unfamiliar and often unacceptable reference-group. 'I'm not like these other people in here' is a natural reaction, often expressed to visitors in a variety of circumstances. The stubborn assertion of individuality, the refusal to accept the group image, may be the spark of personal survival, but all the pressures of the institutional world serve to deny it.

The loss of autonomy is a linked issue. This involves all those features so usefully listed by Russell Barton, but some more subtle ones as well: the control over the use of space described by Foucault; the control over work and leisure activity which Foucault studies at one level, and King and Elliott at another; the control over time, and over the management of privacy and association spelled out by Cohen and Taylor, the slenderness of personal contact found by Townsend.

While Townsend and some other writers associate the loss of autonomy with the large size of institutions, Cohen and Taylor find very similar features in 'E' Wing, which has no more than twenty prisoners. The assumption that small size necessarily equals homeliness and the preservation of personal values might be worth further study. In our experience, the problem is primarily one of staff attitudes.

Depersonalisation can be the consequence of loss of liberty, 'spoiled identity' and loss of autonomy. We found Goffman's analysis of role-stripping more relevant than Cohen and Taylor did, and have suggested some of the reasons why. There is ample evidence that depersonalisation can also be achieved through the excessive administration of drugs, through the imposition of rigid routines, through a simple assumption that systems take precedence over individuals, and through neglect or distortion of personal appearance. Russell Barton's insistence on hairdressing and cosmetics for his women patients, the AEGIS group's enquiries about teeth and spectacles, and Haney, Banks and Zimbardo's somewhat grotesque modifications of the appearance of 'guards' and 'prisoners' are all part of the same story.

Finally, the account of low material standards recurs in the literature. Goffman's account of the pathetic 'make-do's' at St Elizabeth's rings true to the reality of the institutional situation. We have no doubt that, even if long-term institutions were as well equipped as four-star hotels, the effect of the four factors we have outlined above would still be highly damaging. The basic recognition 'I cannot get out. I am like these people I see around me. I cannot make my own decisions' is not really modified by spring mattresses and cheerful curtains; but when bleakness, deprivation and squalor are added to helplessness, any institution becomes a punishment block. The official view in British prisons is still that deprivation of liberty is the punishment — conditions in prison should not add to it. The state of the prisons does not bear this out; and, despite the upgrading which has taken place in geriatric wards, mental hospitals and mental handicap hospitals in Britain, there are still too many hospitals where out-dated architecture and dismal conditions make the premises totally unsuitable. We have seen conditions in other countries, including France and the United States, which are very much worse.

Towards a new analysis

We have learned some negative lessons from this study:

from Goffman, that it is a great deal easier to point to similarities than to toil over differences;

from Foucault, that mystification can be self-defeating;

from Szasz, that semantic games need careful unravelling;

from the British school, that empirical analysis does not wear as well as theoretical analysis;

from Rothman, that historians should not ask simple questions in the expectation of getting simple answers;

from Kittrie, that advocates are not judges (the fact that some of them become judges is one of the mysteries of the legal profession);

from Cohen and Taylor, that it does not do to protest too much;

from Haney, Banks and Zimbardo, that objectivity and enthusiasm to get particular results do not mix;

from King and Elliott, that there may be more than one explanation of a course of events.

But we have also learned many positive lessons, and for these we are grateful:

from Goffman, a new approach, new concepts, and the importance of looking at social dynamics rather than managerial directives;

from Foucault, that some organisations may be designed to fail, and that appearance is not the same as reality; that power and powerlessness are central to the study of institutions;

from Szasz, to read everything he writes twice;

from Russell Barton, some sensible and down-to-earth ideas on practice;

from Townsend, the technique of systematising a measure of quality (through the Quality Scale and the Incapacity Scale), and an object-lesson in the application of research findings to social reform;

from Terence and Pauline Morris, the ability to use theory in order to raise new questions;

from AEGIS, an object-lesson in pressure-group tactics;

from Rothman, the importance of asking 'How did we get where we are?' and of getting the story straight;

from Kittrie, the necessity of enquiring into gate-keeping — who controls who goes in and out; and a Human Rights perspective;

from Cohen and Taylor, many useful pointers to the personal experience of confinement, and the courage to try unorthodox approaches when orthodox ones fail to produce results;

from Haney, Banks and Zimbardo, the possiblity of using simulation models, even if this one went wrong;

from King and Elliott, the value of meticulous recording, and of dealing honestly with both staff and inmates.

We hope that we have learned to be modest in our own ambitions for future work on institutions; to avoid what Etzioni once called 'Utopian aims seen from Olympian heights'; to concentrate on the basic needs and rights of individuals; and to be concerned with the art of the possible — with middle-range idea-and-reality theory which can be operationalised into a theory of practice.

Institutions are at once a threat and a portent: a symbol of liberty lost and affliction accepted. If they are to remain part of our society, it is time for some fresh thinking.

APPENDIX I
Defining 'institutions'

Sociologists use the term 'institution' to refer to a generalised social response to a human situation: marriage, the family, religion are all 'institutions'. They may also use it to refer to more specific responses — the armed forces, the police or a television station are also 'institutions'. The clergy use the word in a sense very close to its Latin root, to describe the ritual act of placing a clergyman in his seat in church as a symbol of his responsibility for the cure of souls. Social policy analysts use it differently again — with reference to residential establishments such as prisons and hospitals, particularly large establishments with long-stay populations. That is the sense in which the term is used in this study.

The three meanings are clearly connected, but there is inevitably a certain amount of confusion. This is increased for social policy writers by the fact that their colleagues tend to import a value-judgment into their use of 'institution'. The term is often used as a criticism rather than as a description. Some writers prefer to avoid it altogether, referring to 'clients' or 'residents' in 'homes' or 'residential care'.[1] This may be appropriate in relation to accommodation administered by Social Services Departments, but it is difficult to subsume prisons and prisoners under such categories, and the more euphemistic terms may obscure the survival of depersonalising conditions in different administrative frameworks.

While the English language offers us no easy solution to these semantic problems, German is more precise. The word *Einsetz* means something which is set up or pledged — a way of doing things. This covers the generalised use of 'institution' in sociology. Max Weber defines another term, *Betriebsverband*, as meaning 'an associative social relationship characterised by an administrative staff devoted to such continuous purposive activity',[2] and this would apply to the armed forces or the police. He also defines *Anstalt* as meaning 'a corporate group, the established order of which has, within a given sphere of activity, been successfully imposed on every individual who conforms to certain specific criteria'.[3]

206

Betriebsverband emphasises purpose, process and staff, and can be held to relate to residential institutions (as to television stations) when studied as social systems. *Anstalt* puts the emphasis on the exercise of authority, and on conformity to authority's demands, and is more relevant to residential institutions when studied in relation to problems of power and powerlessness.

Talcott Parsons, who translated Weber's *On Charisma and Institution Building*, and had a good ear for the nuances of meaning in both German and English, uses the term 'social organisation' in his own writing about mental hospitals and similar establishments, though he stresses the *Betriebsverband* element — 'the relatively clear primacy of a specific collective goal'.[4] The movement away from structural-functionalist interpretations has shifted the interest of social scientists closer to *Anstalt*.

Goffman avoids the problem of definition by simply referring to 'social establishments . . . places such as rooms, suites of rooms, buildings or plants in which activity of a particular kind regularly goes on'.[5]

Despite the difficulties, we have used 'institution' as the best generic term we have. It is not used pejoratively. It simply means any long-term provision of a highly-organised kind on a residential basis with the expressed aims of 'care', 'treatment' or 'custody'. This broad definition makes it possible to examine both *Betriebsverband* and *Anstalt* factors: administration, process, architecture, social dynamics and power relationships.

APPENDIX II
Statistics on institutions

1. *Resident populations of institutions, England and Wales* (thousands)

	1960–1	1978–80
mental hospitals	137.1	79.2
mental handicap hospitals	61.2	46.7
prisons etc.	27.1	43.8
special hospitals	2.2	2.1
geriatric hospitals and units	54.6	55.8
local authority Homes etc.	84.6	152.4
	366.8	380.0

Sources: official statistics summarised by K. Jones and A. J. Fowles, 'People in Institutions: Rhetoric and Reality', in C. Jones and J. Stevenson (eds) *The Year Book of Social Policy in Britain, 1982*, London, Routledge & Kegan Paul, 1983.

2. *Resident populations of institutions, United States of America*

	1960–1	1977–80
mental hospitals	609,795	171,483
mental retardation facilities	168,486	131,721
federal and state prisons	213,142	301,000
	991,423	604,204

Source: *Statistical Abstract of the United States*, US Department of Commerce, Bureau of the Census, 83rd edition, 1962, table 98, p. 83 and table 211 p. 161; 102nd edition, 1981, table 188, p. 117 and table 329, p. 189.

The US figures do not include the population of local jails, private nursing homes, hostels or after-care facilities.

NOTES

Introduction

1 For definition of 'institution', see Appendix I.
2 F. Basaglia, 'Problems of Law and Psychiatry: the Italian experience', *International Journal of Law and Psychiatry*, 3, 1, 1980.
3 D. Melossi and M. Pavarini, *Carcere e fabbrica*, Bologna, Societa editrice il Mulino, 1977, translated as *The Prison and the Factory: origins of the penitentiary system*, London, Macmillan, 1981.
4 See Appendix II.
5 ibid.
6 Personal information from the US Federal Bureau of Prisons.
7 J. P. Morrissey and H. H. Goldman, 'The Enduring Asylum: in search of an international perspective', *International Journal of Law and Psychiatry*, 4, 1981, pp. 13-34.
8 A. T. Scull, *Decarceration: community treatment and the deviant — a radical view*, Englewood Cliffs, N.J., Prentice-Hall, 1977.

1 Goffman: the radical

1 J. Ditton (ed.), *The View from Goffman*, London, Macmillan, 1980, p. 13.
2 See E. Lemert, *Social Pathology*, New York, McGraw-Hill, 1951. Goffman (*Asylums*, Anchor Books edition, New York, Doubleday, 1961, p. 129, footnote 4) expressly draws his readers' attention to pp. 74-6 of Lemert's work.
3 H. S. Becker (ed.), *The Other Side: perspectives on deviance*, New York, Free Press, 1964.
4 op. cit., pp. 9-21; first published in *Social Problems* 9, 1962, pp. 307-14.
5 Goffman, *Asylums*, 1961 edition, p. xiii.
6 op. cit., pp. 5-6.
7 op. cit., p. 9.
8 op. cit., p. 7.

9   op. cit., p. 16.
10   op. cit., pp. 35-7.
11   op. cit., pp. 61-4.
12   op. cit., p. 109.
13   op. cit., p. 135.
14   op. cit., p. 149.
15   op. cit., p. 320.
16   op. cit., p. 367.
17   op. cit., p. 383.
18   op. cit., p. 384.

2 Foucault: the excavator

1   Michel Dion, *Revue Française Sociologique*, 10, 2, 1969, p. 228.
2   The original edition was entitled *Folie et déraison, Histoire de la folie à l'âge classique*, Paris, Plon, 1961.
3   *Madness and Civilisation*, trans. Richard Howard, New York, Pantheon, and London, Tavistock, 1972. This is based on the Gallimard edition, with some additions.
4   For D. J. Rothman, see chapter 8; Michael Ignatieff's *A Just Measure of Pain* was published by Pantheon, New York, in 1978; A. T. Scull's *Museums of Madness* was published by Allen Lane, London, 1979.
5   *Surveiller et Punir*, Paris, Gallimard, 1975. English edition *Discipline and Punish*, trans. Alan Sheridan, New York, Pantheon, and London, Allen Lane, 1977.
6   Alan Sheridan, *Michel Foucault: the will of truth*, New York and London, Tavistock, 1980, p. 2.
7   Philippe Robert, 'Le prison et la sociologie criminelle en France', *L'Année Sociologique*, 25, 1974, pp. 469-78. The quotation comes from p. 473.
8   P. Lazlett, review of *Discipline and Punish*, *New Society*, 1 December 1977, p. 494.
9   Foucault, *Madness and Civilisation*, p. 35.
10   op. cit., p. 39.
11   The English edition is *The Ship of Fools*, trans. Alexander Barclay, London, Cass, 1966. For a commentary on Brant's verse, see John G. Robertson, *A History of German Literature*, London, Blackwood, 1931, pp. 158-9.
12   See Walter S. Gibson, *Hieronymus Bosch*, London, Thames & Hudson, 1973, pp. 41-4.
13   N. N. Kittrie, *The Right to be Different*, Baltimore and London, Johns Hopkins University Press, 1971, p. 57.
14   M. J. Dear and S. M. Taylor, *Not on our street*, London, Pion Ltd., 1982, p. 40.
15   W. B. Maher and B. Maher, 'The Ship of Fools: *Stultifera Navis* or *Ignis Fatuus?*', *American Psychologist*, vol. 37, no. 7, July 1982, pp. 756-61.

16 Foucault, *Madness and Civilisation*, p. 266.
17 op. cit., ch. IX, pp. 241–78.
18 op. cit., pp. 242–3.
19 ibid.
20 S. Tuke, *A Description of the Retreat*, 1813, p. 148.
21 op. cit., p. 141.
22 op. cit., p. 142.
23 Foucault, *Madness and Civilisation*, p. 243.
24 op. cit., p. 247.
25 op. cit., p. 249.
26 op. cit., p. 251.
27 op. cit., p. 271.
28 ibid.
29 op. cit., pp. 252–3.
30 R. Semelaigne, *Philippe Pinel et son oeuvre au point de vue de la médicine mentale*, Paris, Réunis, 1888.
31 Foucault, *Madness and Civilisation*, p. 261.
32 op. cit., p. 265.
33 D. Macrae, Introduction to R. Boudon, *The Use of Structuralism*, London, Heinemann, 1971.
34 op. cit., p. viii.
35 Sheridan, op. cit., p. 16.
36 op. cit., p. 6.
37 Foucault, *Discipline and Punish*, p. 17.
38 op. cit., p. 92.
39 op. cit., p. 304.
40 M. Cranston, *The Mask of Politics*, London, Allen Lane, 1973, p. 150.

3 Szasz: the iconoclast

1 *The Myth of Mental Illness* (1961)
   Liberty, Law and Psychiatry (1963)
   Psychiatric Justice (1965)
   The Ethics of Psychoanalysis (1965)
   Ideology and Insanity (1970)
   The Manufacture of Madness (1970)
   The Age of Madness (ed.) (1973)
   Ceremonial Chemistry (1974)
   Heresies (1976)
   Karl Kraus and the Soul-Doctors (ed.) (1976)
   Schizophrenia (1976)
   Psychiatric Slavery (1977)
   The Theology of Medicine (1977)
   The Myth of Psychotherapy (1978)
   Dates given are those of first publication in the United States. The lengthy sub-titles of most of these works have been omitted. Dr Szasz is also the author of other books, including *Pain and Pleasure* (1957) and *Sex: facts, frauds and follies* (1981).

2   *The Myth of Mental Illness: foundations of a theory of personal conduct*, London, Paladin Press, 1972, p. 9.
3   According to *Who's Who in America*, he was still at Syracuse in 1981.
4   *The Myth of Mental Illness*, p. 10.
5   op. cit., p. 25.
6   op. cit., p. 85.
7   ibid.
8   op. cit., p. 173.
9   op. cit., p. 182.
10 ibid.
11 op. cit., p. 199.
12 op. cit., p. 174.
13 ibid.
14 *Law, Liberty and Psychiatry: an inquiry into the social uses of mental health practices*, New York, Macmillan, 1963, pp. 6–7.
15 op. cit., p. 38.
16 op. cit., p. 4.
17 op. cit., pp. 40–1.
18 op. cit., pp. 48–53.
19 op. cit., pp. 59 and 71.
20 op. cit., p. 108. The discussion of psychiatry and the criminal law covers chapters 8–11.
21 See Chapter 10 in this volume.
22 *Law, Liberty and Psychiatry*, p. 255.
23 *The Myth of Psychotherapy: mental healing as religion, rhetoric and repression*, New York, Anchor Press, Doubleday, 1978, ch. 10.
24 *Law, Liberty and Psychiatry*, p. 12.
25 *The Myth of Mental Illness*, ch. 2, pp. 50–64.
26 op. cit., p. 54.
27 A. A. Luce, *Logic*, London, Hodder & Stoughton, 1958, pp. 22–3.
28 *Schizophrenia: the sacred symbol of Psychiatry*, London, Oxford University Press, 1979, p. 7.
29 *The Myth of Mental Illness*, p. 58.
30 C. Singer, *A Short History of Medicine*, London, Oxford University Press, 1928, reprinted 1944, p. 23.
31 Singer, op. cit., pp. 31–3.
32 op. cit., pp. 32–3.
33 op. cit., pp. 53–60.
34 F. N. L. Poynter and K. D. Keele, *A Short History of Medicine*, London, Mills & Boon, 1961, p. 73 and ch. 6, *passim*.
35 E. Goffman, *Asylums*, New York, Anchor Books, Doubleday, 1961, pp. 323–66.
36 See, for example, Z. J. Lipowski, D. R. Lipsett and P. C. Whybrow (eds), *Psychosomatic Medicine: current treatment and clinical applications*, New York, Oxford University Press, 1977; F. Alexander, *Psychosomatic Medicine: its principles and applications*, London, Allen & Unwin, 1950; O. W. Hill, *Modern Trends in Psychosomatic Medicine 2*, London, Butterworth, 1970.

37 *Report of Royal Commission on Lunacy and Mental Disorder.*
    London, HMSO, 1926.
38 *Law, Liberty and Psychiatry*, p. 38.
39 op. cit., p. 47.
40 op. cit., p. 249.
41 op. cit., p. 250.
42 *The Manufacture of Madness: a comparative study of the Inquisi-
    tion and the mental health movement*, London, Routledge &
    Kegan Paul, 1971, p. 4.
43 op. cit., p. xxv.
44 op. cit., p. 289.
45 op. cit., pp. xxiii–xxv.
46 See Murray Levine, *The History and Politics of Community
    Mental Health*, London, Oxford University Press, 1981.
47 *The Manufacture of Madness*, p. xvii.
48 *Ideology and Insanity: essays on the psychiatric dehumanisation
    of Man*, New York, Anchor Press, Doubleday, 1970, p. 23.
49 op. cit., pp. 188–9.
50 *The Ethics of Psychoanalysis*, p. 165.
51 *The Manufacture of Madness*, p. 15.
52 *The Myth of Psychotherapy*, p. xvi.
53 op. cit., p. 207.
54 *The Myth of Mental Illness*, chapter 11, pp. 207–21 *passim*.
55 See T. S. Szasz, *The Ethics of Psychoanalysis*, London, Routledge
    & Kegan Paul, 1974, p. 94. Eric Berne's *Games People Play*,
    which might have provided a better source, was first published in
    1966, but Szasz makes no reference to it.

4 Russell Barton: the medical interpreter

 1 W. Russell Barton, *Institutional Neurosis*, Bristol, John Wright &
    Sons, 1959, second edition, 1966, p. 5.
 2 op. cit., p. 13.
 3 op. cit., p. 14.
 4 op. cit., p. 11.
 5 op. cit., p. 13.
 6 op. cit., p. 14.
 7 op. cit., p. 15.
 8 op. cit., p. 13.
 9 op. cit., p. 15.
10 op. cit., p. 16.
11 op. cit., p. 17 and ch. 2 *passim*.
12 op. cit., pp. 30–1.
13 op. cit., p. 29.
14 A. H. Stanton and M. S. Schwartz are the authors of *The Mental
    Hospital*, New York, Basic Books, 1954, which stresses the
    therapist's responsibility for every aspect of the patient's care in
    hospital, coining the phrase 'the other 23 hours' to cover the time

in which the patient was not involved in face to face contact with his psychiatrist, but which nevertheless affected his prospects of recovery.

15 M. Greenblatt, D. J. Levinson and R. H. Williams edited a symposium *The Patient and the Mental Hospital*, which incorporated sociological and organisational insights into a consideration of psychiatric management. (Glencoe, Illinois, Free Press, 1957.)

16 I. Goncharov, *Oblomov*, trans. David Magarshack, Harmondsworth, Penguin, 1954.

17 A. Myerson, 'The "Total Push" Method in Schizophrenia', *American Journal of Psychiatry*, 95, 1939, pp. 1197-204.

18 B. Bettelheim and E. Sylvester, 'A Therapeutic Milieu', *American Journal of Orthopsychiatry*, 18, 1948, pp. 191-206.

19 See *Institutional Neurosis*, p. 7 and Goffman, *Asylums*, New York, Anchor Books, Doubleday, 1961, pp. 4-5.

20 See *Institutional Neurosis*, p. 13 and *Asylums*, p. 5.

21 See *Institutional Neurosis*, p. 13 and *Asylums*, p. 6.

22 See *Institutional Neurosis*, p. 17 and *Asylums*, p. 5.

23 World Health Organisation, *Report of Third Expert Committee on Mental Health*, Technical Report Series no. 73, London, HMSO, 1953.

24 Maxwell Jones produced his first account of the therapeutic community, *Social Psychiatry*, for the Tavistock Press in 1952.

5 Townsend: the reformer

1 P. Townsend, *The Last Refuge: a survey of residential institutions and Homes for the Aged*, London, Routledge & Kegan Paul, 1962, p. 4.

2 op. cit., p. 32.

3 op. cit., p. 79.

4 op. cit., pp. 328-9.

5 op. cit., p. 105.

6 op. cit., p. 177.

7 op. cit., ch. 8 *passim*. The scale is given on pp. 210-12, and explained in Appendix 3, pp. 477-91.

8 op. cit., ch. 10, *passim*. The scale is given on p. 259, and explained in Appendix 2, pp. 464-76.

9 op. cit., p. 412.

10 op. cit., p. 429.

11 See Ministry of Health, *Health and Welfare: the Development of Community Care*, London, HMSO, Cmnd 1973, 1963.

12 Central Statistical Office, *Social Trends, 1982*, London, HMSO, p. 239.

13 See the editorial introduction to K. Jones (ed.), *The Year Book of Social Policy in Britain 1973*, where this concept of social policy is more fully explored.

14 op. cit., p. 336.

15 Reports of the Institute of Community Studies are published by

Routledge & Kegan Paul. Early publications in this series include Michael Young and Peter Willmott, *Family and Kinship in East London*, 1957, Peter Marris, *Widows and their Families*, 1958, Michael Young and Peter Willmott, *The Evolution of a Community: a study of Dagenham after forty years*, 1963, in addition to Townsend's two major studies of old people cited in the text.

16 op. cit., p. 310.
17 op. cit., p. 335.
18 op. cit., p. 421.
19 op. cit., p. 330.
20 R. Sommer and H. Osmund, 'The Schizophrenic No-Society', *Psychiatry*, 25, 3, August 1962, pp. 244-55.

6 The Morrises: building on theory

1 T. and P. Morris, *Pentonville: a sociological study of an English prison*, London, Routledge & Kegan Paul, 1963.
2 op. cit., pp. xiii-xiv.
3 op. cit., p. 5.
4 op. cit., p. 4.
5 Gresham Sykes, *Society of Captives; the study of a maximum security prison*, Princeton University Press, 1958.
6 *Pentonville*, pp. 1 and 3.
7 Talcott Parsons, 'The Mental Hospital as a Social System', in M. Greenblatt, D. J. Levinson and R. H. Williams (eds.), *The Patient and the Mental Hospital*, Glencoe, Illinois, Free Press, 1957.
8 Sykes, *Society of Captives*, xiv-xv.
9 op. cit., ch. 6 *passim*.
10 op. cit., p. 49.
11 op. cit., p. 57.
12 op. cit., p. 52.
13 op. cit., p. 271.
14 op. cit., p. 14.
15 op. cit., pp. 99-100.
16 Sykes, *Society of Captives*, ch. 4 *passim*.
17 T. and P. Morris, *Pentonville*, pp. 164-5.
18 ibid.
19 Sykes, *Society of Captives*, p. 68.
20 T. and P. Morris, *Pentonville*, p. 166.
21 op. cit., p. 170.
22 Sykes, *Society of Captives*, p. 77.
23 T. and P. Morris, *Pentonville*, pp. 168-9.
24 D. Clemmer, *The Prison Community*, New York, Rinehart, 1st edn 1940.
25 op. cit., p. 299.
26 *Pentonville*, p. 170.
27 op. cit., pp. 294-5.

28 R. K. Merton, 'Social Structure and Anomie', in *Social Theory and Social Structure*, Glencoe, Illinois, Free Press, 1949.
29 See page 16.
30 T. and P. Morris, *Pentonville*, p. 171.
31 op. cit., p. 170. For Russell Barton's views, see ch. 4 in this volume.
32 Sykes, *Society of Captives*, p. 133.
33 T. and P. Morris, *Pentonville*, pp. 272-92.
34 P. Morris and F. Beverley, *On Licence: a study of parole*, London & New York, Wiley and Sons, 1975.
35 P. Morris, *Prisoners and their Families*, London, Allen & Unwin, 1965.
36 P. Morris, *Put Away: a sociological study of institutions for the mentally retarded*, London, Routledge & Kegan Paul, 1969.
37 See chapter 5.
38 P. Morris, *Put Away*, p. 307.
39 K. Jones, *A History of the Mental Health Services*, London, Routledge & Kegan Paul, 1972, p. 207.
40 Department of Health and Social Security, *Report of the Committee on Nursing* (chairman, Professor Asa Briggs), London, HMSO, Cmnd 5115, 1972, paras 557-65 and recommendation 74; *Report of the Committee on Mental Handicap Nursing and Care*, London, HMSO, Cmnd 7468, vol. I, 1979; K. Jones, J. Brown et al., *Opening the Door: a study of new policies for the mentally handicapped*, London, Routledge & Kegan Paul, 1975, p. 192 and ch. 8 *passim*.
41 P. Morris, *Put Away*, p. 307.
42 Jones, Brown, *et al.*, *Opening the Door*, p. 40.
43 op. cit., p. 96.
44 P. Morris, *Put Away*, p. 21.

7 AEGIS: the disappearing pressure group

1 B. Robb (ed.), *Sans Everything: a case to answer*, London, Nelson, 1967.
2 op. cit., p. 14.
3 op. cit., p. 47.
4 op. cit., pp. 69-112.
5 A Dominican monk and author of *God and the Unconscious*, London, Harvill Press, 1952, which has a foreword by C. G. Jung.
6 *Sans Everything*, pp. 111-12.
7 Ministry of Health, *Findings and Recommendations following Enquiries into Allegations concerning the Care of Elderly Patients in Certain Hospitals*, London, HMSO, 1968.
8 op. cit., pp. 40-1.
9 op. cit., p. 27.
10 op. cit., p. 28.
11 *Sans Everything*, pp. 77, 89, and p. 97.
12 op. cit., p. 146.

13 op. cit., p. 71 establishes the year as 1965, and subsequent events run from January to June. A bed became available in the convent on 23 June (p. 102) and Mrs Robb visited 'in mid-November' (p. 109).

14 *Findings and Recommendations*, pp. 35–6.

15 Fabian Tracts 361–2, 1968.

16 *Sans Everything*, p. 144 (Lord Strabolgi's reference) and p. 146 (Prior Daniel Woolgar's reference).

17 *The Times*, 10 November 1965.

18 *Sans Everything*, p. xiii.

19 op. cit., pp. 124–7.

20 op. cit., pp. 115–23.

21 op. cit., p. xi.

22 op. cit., pp. 128–35.

23 F. Stacey, *The British Ombudsman*, London, Oxford University Press, 1971, p. 177.

24 The main hospital inquires are listed in V. Beardshaw, *Conscientious Objectors at Work*, London, Social Audit, 1981, appendix A.

8 Rothman: the puzzled historian

1 David J. Rothman, *The Discovery of the Asylum: social order and disorder in the New Republic*, Boston, Little, Brown, 1971.

2 David J. Rothman, *Conscience and Convenience: the asylum and its alternatives in Progressive America*, Boston, Little, Brown, 1971.

3 A. von Hirsch (ed.), *Doing Justice: the choice of punishments*, Report of the Committee for the Study of Incarceration, New York, Hill and Wang, 1976.

4 D. J. Rothman, 'Decarcerating Prisoners and Patients', *Civil Liberties Review*, 1, 1, Fall 1973, pp. 8–30 and 'Behaviour Modification in Total Institutions', *Hastings Center Report*, 5, 1, (February 1975), pp. 17–24.

5 Rothman refers to Goffman's work in 'The State as Parent', pp. 67–96 in W. Gaylin *et al.* (eds), *Doing Good: the limits of benevolence*, New York, Pantheon Books, 1978, and to Szasz in 'Decarcerating Prisoners and Patients', p. 18.

6 *Discovery of the Asylum*, p. xvii.

7 op. cit., p. xviii.

8 *Conscience and Convenience*, p. 11.

9 *Discovery of the Asylum*, pp. 82–3.

10 op. cit., p. 105.

11 op. cit., p. 133.

12 op. cit., p. 138.

13 *Conscience and Convenience*, p. 12.

14 *Discovery of the Asylum*, p. xiii.

15 *Conscience and Convenience*, pp. 4–5.

16 *Discovery of the Asylum*, p. 294.

17 op. cit., p. 295.
18 *Conscience and Convenience*, p. 82. The reference is to Anthony Platt, *The Child Savers*, Chicago University Press, 1969.
19 Rothman's knowledge of English precedents is somewhat sketchy. For instance, his discussion of the Retreat at York involves a reference to Samuel Tuke as 'one of the leading students of mental illness in England' and to 'his well known colleague, Henry Maudsley'. Samuel Tuke followed his grandfather into the grocery business, and retired from active life when the future Sir Henry Maudsley (a distinguished alienist) was fourteen years old (*Discovery of the Asylum*, p. 113; *Dictionary of National Biography*).

9 Kittrie: the advocate

1 N. N. Kittrie, *The Right to be Different: deviance and enforced therapy*, Baltimore and London, Johns Hopkins University Press, 1971, pp. xx–xxi.
2 op. cit., p. xxi.
3 J. S. Mill, *On Liberty*, 1859, in J. S. Mill, *Utilitarianism, Liberty and Representative Government*, Everyman edition, London, J. M. Dent and Sons Ltd., 1910, pp. 72–3. Quoted in Kittrie, *The Right to be Different*, pp. 77 and 356.
4 Kittrie, op. cit., p. 356.
5 op. cit., pp. 4, 349 and 362.
6 op. cit., pp. 79–80.
7 A. V. Dicey, *Law of the Constitution*, London, Macmillan, 1885, eighth edn, 1931 pp. xliii–xlviii.
8 Kittrie, *The Right to be Different*, p. 9.
9 op. cit., p. 39.
10 op. cit., pp. 10–11, quoting Charles Reich, Individual Rights and Social Welfare: the emerging legal issues. 74 *Yale Law Journal*, 1245, 1965.
11 *The Right to be Different*, pp. 402–4.
12 William of Ockham's dictum is usually quoted as 'Entities must not be multiplied without necessity', though P. Boehner in *Ockham, Philosophical Writings*, London, Nelson, 1957, pp. xx–xxi, disputes this meaning.
13 *The Right to be Different*, pp. 408-9.
14 op. cit., pp. xvi–xix.
15 op. cit., p. 51.
16 J. S. Mill, *On Liberty*, p. 73.
17 op. cit., p. 138.
18 Kittrie, *The Right to be Different*, p. 383.
19 Mill, *On Liberty*, p. 151.
20 R. W. Leage, *Roman Private Law*, London, Macmillan, 1906, pp. 109 and 280.
21 See A. V. Dicey, *Law of the Constitution*, pp. 12–15, where Dicey

specifically challenges the applicability of Anglo-Saxon precedents; S. F. C. Milsom, *Historical Foundations of the Common Law*, London, Butterworth, 1969, p. 26.

22 Kittrie, *The Right to be Different*, p. 9.
23 John Locke, *Of Civil Government*, Book II, para 26. Everyman edition, London, J. M. Dent and Sons, Ltd., 1924, pp. 130. See commentary by Maurice Cranston in *What are Human Rights?* Oxford, Bodley Head, 1973, p. 2. If, as Cranston thinks, Locke was a disciple of the Stoics, the Stoic philosophy had lain dormant since the collapse of classical Greece.
24 Henry de Bracton, *De Legibus et Consuetudinibus Angliae*, trans. S. E. Thorne, ed. G. E. Woodbine, Cambridge, Mass., Harvard University Press, 1977, pp. 408, 410.
25 Blackstone, *Commentaries*, p. 427; Kittrie, *The Right to be Different*, p. 5.
26 op. cit., p. 460.
27 P. Parsloe, *Juvenile Justice in Britain and the United States*, London, Routledge & Kegan Paul, 1978, p. 62.
28 See chapter 8, note 5 in this volume.
29 Lord Denning, M.R., in R. v. Sec. of State for Home Affairs, *ex parte* Bhajan Singh. Quoted by Sir Norman Anderson, *Liberty, Law and Justice*, London, Stevens, 1968, pp. 66-7.
30 Kittrie, pp. 79-80.
31 op. cit., p. 217.
32 B. Abel-Smith and R. Stevens, *In Search for Justice: society and the legal system*, London, Allen Lane, 1968, p. 354.
33 For a fuller discussion of the disparity between the legal and psychiatric discourses, see K. Jones, 'The Limitations of the Legal Approach to Mental Health', *International Journal of Law and Psychiatry*, 3, 1, 1980, pp. 1-15.
34 Kittrie, *The Right to be Different*, p. 81.
35 op. cit., pp. 82-3.
36 op. cit., p. 4.
37 op. cit., p. 5.
38 T. Szasz, *Law, Liberty and Psychiatry: an inquiry into the social use of mental health practices*, New York, Macmillan, 1963, p. 212.
39 Kittrie, *The Right to be Different*, p. 8, note 2; p. 10, note 1; p. 46.
40 op. cit., p. 101.
41 op. cit., pp. 354-5.
42 op. cit., p. 355.
43 op. cit., p. 41.
44 op. cit., p. 355.
45 op. cit., p. 101.
46 op. cit., p. 164.
47 A. T. Scull, *Decarceration*, Englewood Cliffs, N.J., Prentice-Hall, 1977, pp. 48-55.
48 Kittrie, *The Right to be Different*, pp. 325-6 and 334.

49 op. cit., p. 168.
50 op. cit., p. 260.

10 Cohen and Taylor: the infiltrators

1 Stanley Cohen and Laurie Taylor, *Psychological Survival: the experience of long-term imprisonment*, Harmondsworth, Pelican Books, 1972, p. 29.
2 *New Society*, 11 January 1973.
3 Cohen and Taylor, *Psychological Survival*, p. 30.
4 *Report of the Inquiry into Prison Escapes and Security by Admiral of the Fleet the Earl Mountbatten of Burma*, London, HMSO, Cmnd 3175, December 1966.
5 *The Regime for Long-Term Prisoners in Conditions of Maximum Security*, Report of the Advisory Council on the Penal System (The Radzinowicz Report), London, Home Office, HMSO, 1968.
6 Cohen and Taylor, *Psychological Survival*, p. 13.
7 op. cit., p. 61.
8 Radzinowicz Report, para 147.
9 This paragraph is based on scattered comments by Cohen and Taylor, *Psychological Survival*, pp. 181, 31 and 33.
10 This is the title of Howard Becker's article reproduced in H. S. Becker, *Sociological Work*, London, Allen Lane, 1971.
11 *Psychological Survival*, p. 58.
12 op. cit., p. 66.
13 op. cit., p. 186.
14 op. cit., p. 33.
15 op. cit., p. 66.
16 op. cit., p. 33.
17 op. cit., p. 182.
18 D. Matza, *Becoming Deviant*, Englewood Cliffs, N.J., Prentice-Hall, 1969.
19 H. Becker (ed.), *The Other Side: perspectives on deviance*, Glencoe, Illinois, Free Press, 1964, Introduction.
20 Cohen and Taylor, *Psychological Survival*, pp. 159–60.
21 op. cit., p. 148.
22 op. cit., p. 43.
23 ibid.
24 See pp. 13–14.
25 *Psychological Survival*, p. 131.
26 op. cit., p. 178.
27 *New Society*, 23 October 1975.
28 Cohen and Taylor, op. cit., pp. 134–46.
29 T. Mathiesen, *The Defences of the Weak: a sociological study of Norwegian correctional institutions*, London, Tavistock, 1965.
30 op. cit., p. 136.
31 Radzinowicz Report, para 22.
32 Cohen and Taylor, *Psychological Survival*, p. 41.

33 See Maurice Farber in Kurt Lewin (ed.), *Studies in Authority and Frustration*, University of Iowa Studies in Child Welfare, xx, iv, and John Irwin, *The Felon*, Englewood Cliffs, N.J., Prentice-Hall, 1970.

34 Cohen and Taylor, *Psychological Survival*, pp. 166–78.

35 See, for example, the discussion by Anthony Kenny in *Freewill and Responsibility*, London, Routledge & Kegan Paul, 1978, or H. L. A. Hart, *Punishment and Responsibility*, Oxford, Clarendon Press, 1968.

36 Cohen and Taylor, *Psychological Survival*, pp. 201–7; L. Taylor, 'Ethics and Expediency in Penal Practice', chapter 17 in J. C. Freeman (ed.), *Prisons Past and Future*, London, Heinemann, 1978, pp. 199–206.

37 S. Cohen and L. Taylor, Prison Research: a cautionary tale, *New Society*, 30 January 1975.

38 *New Society*, 6 February 1975: letter from P. H. Kerr. See also correspondence in *New Society* on 20 February and 6 March 1975, and Laurie Taylor's reply on 20 March.

39 Cohen and Taylor, *Psychological Survival*, p. 199, paraphrasing the Radzinowicz Report, para 204.

40 L. Taylor, 'Ethics and Expediency in Penal Practice', in *Prisons Past and Future*, Freeman, pp. 199–206.

11 Haney, Banks and Zimbardo: the experimentalists

1 Craig Haney, Curtis Banks and Philip Zimbardo, 'Interpersonal Dynamics in a Simulated Prison', *International Journal of Criminology and Penology*, 1, 1973, pp. 69–97.

2 Larry O. Gostin, *A Human Condition*, MIND, 14 Harley Street, London, W1, vol. II, 1977, pp. 125–6.

3 op. cit., p. 129.

4 One cell presumably contained four prisoners, not three.

5 S. Milgram, 'Some Conditions of Obedience and Disobedience to Authority', *Human Relations*, 18, 1, 1965, pp. 57–76.

12 King and Elliott: the analysts of failure

1 Roy D. King and Kenneth W. Elliott, *Albany: birth of a prison – end of an era*, London, Routledge & Kegan Paul, 1977, pp. ix.

2 op. cit., pp. 76–7.

3 op. cit., p. 77.

4 *Penal Practice in a Changing Society*, London, Home Office, HMSO, Cmnd 145, 1959.

5 *Albany*, p. 90.

6 op. cit., picture 8.

7 op. cit., p. 92.

8 Presumably the provision of flush toilets was vetoed on the grounds

of expense. Another reason for the perpetuation of 'slopping out' even in new prisons such as H.M.P. Frankland is that the British prison authorities take the view that prisoners might endanger security by blocking the outlets and flooding the cells. This problem does not seem to occur in US prisons, where, whatever the other privations, individual flush toilets are generally provided.

9 *Albany*, p. 75.
10 op. cit., p. 107.
11 op. cit., p. 137.
12 op. cit., pp. 154–5.
13 op. cit., p. 164.
14 op. cit., p. 171.
15 op. cit., p. 29.
16 op. cit., p. 30.
17 op. cit., p. 281.
18 op. cit., p. 243.
19 op. cit., pp. 126–7.
20 op. cit., p. 342.
21 *Penal Practice in a Changing Society*, Home Office, HMSO, 1959, para. 46.
22 op. cit., para. 75.
23 King and Elliott, *Albany*, p. 336.
24 Home Office, *People in Prison*, London, HMSO, 1969, para. 56.
25 J. E. Hall Williams, *Changing Prisons*, London, Peter Owen, 1975, p. 127.
26 op. cit., p. 129.
27 King and Elliott, *Albany*, p. 340.
28 *Report of the Inquiry into Prison Escapes and Security by Admiral of the Fleet Earl Mountbatten of Burma*, London, HMSO, Cmnd 3175, para. 322.
29 Advisory Council on the Penal System, *The Regime for Long-term Prisoners in Conditions of Maximum Security*, London, HMSO, 1968, para. 20.
30 King and Elliott, *Albany*, p. 347.
31 op. cit., p. 350.
32 Maxwell Jones, *Social Psychiatry in Practice: the idea of the therapeutic community*, Harmondsworth, Penguin, 1968, p. 133.
33 Maxwell Jones, *Social Psychiatry in Practice*, pp. 135–44.

Conclusion

1 Alan Sheridan, *Michel Foucault: the will to truth*, London and New York, Tavistock, 1980, p. 96. The reference is to Foucault's concern with statements on such subjects as medicine, economics and grammar in *L'archéologie du savoir*, Paris, Gallimard, 1969. The English version is *The Archaeology of Knowledge*, trans. A. Sheridan, London, Tavistock and New York, Pantheon, 1972, pp. 28–9.

2 E. Goffman, *Stigma: notes on the management of spoiled identity*, Englewood Cliffs, N.J., Prentice Hall, 1963.

Appendix I Defining 'institutions'

1 See, for example, the Discussion Document on *Training for Residential Work* issued by the Central Council for Training and Education in Social Work, London, 1973.
2 M. Weber, The Concept of Legitimate Order, trans. A. R. Henderson, and Talcott Parsons, in *On Charisma and Institution Building*, ed. S. N. Eisenstadt, Chicago University Press, 1968, p. 15.
3 ibid.
4 Talcott Parsons, 'The Mental Hospital as a Type of Organisation', in M. Greenblatt, D. J. Levinson and R. H. Williams (eds), *The Patient and the Mental Hospital*, Glencoe, Illinois, Free Press, 1957, p. 108.
5 E. Goffman, *Asylums*, New York, Anchor Books, Doubleday, 1961, p. 3.

BIBLIOGRAPHY

Abel-Smith, B., and Stevens, R., *In Search of Justice: society and the legal system*, London, Allen Lane, 1968.

Advisory Council on the Penal System, *The Regime for Long-Term Prisoners in Conditions of Maximum Security*, London, HMSO, 1968.

Alexander, F., *Psychosomatic Medicine: its principles and applications*, London Allen & Unwin, 1950.

Anderson, N., *Liberty, Law and Justice*, London, Stevens, 1978.

Barton, W. Russell, *Institutional Neurosis*, Bristol, John Wright & Sons, 1959.

Basaglia, F., 'Problems of Law and Psychiatry: the Italian experience', *International Journal of Law and Psychiatry*, 3, 1, 1980, pp. 17-36.

Beardshaw, V., *Conscientious Objectors at Work*, London, Social Audit, 1981.

Becker, H.S. (ed.), *The Other Side: perspectives on deviance*, Glencoe, Illinois, Free Press, 1964.

Becker, H.S., *Sociological Work: method and substance*, London, Allen Lane, 1971.

Benaim, S., 'The Italian Experience', *Bulletin of the Royal College of Psychiatrists*, January 1983, pp. 7-10.

Berne, E., *Games People Play: the psychology of human relationships*, London, Deutsch, 1966.

Bettelheim, B., and Silvester, E., 'A Therapeutic Milieu', *American Journal of Orthopsychiatry*, 18, 1948, pp. 191-206.

Blackstone, W.E., *Commentaries on the Laws of England*, 1783.

Boehner, P., *Ockham, Philosophical Writings*, London, Nelson, 1957.

Boudon, R., *The Uses of Structuralism*, London, Heinemann, 1971.

Bracton, H. de, *De Legibus et Consuetudinibus Angliae*, trans. S. E. Thorne, ed. G. E. Woodbine, Cambridge, Mass., Harvard University Press, 1977.

Brant, S., *Narrenschyff, The Ship of Fools*, trans. Alexander Barclay, London, Cass, 1966.

Central Council for Education and Training in Social Work, *Training for Residential Work: a discussion document*, London, CCETSW, 1973.

Central Statistical Office, *Social Trends, 1982*, London, HMSO.

Clemmer, D., *The Prison Community*, New York, Rinehart, 1940.

Cohen S., and Taylor, L., *Psychological Survival: the experience of long-term imprisonment*, Harmondsworth, Pelican, 1972.

Cranston, M., *What Are Human Rights?*, London, Bodley Head, 1973.

Cranston, M., *The Mask of Politics and Other Essays*, London, Allen Lane, 1973.

Dear, M.J., and Taylor, S.M., *Not on our street*, London, Pion, 1982.

Dicey, A.V., *Law of the Constitution*, London, Macmillan, 1885.

Dion, M., Review of Goffman's *Asylums*, *Revue Française Sociologique*, 10, 2, 1969, p. 228.

Ditton, J. (ed.), *The View from Goffman*, London, Macmillan, 1980.

Eisenstadt, S.N. (ed.), *On Charisma and Institutional Building*, Chicago University Press, 1968.

Erikson, K., 'Notes on the Sociology of Deviance', *Social Problems*, 9, 4, Spring 1962, pp. 307-14.

Foucault, M., *Folie et Déraison. Histoire de la folie à l'âge classique*, Paris, Plon, 1961; shorter version — *Histoire de la folie*, Paris, U.G.E., 1961; English version — *Madness and Civilisation*, trans. Richard Howard, New York, Pantheon, 1965 and London, Tavistock, 1967.

Foucault, M., *Surveiller et Punir: naissance de la prison*, Paris, Gallimard. 1975; *Discipline and Punish: the birth of the prison*, trans. Alan Sheridan, London, Allen Lane, 1977.

Fowles, A.J., with Jones, K., 'People in Institutions: rhetoric and reality', *Year Book of Social Policy in Britain 1982*, London, Routledge & Kegan Paul, 1983.

Gaylin, W. *et al.* (eds), *Doing Good: the limits of benevolence*, New York, Pantheon, 1978.

Gibson, W.S., *Hieronymous Bosch*, London, Thames & Hudson 1973.

Goffman, E., *Asylums: essays on the social situation of mental patients and other inmates*, New York, Anchor Books, Doubleday, 1961.

Goffman, E., *Stigma: notes on the management of spoiled identity*, Englewood Cliffs, N.J., Prentice-Hall, 1963.

Goncharov, I., *Oblomov*, trans. David Magarshack, Harmondsworth, Penguin, 1954.

Gostin, L.O., *A Human Condition vol. II*, MIND, 1977.

Greenblatt, M., Levinson, D.J., and Williams, R.H. (eds), *The Patient and the Mental Hospital*, Glencoe, Illinois, Free Press, 1957.

Haney, C., Banks, C., and Zimbardo, P., 'Interpersonal Dynamics in a Simulated Prison', *International Journal of Criminology and Penology*, 1, 1973, pp. 69-97.

Hall Williams, J.E., *Changing Prisons*, London, Peter Owen, 1975.

Hart, H.L.A., *Punishment and Responsibility: essays in the philosophy of law*, Oxford, Clarendon Press, 1968.

Health, Ministry of, *Findings and Recommendations following Enquiries into Allegations concerning the Care of Elderly Patients in Certain Hospitals*, London, HMSO, 1968.

Health, Ministry of, *Health and Welfare: the development of community care*, London, HMSO, Cmnd 1973, 1963.

Health and Social Security, Department of, *Report of the Briggs Committee on Nursing*, London, HMSO, Cmnd 5115, 1972.

Health and Social Security, Department of, *Report of the Jay Committee on Mental Handicap Nursing and Care*, London, HMSO, Cmnd 7468, vol. 1, 1979.

Hill, O.W., *Modern Trends in Psychosomatic Medicine 2*, London, Butterworth, 1970.

Hirsch, A. von (ed.), *Doing Justice: the choice of punishments*, Report of the Committee for the Study of Incarceration, New York, Hill and Wang, 1976.

Home Office, *Penal Practice in a Changing Society*, London, HMSO, Cmnd 145, 1959.

Home Office, *Report of the Inquiry into Prison Escapes by Admiral of the Fleet the Earl Mountbatten of Burma*, London, HMSO, Cmnd 3175, 1966.

Ignatieff, M., *A Just Measure of Pain: the penitentiary in the industrial revolution, 1750-1850*, New York, Pantheon, 1978.

Irwin, J., *The Felon*, Englewood Cliffs, N.J., Prentice-Hall, 1970.

Jones, K., *A History of the Mental Health Services*, London, Routledge & Kegan Paul, 1972.

Jones, K., (ed.), *The Year Book of Social Policy in Britain, 1973*, London, Routledge & Kegan Paul, 1974.

Jones, K., 'The Limitations of the Legal Approach to Mental Health', *International Journal of Law and Psychiatry*, 3, 1, 1980, pp. 1-15.

Jones, K., Brown, J., Cunningham, W. J., Roberts, J., and Williams, P., *Opening the Door: a study of new policies for the mentally handicapped*, London, Routledge & Kegan Paul, 1975.

Jones, K. and Fowles, A.J., 'People in Institutions: rhetoric and reality', in C. Jones and J. Stevenson (eds), *The Year Book of Social Policy in Britain, 1982*, London, Routledge & Kegan Paul, 1983.

Jones, M., *Social Psychiatry*, London, Tavistock, 1952.

Jones, M., *Social Psychiatry in Practice: the idea of the therapeutic community*, Harmondsworth, Penguin, 1968.

Kenny, A., *Freewill and Responsibility*, London, Routledge & Kegan Paul, 1978.

King, R., and Elliott, K.W., *Albany: birth of a prison — end of an era*, London, Routledge & Kegan Paul, 1977.

Kittrie, N.N., *The Right to be Different: deviance and enforced therapy*, Baltimore and London, Johns Hopkins University Press, 1971.

Lazlett, P., Review of *Discipline and Punish*, *New Society*, 1 December 1977, p. 494.

Leage, R.W., *Roman Private Law*, London, Macmillan, 1906.

Lemert, E., *Social Pathology*, New York, McGraw-Hill, 1951.

Levine, M., *The History and Politics of Community Mental Health*, Oxford University Press, 1981.

Lewin, K. (ed.), *Studies in Authority and Frustration*, University of Iowa Studies in Child Welfare, University of Iowa.

Lipowski, Z.J., Lipsett, D.R., and Whybrow, P.C. (eds), *Psychosomatic Medicine: current treatment and clinical applications*, New York, Oxford University Press, 1977.

Locke, J., *Of Civil Government*, Everyman edition, London, J. M. Dent and Sons, 1924.

Luce, A.A., *Logic*, London, Hodder & Stoughton, 1958.

Marris, P., *Widows and Their Families*, London, Routledge & Kegan Paul, 1958.

Mathieson, T., *The Defences of the Weak: a sociological study of a Norwegian correctional institution*, London, Tavistock, 1965.

Matza, D., *Becoming Deviant*, Englewood Cliffs, N.J., Prentice-Hall, 1969.

Melossi, D. and Pavarini, M., *Carcere e fabbrica*, Bologna, Societa editrice il Mulino, 1977, trans. as *The Prison and the Factory: origins of the penitentiary system*, London, Macmillan, 1981.

Merton, R.K., *Social Theory and Social Structure*, Glencoe, Illinois, Free Press, 1949.

Milgram, S., 'Some Conditions of Obedience and Disobedience to Authority', *Human Relations*, 18, 1, 1965, pp. 57-76.

Mill, J.S., *Utilitarianism, Liberty and Representative Government*, Everyman edition, London, J. M. Dent and Sons, 1910.

Milsom, S.F.C., *Historical Foundations of the Common Law*, London, Butterworth, 1969.

Morris, P., *Prisoners and their Families*, London, Allen & Unwin, 1965.

Morris, P., *Put Away: a sociological study of institutions for the mentally retarded*, London, Routledge & Kegan Paul, 1969.

Morris, P. and Beverley, P., *On Licence: a study of parole*, London, Wiley, 1975.

Morris, T. and P., *Pentonville: a sociological study of an English prison*, London, Routledge & Kegan Paul, 1963.

Morrissey, J.P., and Goldman, H.H., 'The Enduring Asylum: in search of an international perspective', *International Journal of Law and Psychiatry*, 4, 1981, pp. 13-34.

Myerson, A., 'The "Total Push" Method in Schizophrenia', *American Journal of Psychiatry*, 95, 1939, pp. 1197-204.

Parsloe, P., *Juvenile Justice in Britain and the United States: the balance of needs and rights*, London, Routledge & Kegan Paul, 1978.

Parsons, T., 'The Mental Hospital as a Social System', in M. Greenblatt, D. J. Levinson and R. H. Williams (eds), *The Patient and the Mental Hospital*, Glencoe, Illinois, Free Press, 1957.

Platt, A.M., *The Child Savers: the invention of delinquency*, Chicago University Press, 1969.

Poynter, F.N.L., and Keele, K.D., *A Short History of Medicine*, London, Mills & Boon, 1961.

Reich, C., 'Individual Rights and Social Welfare: the emerging legal issues', *Yale Law Journal*, 74, 1965, pp. 1245-57.

Robb, B. (ed.), *Sans Everything: a case to answer*, London, Nelson, 1967.

Robert, P., 'La Prison et la Sociologie Criminelle en France', *L'Année Sociologique*, 25 1974, pp. 469-78.

Robertson, J.G., *A History of German Literature*, Edinburgh, Blackwood, 1931.

Rothman, D.J., *The Discovery of the Asylum: social order and disorder in the New Republic*, Boston, Little, Brown, 1971.

Rothman, D.J., 'Decarcerating Prisoners and Patients', *Civil Liberties Review*, 1, 1, Fall 1973, pp. 8-30.

Rothman, D.J., 'Behavior Modification in Total Institutions', *Hastings Center Report*, 5, 1, February 1975, pp. 17-24.

Rothman, D.J., *Conscience and Convenience: the asylum and its alternatives in Progressive America*, Boston, Little, Brown, 1980.

Royal Commission on Lunacy and Mental Disorder, London, HMSO, 1926.

Scull, A.T., *Decarceration: community treatment and the deviant; a radical view*, Englewood Cliffs, Prentice-Hall, 1977.

Scull, A.T., *Museums of Madness: the social organisation of insanity in nineteenth century England*, London, Allen Lane, 1979.

Sedgwick, P., *Psycho Politics*, London, Pluto Press, 1982.

Semelaigne, R., *Philippe Pinel et son oeuvre au point de vue de la médecine mentale*, Paris, Réunis, 1888.

Sheridan, A., *Michel Foucault — the will to truth*, London, Tavistock, 1980.

Singer, C., *A Short History of Medicine*, London, Oxford University Press, 1928, reprinted 1941.

Sommer, R., and Osmund, H., 'The Schizophrenic No-Society', *Psychiatry*, 25, 3, August 1962, pp. 244-55.

Stacey, F., *The British Ombudsman*, London, Oxford University Press, 1971.

Stanton, A.H., and Schwartz, M., *The Mental Hospital*, London, Tavistock, 1954.

Sykes, G., *Society of Captives: the study of a maximum security prison*, Princeton University Press, 1958.

Szasz, T.S., *The Myth of Mental Illness: foundations of a theory of personal conduct*, New York, Dell, 1961.

Szasz, T.S., *Law, Liberty and Psychiatry: an inquiry into the social uses of mental health practices*, New York, Macmillan, 1963.

Szasz, T.S., *Ideology and Insanity: essays on the psychiatric dehumanisation of Man*, New York, Anchor Books, Doubleday, 1970.

Szasz, T.S., *The Manufacture of Madness: a comparative study of the Inquisition and the mental health movement*, London, Routledge & Kegan Paul, 1971.

Szasz, T.S., *Ethics of Psychoanalysis: the theory and method of autonomous psychotherapy*, London, Routledge & Kegan Paul, 1974.

Szasz, T.S., *Ceremonial Chemistry: the ritual persecution of drug addicts and pushers*, London, Routledge & Kegan Paul, 1975.

Szasz, T.S. (ed.), *The Age of Madness: history of involuntary mental hospitalisation*, London, Routledge & Kegan Paul, 1975.

Szasz, T.S., *Heresies*, New York, Anchor Books, Doubleday, 1976.

Szasz, T.S. (ed.), *Karl Kraus and the Soul-Doctors: a pioneer critic and his criticism of psychiatry and psychoanalysis*, Baton Rouge, Louisiana University Press, 1976.

Szasz, T.S., *The Theology of Medicine: the political-philosophical foundations of medical ethics*, Baton Rouge, Louisiana University Press, 1977.

Szasz, T.S., *Psychiatric Slavery: the dilemmas of involuntary psychiatry as exemplified by the case of Kenneth Donaldson*, New York, Free Press, 1977.

Szasz, T.S., *The Myth of Psychotherapy: mental healing as religion, rhetoric and repression*, New York, Anchor Books, Doubleday, 1978.

Szasz, T.S. *Schizophrenia: the sacred symbol of psychiatry*, London, Oxford University Press, 1979.

Taylor, L., 'Ethics and Expediency in Penal Practice', in J. C. Freeman (ed.), *Prisons Past and Future*, London, Heinemann, 1978.

Townsend, P., *The Last Refuge — a survey of residential institutions and Homes for the aged in England and Wales*, London, Routledge & Kegan Paul, 1962.

Tuke, S., *A Description of the Retreat*, York, 1813.

White, V., *God and the Unconscious*, London, Harvill Press, 1952.

World Health Organisation, *Report of the Third Expert Committee on Mental Health*, Technical Report Series no. 73, London, HMSO, 1953.

Young, M., and Willmott, P., *Family and Kinship in East London*, London, Routledge & Kegan Paul, 1957.

Young, M., and Willmott, P., *The Evolution of a Community: a study of Dagenham after forty years*, London, Routledge & Kegan Paul, 1963.

INDEX